Bearing Witness

BEARING WITNESS

A Resource Guide to Literature, Poetry, Art, Music, and Videos by Holocaust Victims and Survivors

PHILIP ROSEN
and NINA APFELBAUM

Greenwood Press
Westport, Connecticut • London

Library of Congress Cataloging-in-Publication Data

Rosen, Philip.
    Bearing witness : a resource guide to literature, poetry, art, music, and videos by
Holocaust victims and survivors / Philip Rosen and Nina Apfelbaum.
      p. cm.
    Includes bibliographical references (p.) and index.
    ISBN 0–313–31076–9 (alk. paper)
    1. Holocaust, Jewish (1939–1945)—Personal narratives—Bio-bibliography. 2.
Holocaust, Jewish (1939–1945), in literature—Bio-bibliography. 3. Holocaust, Jewish
(1939–1945), in art—Catalogs. 4. Holocaust, Jewish (1939–1945)—Songs and
music—Bibliography—Catalogs. 5. Holocaust, Jewish (1939–1945)—Video catalogs. I.
Apfelbaum, Nina. II. Title.
Z6374.H6 R67 2002
[D804.3]
016.94053'18—dc21   00–069153

British Library Cataloguing in Publication Data is available.

Library of Congress Catalog Card Number: 00–069153
ISBN: 0–313–31076–9

First published in 2002

Greenwood Press, 88 Post Road West, Westport, CT 06881
An imprint of Greenwood Publishing Group, Inc.
www.greenwood.com

Printed in the United States of America

The paper used in this book complies with the
Permanent Paper Standard issued by the National
Information Standards Organization (Z39.48–1984).

10 9 8 7 6 5 4 3 2 1

28854

Contents

Preface

The writers, artists, and musicians whose works are profiled in this resource guide were selected on the basis of a number of criteria. Each individual was a victim or a survivor under the Nazi heel or of the repression of an ally of the Nazis—victims and survivors of concentration camps and ghettos, members of partisan groups, those in hiding, Jews disguised as Christians, and other victims of Nazi persecution. We have attempted to provide entries representing a variety of firsthand experiences and responses. Only works by those who were there—eyewitnesses to Holocaust history—are included. Some works cited in this book are collections of testimony, narratives, fiction, art, or poetry; each narrative, poem, or artwork in the collection is a firsthand account or artistic interpretation by a victim or survivor of the Holocaust. We have attempted to include those writers and artists who have achieved a degree of international recognition such as writers Charlotte Delbo, Primo Levi, and Elie Wiesel; poets Nellie Sachs and Paul Celan; painters Norbert Troller and Leo Haas; and composers Viktor Ullmann and Herschel Glik. But this resource also includes the work of less well known, unsung, and unrecognized eyewitnesses to history whose literature or art will help the student and other interested people to gain firsthand knowledge of what it was like to be a victim of Nazi persecution in the Holocaust.

This resource spans the entire period of Nazi aggression and genocide, from the early days of Nazi consolidation of power in Germany to the end of World War II. The experiences of writers and artists from many countries are represented, including those of Gentiles who shared the same fate as Jews. The experience of the Jews of Poland, of whom 3 million were killed by the Nazis, is well represented. Works from a variety of ghettos, especially the Warsaw Ghetto, and from concentration camps, particularly Auschwitz, are also well represented.

To put the literature, art, and music resources into context, an introductory essay describes briefly the historical background of the Nazi persecution and Holocaust. The resource guide is then organized into five chapters:

1. Writers of memoirs, diaries, and fiction
2. Poets
3. Artists
4. Composers and musicians
5. Videos of the Holocaust experience

Each chapter is organized alphabetically by entry, and within the entry alphabetically by title. Entries that fall into two categories are fully annotated in the main section to which they are appropriate and are cross-referenced in the other section.

Chapter 1, Writers, provides a brief overview of Holocaust writing. The entry on each writer contains the following elements: brief biography, including birth (and death) date(s), place of birth and family members, a short overview of the writer's Holocaust experience, and in the case of survivors, their liberation and immediate postwar experience. This is followed by an annotated bibliography of recommended works, which includes complete bibliographic data, capsule description of the work, and age appropriateness. Age appropriateness was determined by the work's content, its vocabulary and its complexity of concepts and sentences. In addition, educational materials that designate age appropriateness, such as the catalogues of the United States Holocaust Memorial Museum, Social Studies School Service, and the Anti-Defamation League, were utilized.

Chapter 2, Poets, begins with an essay on Holocaust poetry. Quite a few poets were Gentiles who empathized with the plight of the Jews. Each entry features a biographical sketch of the poet and discussion of the nature of the poet's work. Entries cite the anthologies where the poet's work can be found, along with complete bibliographic data, the title of the poem, and the page on which it is located.

Chapter 3, Artists, features survivor artists who completed their pieces relating to their Holocaust experience either during the Holocaust or after and includes an introductory essay on Holocaust art and artists. The entry on each artist includes a biographical sketch (although in some cases little information is available) followed by a brief description of the artist's work and a list of artworks and sources where they can be found or institutions where they can be viewed.

Chapter 4, Composers and Musicians, follows the format of the previous chapters. This section contains entries on books, sheet music, and musical scores. Wherever possible composers are named, the compiler of the songs noted, and the sources for obtaining the music given. Many songs arose from the folk, however, not from an individual; and since the mother tongue of Eastern European Jews was Yiddish, many of these songs are in that tongue.

Chapter 5 features a bibliography of annotated videos about the Holocaust experience. The guiding principal in selection was a film's emphasis on the victim-survivor. Documentaries are included if they contain a significant amount of survivor testimony. Following a general introduction, entries are arranged alphabetically by title. Wherever possible, videos by survivor producer-directors are featured. A consideration in selecting videos is a lack of grotesque photos that might be inappropriate for younger viewers. Each video entry includes title, running time, whether in color or black and white, age appropriateness, vendor, and a description of the video. The name of another writer, artist, or musician in an entry is in bold if the person is the subject of another main entry.

The number of Holocaust memoirs, diaries, fiction, poetry, art, music, and videos is great. This resource is not meant to be exhaustive, but it is designed to provide teachers, librarians, students, and those interested in the Holocaust with direction for selecting firsthand accounts and responses to the experience of the Holocaust.

Historical Background of the Holocaust

To understand events of the Holocaust and the literature, art, music, and film that depict them, one must understand the historical context in which they took place. Hitler legally came to power as chancellor in Germany by appointment on January 30, 1933. It did not take long for him to impose laws and decrees that circumscribed the lives of the 500,000 Jews of Germany. Jews were dismissed from all government jobs; Jewish medical professionals could not practice on "Aryans" (the word for Gentile Germans). Jews were exposed to ridicule, humiliation, and random beatings. Racist doctrine alienated the Gentile population from Jews. Boycotts, book burning, and cultural exclusion made Jews who thought they had been accepted into German society feel unwanted and fearful, their lives threatened. Jewish artists and musicians had their works banned as decadent. With the Nuremberg laws enacted in 1935, marriage and social intercourse between Jew and Aryan was prohibited. A new category was invented, "mischling," a half-breed, someone part Jewish, part Aryan. When the Reich annexed Austria in 1938, the discriminatory laws were applied to Austria's 180,000 Jews. On November 9, 1938, a huge government-sponsored riot, now recalled as Kristallnacht, left most synagogues and Jewish institutions burned and sent 30,000 Jews to concentration camps until they could prove they could leave Germany. Whereas a number of Jews found refuge in nearby countries in Western Europe, few were admitted to the United States. Indeed, the Jews became a "refugee problem" as countries closed their immigration doors. Ten thousand Jewish children from Greater Germany (Germany, Austria, and part of Czechoslovakia) were permitted to go to England on the Kindertransport, however, but they had to leave their parents behind. Writers and poets tell of this permanent separation. In 1939 the one means by which Jews made a living, commerce, was taken away. Germany swallowed up Czechoslovakia, and Palestine, the haven promised by the League of Nations as a Jewish homeland and ruled by Great Britain after World War I, was closed to Jewish immigration. Jewish property was confiscated, or sold at a fraction of its worth. Jewish schoolchildren were no longer allowed in public schools. They went to Jewish schools, but they were not safe from Hitler Youth attacks.

With the outbreak of war by the German invasion of Poland in September, 1939, 3.5 million Jews came under totalitarian rule. Meanwhile, the Soviet Union (today, mainly Russia) conquered the eastern half of Poland. There the communists did not murder the Jews; instead, they made anti-Semitism illegal, but they also eliminated the Jews' communal and religious institutions and shipped Zionists and so-called capitalists (those who had small stores) to concentration camps in Siberia known as the Gulag. In the German area of Poland, however, random murder and severe persecution of Jews became the order of the day. All Jewish property was taken away, and in 1940 the Nazis instituted ghettoization. Small Jewish communities were dissolved and their Jewish residents were forced into ghettos, small, partitioned sections of larger towns or cities. Ruthless roundups in the ghettos recruited slave labor for the Reich. Provisions were carefully controlled through a Jewish-self-governing body called the Jewish Council (Judenrat). The Judenrat was created within the ghetto, but its role was to carry out inhuman Nazi decrees. Inadequate housing, privation, great overcrowding, starvation, lack of sanitation, exposure to the elements, and slave labor became common. To add to the misery, the Schutzstaffel (SS) in charge of the ghettos, Hitler's private army responsible for carrying out racial policies, brutalized the residents. The writers and artists wrote of their resentment of the members of the Judenrat and their arm, the Jewish police.

Despite the terrible conditions, writers wrote, poets, musicians and painters composed, religious activities continued, children learned the Jewish tradition or about Palestine (Zionism). Jewish self-help organizations sprang up. Children went over the ghetto walls to smuggle food, medicine, and other supplies. Life continued despite the hardships.

In June 1941 Germany attacked the Soviet Union. Under cover of this war, the Holocaust came into full force. Einsatzgruppen—mobile murder units—followed the German army, murdering tens of thousands of Jews through mass shootings. Quickly overrun were Lithuania, Latvia, and Estonia, which the Soviet Union had annexed in 1940. Overrun as well was the half of Poland conquered by the USSR in 1939, and there the Nazis instituted a reign of terror. Among the local populations were many anti-Semites, who saw in the German victory a chance to unleash their hatred in riots and killing sprees against Jews while the Nazis looked on. A symbol of the ensuing atrocities is Babi Yar, a ravine in the Ukraine just outside Kiev. It was a site of mass murder perpetrated by the Nazis, who were aided by Ukrainian militia. In Lithuania local militia took the opportunity to wipe out whole towns, towns where Jews had lived for centuries. The Ponery forest was one Lithuanian killing site. Hitler's allies, Hungary and Romania, also took the opportunity to persecute their Jews. Hungary forced male Jews into labor battalions and shipped them to the Russian front, whereas Romanian fascists headed by dictator Ian Antonescu deported the Jewish population living in Bukovina, a northwestern province of Romania, into concentration camps freshly built in the southern Ukraine, in an area called Transnistria, a newly created province given to Romania by Hitler between the Bug and Dneister Rivers.

In 1942 the Final Solution—the Nazi program for extermination of all Jews in Europe—was formalized. Concentration camps swelled, and six death camps were set up in Poland. Auschwitz built an annex, Birkenau, the site of four gas chambers and crematoria set up especially for Jews and Gypsies. With over 1.5 million Jews murdered at Auschwitz and Birkenau, a great many artists and writers speak of this place. I. G. Farben, a huge German chemical works, established Monowitz, a plant near Auschwitz. The three places together—Auschwitz (mainly for Gentiles), Birkenau (mainly for Jews and Gypsies), and Monowitz (the slave labor camp)—are generically called by many writers Auschwitz. Two outstanding writers, Primo Levi and Jean Amery, wrote specifically about Monowitz. The other death camps included Treblinka, where most Warsaw Jews were sent—Belzec, Majdanek, Chelmno, and Sobibor were death camps where 90 to 95 percent of the Jews transported there were murdered. Nazi doctors selected who was to live in the camps or serve as slave laborers or die in gas chambers; such selections are mentioned often by artists and writers recalling their experiences in the camps.

Concentration camps incarcerated Jews and political prisoners, as well as Gypsies, homosexuals, Jehovah's Witnesses, communists, resistance fighters, members of underground patriotic organizations, prisoners of war (POWs), and those the Germans deemed "undesirables." Located throughout occupied Europe or in countries controlled by Nazi allies, camps were of several kinds. Those in Western Europe were holding areas, transit places detaining deportees until they could be sent "to the East," meaning to the death camps or to the slave labor camps. Most of the latter were inside Germany proper and located near quarries, factories, mines, or military installations. Often conditions at these camps were so poor that inmates died of exhaustion, disease (very often typhus), or starvation.

Theresienstadt was a special camp. It consisted of two parts, a ghetto created near the town of Terezin and, one mile away, a "Little Fortress," which became a prison and concentration camp. The ghetto contained many so-called privileged Jews, those who were of German background, elderly, veterans of World War I, or prominent individuals and their families. This ghetto was to be a showcase, a false front to confuse the Red Cross, who visited to check on conditions. Inmates were allowed a cultural life, concerts, art shows, lectures, and the like. The painters conspired to secretly depict the true conditions of the ghetto, however, and a number of their creative works survive. Hanging over the heads of all the residents were the ever-present and frequent transports to death at Auschwitz. Only 100 of 15,000 children who were incarcerated at Theresienstadt survived.

Hungary and Italy are special cases. At the beginning of World War II they were allies of Nazi Germany. As a reward, Hitler awarded a section of Czechoslovakia located in the Carpathian Mountains to Hungary. Many Jews there embraced a Hungarian culture. In 1940 Hitler gave Hungary nearly half of Transylvania, a huge area of Romania. When Germany invaded Hungary in 1944, the Hungarian Jews were deported. The last great mass murder of Jews at Auschwitz consisted of Jews from Hungary and the annexed territories. Although from 1938 onward Italy instituted highly discriminatory anti-Semitic laws, the Final Solution was not practiced there. The Italian army in fact protected Jews wherever it occupied territory, most notably in Bosnia, Greece, Albania, and southern France. In September 1943, however, when Italy joined the Allies against the Nazis, Germany invaded Italy and a puppet fascist government was set up under Mussolini. With massive SS aid, deportations began.

The Jews' resistance to their fate took many forms. Military resistance occurred in a number of ghettos, the most well known the Warsaw Ghetto Uprising. The Vilna Ghetto also rose up. Jews formed partisan units in forests, some with local fighters, some in only Jewish units. Often the native partisans were anti-Semitic; consequently, Jews who joined partisan groups withheld the fact that they were Jewish. Jews also flocked to underground movements in their homelands. The French Maquis, the French underground and partisan fighters of various political persuasions, harbored many Jews. Yugoslavia's partisans under their Marshal Tito had Jewish officers. Jews participated in national uprisings such as the Polish Warsaw uprising in August 1944 and the Slovakian National Revolt. Communist units permitted Jews to join, and, indeed, Soviet Partisans enlisted Jewish fighters. Some Jews flew to Moscow and then returned to lead fighters in occupied areas. Parachutists from the Jewish settlement in Palestine were dropped to lead revolts. The best-known parachutist was Hannah Senesh. Finally, there came revolts in concentration camps, with Treblinka and Sobibor shut down after Jewish insurrections. Even in Auschwitz Jews blew up a gas chamber.

Resistance had a spiritual as well as a cultural dimension. Jews kept diaries and memoirs; historians chronicled events in the ghetto. The most well-known chronicle is Emmanuel Ringelblum's Oneg Shabbat archive. Nelly Toll as a child painted while in hiding. Musicians composed songs of woe and defiance. Religious services were held, holidays observed, sacred objects produced, and young and old prayed and learned under the threat of death in ghettos and camps.

There were Righteous Gentiles, Christians who risked their lives to save Jews. About 14,000 have been identified as such at Yad Vashem, the Holocaust memorial in Jerusalem. Some were anti-Nazi native patriots; some were members of the Resistance who saw as their mission the rescue of Jews. The most dramatic example was the entire nation of Denmark, which transported its 7,000 Jews to safety in Sweden. There were others who rescued Jews out of religious, humanitarian, or altruistic motives. Some hid Jews; others supplied Jews in hiding; others supplied Jews with false papers; others, like Varian Fry, led them across mountains to neutral areas and safety. Many of these people have gone unrecognized.

As the Soviet Red Army moved into Poland and the American, British, and Allied armies advanced across France, the Germans moved their slave laborers and concentration camp prisoners into central Germany. The inmates often had to march many, many miles without shelter, provisions, or adequate clothing. These were death marches. The SS guards shot those who could not keep the pace. Liberation came to them and to inmates of concentration camps when the Red Army or the Allied armies chased the guards away. The Red Army liberated first the huge death camps in Poland, including the infamous Auschwitz in January 1945, and in late 1944 and early 1945 relieved the partisans of Belorussia, Latvia, Lithuania, and Poland. American liberators came on the scene mainly in April 1945, but they were unprepared for the horrors they saw and the sorry state of the victims. Most liberated Jews did not want to return to Eastern Europe, and those who did faced anti-Semitism and great danger. Jews who returned to homes in Western Europe often had their property restored and resumed their lives. Yet many chose to be displaced persons—those who would not or could not return to their former homes. Camps for displaced persons were set up in the French and British zones of occupied Germany. Jews preferred to gravitate to the American zone, where they believed conditions more favorable. Jews who returned to communist-controlled areas met up with communist oppression and sought to escape to the West, the American zone.

For Holocaust survivors the Holocaust is never over. The memory of those terrible days is a psychic wound that never quite heals. Most survivors immigrated either to America or to Israel, and in their host countries they have sought through writing, teaching, or speaking to inform about the defining event of the twentieth century, the crime that has no equal.

Bearing Witness

1

Memoirs, Diaries, and Fiction of the Holocaust

INTRODUCTION

Reading the memoirs, diaries and works of fiction written by Holocaust survivors provides another dimension to an understanding of the Holocaust. These works personalize a crime which has has no equal in its enormity and inhumanity in the course of human history. They relate details about the survivors' daily life before the Nazi storm and then during the time of great persecution, and they describe the aftermath not told by history books. They reveal the writers' passion to let the world know their tragic stories and their inner strength to carry on. They also reveal people's determination, ingenuity, compassion, and goodness toward others in the face of absolute evil and terror.

The memoirs and diaries seem to fall into several categories. The largest category is comprised of memoirs written after the Holocaust experience. These memoirs are straight narration, with the writer telling the reader his or her story. Western European writers such as Michael Blumenthal, Victor Klemperer, and Ida Vos, while nominally Jewish, think themselves very assimilated into the Gentile societies of their native land. German Jews in particular point out their long family history in the fatherland. When the Nazi terror strikes, they are shocked to find those neighbors they once thought friendly turn on them, although quite a few remain sympathetic. They try to escape deportation. Olga Drucker narrates the agony of leaving her parents on the platform as she boards the Kindertransport to England alone. Ernest Heppner finds refuge, as do 20,000 other German and Austrian Jews, in Shanghai, China, where Japanese overlords admit them freely. Outside the greater Reich some Jews go into hiding, as do Clara Isaacman in Belgium and Ruth Hartz in France, aided by friends and members of the Underground. Some individuals remain in hiding until they are betrayed to the Gestapo and are sent first to prison, then to a concentration camp. What happens to them is described as unbelievable, unthinkable. Usually the writer befriends someone at the camp or is sent there with her mother and they support each other. Sara Bernstein endures with her sister, for example, and Livia Bitten-Jackson with her mother. One writer must endure a death march toward central Germany: Charlotte Delbo uses prose poetry to describe the horrors of this march. Liberation comes either by the Soviets or the Americans. At Bergen-Belsen, by the British. The liberators at first provide little physical care, but after a short time give aid. Several from the West return home to find a relatively friendly environment and resume life in their native land. Among these are Charlotte Delbo, Fania Fenelon, and Primo Levi, who try to resume life in their former homes. German Jews do not return to Germany, however. And many Jews from Eastern Europe immigrate to Britain, to Australia, or to the United States, the preferred place.

Survivors from Eastern Europe are more likely to be religious, and if not strictly observant, then at least formally traditional. They generally live in a Jewish area and are less integrated into Gentile society. Writers tend to idealize their family life, which emerges as a placid picture of happiness and tranquility before the Nazi storm. They do mention anti-Semitism, but more as a cultural mindset than a violent antagonism. With the Nazi onslaught, these writers are surprised at the strength of their neighbors' anti-Semitism, now expressing itself in violence and collaboration with the occupier. As in the West, some Eastern European Jews escape by hiding, as Jerzy Kosinski shows in the autobiographical novel *The Painted Bird*.

Most Eastern European writers describe facing Nazi savagery before they enter a ghetto. The travails of the ghetto follow, and then the pain of deportation. Through them we see the horrors of the concentration camp. Many of the writers are moved to several camps and also endure a death march. Unlike writers from Western Europe, Eastern European writers who return to their country of birth face severe anti-Semitism and a repressive communist regime. Typical of such Eastern European writers are Eddie Gastfriend, Henry Orenstein, and George Topas. Some Eastern European Jews seek displaced persons camps in the American Zone of Occupation in Germany and make a great effort to get to America. Others choose to immigrate to the Jewish settlement in Palestine (now Israel). Most of the writers, both diarists and memoirists alike, are interested in telling their story "so the world should know." Most Eastern European as well as Western Jewish survivors go on to receive higher education and become professionals in the postwar period.

Fiction writers such as Elie Wiesel write their novels in the first person, as if writing a memoir; and thus their stories capture the terror of the Holocaust. Aharon Appelfeld avoids vivid details of the Holocaust and instead writes fiction about middle-class Jews often living in 1939, a prelude to the Holocaust, who reside in what was once the Austro-Hungarian Empire—Jews who are effete, highly assimilated, and naïve enough to believe they can conceal their Jewishness. He also writes about the aftermath and not the horrors themselves. Arnost Lustig uses the novel and short fiction story to describe life in Theresienstadt and the death camps. Tadeuz Borowski uses the short story to recount the horrors of the gas chambers. Ida Fink uses the short fictional story to detail Nazi terror. Thus, writers of fiction focus exclusively on the Jewish experience.

Indeed, very few of the writers examine the mind of the Nazi perpetrator. Even such intellectuals as Charlotte Delbo, Jean Amery, Leon Wells, and Primo Levi, whose experiences take them into the depths of the death machine, say little of the Nazis' motives. When Primo Levi asks, "Why [the senseless torture and privation]," he accepts the answer, "Here there is no reason why." He fails to acknowledge Nazi brainwashing—that to the Nazi, murdering Jews is therapeutic for the Reich.

Camp survivors each seem to have a special skill that aids them. Two writers, Miklos Nyiszli and Gisella Perl, are medical doctors. George Topas and Henry Orenstein pretend to be, respectively, a chemist and a mathematician, based on their high school education, and as a result receive research work detail. Morris Wysograd has artistic skill and is able to get better treatment when he paints privately for his captors. Norbert Troller is a member of an artistic staff at Theresienstadt and manages relatively well until caught smuggling to the outside world paintings revealing the poor conditions at the camp. A chemist in civilian life, Primo Levi has a related job at I. G. Farben's plant in Poland.

Jewish partisans who write of their resistance come mostly from Eastern Europe. They describe their special efforts to join partisan groups. When joining Gentile partisans, they try to hide that they are Jews for fear of murderous anti-Semitism. They describe the suspicious nature of Soviet partisans and the danger from their comrades in arms. Faye Schulman's memoir underscores Russian paranoid nature: When Jews are liberated, communist officials see treason and crime everywhere, and so she seeks to flee from their rule. Many liberated Jews go to the West, and some become part of the Bricha movement, fleeing secretly underground to Palestine. Alicia Appleman-Jurman's story typifies this group. Then they go to Palestine and find a life in Israel. The Warsaw, Bialystok, and Vilna Ghettos produced resisters who were avid Zionists such as Zivia Lubetkin, Chaika Grossman, Abba Kovner, Yitzhak Arad, and Yitzhak Zukerman. They tell of problems with fellow Jews, Judenrat members, and native collaborators.

Some writers frame their narrative or diary in a religious context or take a larger worldview. Corrie Ten Boom is a Christian evangelical. The diarist Moshe Flinkler is a very Orthodox Jew and views events through his religious prism. Yaffa Eliach edits an anthology of the writings of ultra religious Jews who retain their faith. David Swierakowiak, a Marxist, is very critical in his diary of the ghetto's class system. Viktor Frankl comes to the conclusion while in the concentration camp that mental health depends on finding meaning in life. Bruno Bettelheim sees the camp routine as part of the destruction of individual autonomy, which is extended into regular civilian life.

Three diarists provide historians with excellent material on life inside ghettos. Included in this group are Chaim Kaplan, who wrote *Scroll of Agony*, Emmanuel Ringelblum, author of *Notes from the Warsaw Ghetto*, and Avraham Tory, who wrote about the Kovno ghetto. Etty Hillesum provides the reader with an insight into life in the Dutch camp Westerbork.

A number of writers were preteens or teenagers when they endured the horrors of Nazi aggression. They credit their survival to the ingenuity and courage of their mothers, who shared the experience with them. Elli Bitten-Jackson, an Orthodox Jew, saw redemption out of her experience. Ruth Hartz owes her life to her mother's farsightedness in providing hiding places. Often writers who were very young during the Holocaust write for the preteen–early teen audience. Such writers include Ruth Sender, Doris Orgel, Uri Orlev, Renee Roth-Hano, Nelly Toll, Marion Wolff, and Aranka Siegal.

Righteous Gentiles have won a place in Holocaust literature. Such righteous individuals include Miep Gies, Irene Opdyke, Varian Fry, Corrie Ten Boom, and Wladyslaw Bartoszewski, the founder of Zegota, the Polish underground agency to aid Jews. Anthologies of testimonies by Gentile rescuers examined in this reference include Gay Block and Malka Drucker's *Rescuers* and work by Marak Halter, who dubs rescuers "The Just." Also, a number of Jews who survived by hiding owe their existence to the righteous. Renee Roth-Hano and Ruth Hartz owe their lives to Catholic nuns. Clara Isaacman and Nelly Toll are indebted to those who risked their lives to hide them. Primo Levi survived because an Italian worker provided him with food and other supplies in Monowitz.

The personal stories of survivors provide the reader with what the history books and essays do not tell—the survivors' emotions, thoughts, hopes and dreams, and their reactions to the terror and horror they experienced.

AMERY, JEAN
(1912–1978)

The essayist was born Hans Mayer in Vienna to a family that could trace its roots in the Austro-Hungarian Empire to the seventeenth century. Amery's Jewish father died fighting in World War I. His widowed Catholic mother managed an inn until she married another Jewish man, one from Eastern Europe. Upon annexation of Austria by Germany in 1938, Jean fled to Belgium. With the Nazi conquest of Belgium, he joined the anti-Nazi Resistance. Caught by the Gestapo, he was sent to Gurs, a concentration camp near the French-Spanish border run by the collaborationist Vichy government of France. Escaping from Gurs, he rejoined the Resistance, but was captured again. Amery was sent to the Belgian camp, Breendenk, then to Monowitz, a satellite work camp of the Auschwitz complex, a place where he befriended writer Primo Levi. In 1945 he was deported to Bergen-Belsen in northern Germany, suffering two years of incarceration in camps. Liberated by the British, he returned to Brussels, where he married. He made his living as a freelance political and cultural essayist. In October 1978 the survivor committed suicide.

At the Mind's Limit: Contemplations by a Survivor on Auschwitz and Its Realities. Sidney and Stella Rosenfeld, translators. Bloomington. Indiana University Press, 1996. 128 pp. ISBN: 0253211735. Adult. Memoir.

This anthology consists of a series of five autobiographical essays that are a retrospective chronicle of the author's intellectual and physical existence during the war years, 1940–1945. Half-Jewish, Amery decides to throw in his lot with the Jews. He tells of his arrest and torture in the Belgian camp, Breendonk, then in Auschwitz-Monowitz. As an intellectual he feels isolated, alienated, and cynical, losing faith in the so-called Christian civilized world, a world he believes is hopelessly anti-Semitic and, at best, indifferent to Jewish suffering. Amery detects a predisposition to genocide. He sees signs of the virulent anti-Semitism of the 1960s under the guise of anti-Zionism and does not rule out a new Holocaust. He bemoans that he cannot identify as a religious or even cultural Jew, but merely as a Jewish victim. Like Primo Levi, his companion at Monowitz, he shows his despair, and one might predict his imminent suicide.

APPELFELD, AHARON
(1932–   )

The prolific Holocaust writer was born in Bukovina, a large province of Romania. His parents were wealthy assimilated Jews; this meant they ignored their Jewish traditions and immersed themselves in the German culture of the city of Czernowitz, a region that before World War I belonged to the Austro-Hungarian Empire. At the age of 9, he escaped with his father from the German and Romanian forces who had murdered his mother and grandmother. Arrested later, father and son were deported by Romania, a Nazi ally, to an area in southeastern Ukraine called Transniestra. Many Jews died in concentration camps there, but the 9-year-old escaped and lived by his wits in the countryside. In 1944 the Red Army, the military arm of the Soviet Union, reconquered the area. For a while the 12-year-old Appelfeld worked in an army field kitchen. Unhappy with communist rule, he fled to the Jewish settlement in Palestine in 1946. There he joined the settlement's military forces, fought, and then completed his high school and college education. He married and fathered five children. Appelfeld embraced Orthodox Judaism and lived in a religious section of Jerusalem. Currently he is a professor of literature at Ben Gurion University and an author, many of whose books touch on the Holocaust and Jewish identity.

The Age of Wonders. Dalya Bilu, translator. Boston: David R. Godine, 1989. 270 pp. ISBN: 0879237988. Ages 16–up. Fiction.

The protagonist of this fictional tale is Bruno, a Jewish boy, then man, frantically trying to assimilate. He returns to his boyhood haunts with his wife and recreates scenes of prewar (pre-Holocaust) Vienna and Prague. The prose looks at this period through a child's eyes and includes flashbacks and flashforwards to events from the Holocaust—ghettoization and deportation, but without detail. Bruno recalls that his father was unsuccessful in evading the Nazis despite his assimilation and attempts to conceal his Jewish background. Bruno hears from Gentiles how Jews tried to flee the Nazis, but were unsuccessful. A popular theme with Appelfeld is the struggle of converted Jews and half-Jews with their identity and against anti-Semitism.

Badenheim 1939. Dalya Bilu, translator. Cambridge, Mass.: Godine, 1998 (reissue). 160 pp. ISBN: 0879237996. Ages 16–up. Fiction.

This tale about the false tranquility of assimilated Austrian Jews was Appelfeld's first novel, published in English in 1974. The story is set in

1939, just before the Austrian Jews' deportations to Poland. Summer vacationers at a fashionable spa, the protagonists are wealthy Viennese Jews who refuse to believe that the Nazis mean them harm. They are in denial and preoccupied with petty recreational affairs as the impending doom closes in on them. A so-called Sanitation Department forces them to sign a Jewish register and holds them as virtual prisoners at the resort, Badenheim. The guests blind themselves to the blatant anti-Semitism they experience and to the true meaning of deportation. They struggle to convince themselves that everything is perfectly normal despite the vice of oppression closing in. This self-deception continues as they board cattle cars for the trip to doom in Poland.

For Every Sin. Jeffrey M. Green, translator. New York: Grove/Atlantic, 1996. 178 pp. ISBN: 0802134467. Ages 16–up. Fiction.

Young Theo Braun has survived four years in concentration camps. In this novel, told in the first person, he tries to forget the horrible memories of the camps and avoid fellow survivors, who will restore the memories. Hoping to recapture his life before World War II and the Holocaust, Theo seeks out old haunts while returning to his former home near Vienna. As he plods his way on foot, he meets along the road gatherings of fellow refugees, survivors who beckon to him to share coffee, cigarettes, and companionship. At first he tries to avoid them, but he recognizes his own need for friendship and community. Theo realizes that he cannot isolate himself, that he cannot return to the past, and that he needs to be with his fellow sufferers and brethren.

The Healer. New York: Grove/Atlantic Press, 1994. 224 pp. ISBN: 0892133576. Ages 16–up. Fiction.

Felix Katz is an assimilated Jew embracing Viennese culture, a common character in Appelfeld's novels. His daughter, Helga, has an emotional problem that resists conventional cures. Felix decides on unconventional treatment and agrees to journey with his family to the Carpathian Mountains to seek out a wonder rabbi, a holy man renowned as a healer. His wife and son accompany him and his disturbed daughter. When they reach the rabbi's village, they are repelled by the rabbi's solution—immersion in Hebrew and the prayerbook—an approach at great odds with Katz's rejection of Jewish tradition. His daughter and wife do wish to return to their Jewish roots and remain with the rabbi. Felix and his son, however, decide to return to Vienna. On the way home on the train Felix engages in conversation with a Gentile police officer, who, upon discovering his surname, remarks that it "annoys" him. Katz now has a hint of the dangers to come.

The Immortal Bartfuss. New York: Grove/Atlantic, 1994. 138 pp.
ISBN: 0802133584. Ages 16–up. Fiction.

Appelfeld in this novel portrays a Holocaust survivor whom he calls
immortal because of his experiences in the concentration camps. Bartfuss
is struggling between his desire to forget the horror and the need to
remember. He is now an old man, nearing the end of his life, troubled
and locked into a bad marriage. He lives with a woman who has no
understanding of his dilemma. Also, his two daughters are unsympath-
etic. Bartfuss is a transplanted Budapest native. Scenes take place first in
Italy, then in Jaffa, Israel. The story unfolds in the first person through
the eyes of Bartfuss. The work is a character portrayal of an emotionally
scarred man who has great difficulty with intimacy and is alienated from
those around him, another victim of the Holocaust.

The Iron Tracks. Jeffrey M. Green, translator. New York: Schocken
Books, 1999. 195 pp. ISBN: 080210997. Ages 16–up. Fiction.

Erwin Siegelbaum was finally freed from a concentration camp and
seeks revenge. He hopes that one day he will find the Nazi officer, Nach-
tigal, who murdered his parents. He has been traveling for forty years,
mainly over the rails of postwar central Europe. Erwin greets old friends
and returns to familiar hotel rooms. His comrades are Jewish men without families, but with memories, traveling the same routes. Like Erwin
they cull Jewish religious objects—candlesticks, prayerbooks, kiddish
cubs, and the like. In this novel, written in the first person, Erwin relates
his reflections about people he encounters and how their experiences and
attitudes have affected their spiritual selves. They and the protagonist
seek to know what to do with the lives that have been spared.

Katerina. Jeffrey M. Green, translator. New York: Random House,
1992. 212 pp. ISBN: 067946107. Ages 16–up. Fiction.

Katerina is a Gentile peasant woman who has worked for Jewish families and comes to identify with them. Her own parents mistreated her,
so she ran away. She experiences the pogroms that Jews endure and
survives. Katerina has two children out of wedlock by non-Jews. One
she gives away, and the other she tries to raise as a Jew. When the son
is brutally murdered by a Gentile, Katerina kills him. For this she is
imprisoned over forty years. She is released during World War II when
the Germans enter the Slovak area of Ruthenia. She witnesses the Gentiles' glee on the murder of the Jews.

Appelfeld's view of the Gentiles in his novels is not flattering. It speaks
of their undisciplined behavior. Through the eyes of the protagonist, he
describes different kinds of Jews. Appelfeld contrasts their behavior—

gentleness, struggling with their own faith, ambivalence and self-loathing, and skill in commerce—with the life of neighboring, often murderous peasants.

The Retreat. Dalya Bilu, translator. New York: Schocken Books, 1998. 165 pp. ISBN: 0805210962. Ages 16–up. Fiction.

As in Appelfeld's *Badenheim 1939*, the setting is the Austrian countryside at a spa hotel filled with assimilated Viennese Jews. The resort in this novel has become a school for Jewish assimilation where the patrons are taught proper eating habits and how to talk, look like, and engage in activities like their Gentile compatriots. Included are outdoors athletics and "wholesome" exercise, along with mind-dulling card games, gambling, and dining. Hitler is on the march, although he is not mentioned, and the reader knows the customers are blind to their fate. An aging actress, Lotte, no longer able to find work, twice divorced, and alienated from an acquisitive daughter, believes the retreat is a spiritual center. Lotte soon recognizes the vapidness, yet stays on, reflecting on her past and hoping to postpone a very uncertain future.

APPLEMAN-JURMAN, ALICIA
(1930–)

Alicia Appleman was born in Buczacy, Poland, the only daughter among four brothers in an Orthodox Jewish family. Her father made a living in the fabric business. She attended public school where she endured Polish folk anti-Semitism. In September 1939, when Alicia was 9, the Red Army conquered the region. Her brother Moise died in a Soviet prison on trumped-up charges. After surviving communist rule, in 1941 the Nazis overran her town. Her family eluded them, though they all later died at the hands of the Nazis. Alicia aided Soviet partisans, and with the Red Army's reconquest of Poland she established a Jewish orphanage and escape routes to Palestine for Jewish children. At war's end she immigrated to Palestine and worked on a kibbutz. In 1948 Alicia met an American volunteer aiding in the Israeli War of Independence and married. In 1952 the family immigrated to California where she now lives with her husband and two children and works as a writer and lecturer.

Alicia, My Story. New York: Bantam Books, 1988. 433 pp. ISBN: 0553282182. Ages 14–up. Memoir.

Alicia Appleman-Jurman's autobiography covers the period 1938 to 1947. She experiences the difficulties of living under the totalitarian dictatorships of Soviet communism and German Nazism. Most of her memoir deals with surviving the horrors of the Holocaust in Poland. She and her four brothers narrowly escape death, although her eldest brother is killed by Soviets while in prison on false charges. As her narrative progresses, her father, brothers, and finally her mother perish at the hands of the Nazis. The work reveals details of life in ghettos and in hiding and the severe anti-Semitism of both the Poles and Ukrainians. She covers the so-called "liberation" by the Russians and their malevolent rule over the former Polish citizens. Fortunately she had aided some Soviet partisans and was allowed to set up an orphanage for Jewish children. Alicia then becomes involved with the secret flight from Europe to Palestine called the Bricha. She finally takes flight on a Jewish blockade-runner, trying to get by British destroyers blocking Jewish immigrants to Palestine. Alicia ends up in Cyprus, a huge British internment camp for Jews.

ARAD, YITZHAK (ISAAC RUDNICKI)
(1926–   )

Isaac Rudnicki was born in Warsaw, Poland, to Orthodox Jewish parents. He lived with his father, a cantor; his mother, a homemaker; and his sister, Rachel, close to him in age. When he was 13, the Germans captured Warsaw (1939). He witnessed the cruelty of the occupiers and escaped to the Soviet Zone of Occupation in Swienciany, Lithuania. The Nazis murdered his parents. In 1941 the Germans launched their attack on the Soviet Union and occupied Swienciany. Witnessing mass murders by Nazi mobile killing units, Rudnicki fled to nearby forests and became an underground fighter, a partisan. After a number of daring exploits, he discovered that his sister, Rachel, also fought as a partisan. The war ended with a Soviet victory over the German forces. Returning to Poland and meeting with anti-Semitism, he joined Bricha, the secret movement to Jewish Palestine. When the British blockaded transports attempting to deliver refugees to Palestine, he jumped ship and swam ashore to safety, Isaac soon joined Palmach, the elite advanced forces of the Jewish Underground. In 1948, while fighting against Arab invasion, he married a fellow soldier, Michal. Rudnicki, now Yitzhak Arad, a more Hebrew name, fought in all Israel's wars and rose to the rank of brigadier general. After retirement he became the director of Yad Vashem, the Holocaust memorial museum in Jerusalem, and authored historical books.

The Partisan: From the Valley of Death to Mount Zion. New York: Holocaust Library, and U.S. Holocaust Museum (Washington, DC), 1979. 288 pp. ISBN: 0896040100. Ages 16–up. Memoir.

The Partisan deals with three themes—life in two ghettos, the writer's life as a partisan, and the author's participation in the 1948–1949 Israeli War of Independence. The memoir starts with Isaac Rudnicki's participation in the defense of Warsaw against the German attackers. Then, he witnesses the occupation by the Germans and the increasing persecution of the Jews. He tells of his escape to Swienciany, Lithuania, under Soviet occupation. He studies in a Zionist school and participates in the "illegal" Zionist movement. He writes of the Soviets' attempts to wipe out Jewish religion and culture. Two years later the Einsatzgruppen, Nazi mobile killing units, enter the town and commit mass murder and crimes against humanity. A ghetto and a Jewish council are established, both of which Rudnicki opposes. Leaving the ghetto, he joins Soviet-leaning Lithuanian partisans. Nationalist partisans are anti-Semitic, however. As a young Underground fighter, he is sent on many missions, including the derailing of thirteen German army trains. He is happy to find that his sister, Rachel, is also a partisan.

Upon the victories of the regular Soviet army, Rudnicki returns to Poland, but he encounters much hostility since Polish nationalists consider the Jews pro-Russian and communist. Rudnicki searches out Palestine-led Bricha agents and seeks immigration to the Jewish settlement in Palestine. The last fourth of the memoir deals with Isaac, now Yizhak Arad, a Palestinian Hebrew name, and his adventures as a member of the Palmach, the elite fighting units of the Jewish Palestine settlement and their struggle during the 1948–1949 War of Independence.

AUERBACHER, INGE
(1934–   )

An only child, Inge Auerbacher lived in Kippenheim in the Black Forest of Germany. Her parents were descended from Jewish families who traced their roots back over 200 years in Germany. They were wealthy; her father owned a textile firm and, like most German Jews, assimilated into German society. On the night of Inge's fourth birthday (November 9, 1938), Kristallnacht, government-orchestrated riots against Jews, broke out. Her father, Berthold, was sent to Dachau. When he was released, the family moved to the grandparents' house in the country, where with her family Inge suffered the indignities heaped on Jews. Then in 1942 she and her parents were transported to the Theresienstadt ghetto–concentration camp in Czechoslovakia. There the family dwelled in the disabled World War I veterans section. She was 10 years of age when the Soviet Red Army liberated her and her parents on May 8, 1945. One year later the family immigrated to New York City. The young survivor attended Queens College and in 1955 graduated with a degree in chemistry. She now devotes her time to lecturing, writing poetry, and creating music on Holocaust themes. Auerbacher still suffers from persistent tuberculosis contracted from the poor conditions at Theresienstadt.

Beyond the Yellow Star to America. Unionville, N.Y.: Royal Fireworks Press, 1995. 224 pp. ISBN: 0880922532. Ages 12–up. Memoir.

Auerbacher tells of the aftermath of her experiences at Terezin, particularly focusing on her life in America. Her memoir contains flashbacks to events in 1942–1945. She includes her poem "We Shall Never Forget." Inge narrates how she and her parents came to New York as regular quota immigrants. (At that time American immigration laws permitted 27,000 Germans under its quota.) Diagnosed with tuberculosis, she is confined to a hospital for two years. Undeterred, the young woman graduates Queens College as a chemist and is employed at Mount Sinai Hospital in Elmhurst. Her brief return to Germany for a visit is not a happy one, for she is met with hostility. Auerbacher tells how she presents an optimistic spirit and spends most of her time in educational institutions expounding her experiences under the heel of Nazi Germany.

I Am a Star. New York: Puffin, 1993. Illustrated by Israel Berenbaum. 80 pp. ISBN: 0140364013. Ages 12–up. Memoir.

This memoir is an eyewitness account of a child survivor of the ghetto Theresienstadt (Terezin in Czech), a place of imprisonment for the author from ages 7 through 10, 1942–1945. Inge describes the horrendous conditions there—the inadequate food, the poor sanitation, the inadequate heating, the crowding, and the infestation of disease-carrying vermin. She tells of the constant fear of deportation to death camps in Poland. (Of the 15,000 children imprisoned at Terezin, Inge was among the 100 who survived.) Auerbacher relates how the SS deceived the International Red Cross in 1944 upon its inspection in June 1944. Her personal narrative is amply illustrated with photos and drawings. Her poem with music score entitled "We Shall Never Forget" is included. The account ends with liberation on May 8, 1945, by the Soviet Red Army.

BARTOSZEWSKI, WLADYSLAW
(1922–)

Wladyslaw Bartoszewski was a Roman Catholic who shared the plight of the trapped Jews in the Warsaw Ghetto. After being arrested and sent to a concentration camp, he returned to Warsaw. Sympathetic with the plight of the Jews, he served as liaison between the Polish Underground and Jewish Resistance leaders. Bartoszewski was one of the founders of Zegota, the Council for Aid to the Jews. He participated in two uprisings, the Jewish Warsaw Uprising in April 1943 and the citywide Polish one of August 1944. After World War II he became a professor of history at the Catholic University in Lublin and an author of eighteen books, largely dealing with Poles and Jews under Nazi rule. Professor Bartoszewski has been awarded the Righteous of the Nations Award from the Jewish memorial agency in Jerusalem, Yad Vashem, for risking his life to save Jews.

The Warsaw Ghetto: A Christian Testimony. Boston: Beacon Press, 1987. 103 pp. ISBN: 0807056022. Ages 15–up. Memoir.

Bartoszewski provides the reader with a unique perspective on events in the Warsaw Ghetto. He tells how the Germans sought to destroy the Polish intelligentsia (he was a college student) and gives other background information on Nazi plans and policies in Poland. He quotes conversations with various Jewish leaders of the ghetto—Marek Edelman, Adolf Berman, and Adam Czernikow. He tells of his efforts on behalf of the Council for Aid to Jews and his meeting with the heroic Jan Karski, the Gentile Polish courier who alerted the Allies. In the epilogue Bartoszewski relates what happened to each of the main resisters of the Warsaw Ghetto. Mixed in with his personal narrative is objective history of the Holocaust in Poland and those Righteous Gentiles who tried to aid the doomed Jews at the risk of their own lives.

BERNBAUM, ISRAEL
(?–1988)

Bernbaum was born in Warsaw, Poland, to traditional Jewish parents. When the Nazis conquered his hometown, he managed to escape to the Soviet section of Poland. From there he went into the Soviet Union (today Russia) and spent the war years there. Bernbaum married, and after the war the couple lived in Paris, where he began art studies. In 1957 the Bernbaums came to the United States and had three sons. Bernbaum worked as a dental technician while he received his bachelor of arts degree from Queens College in New York City in 1973. He began a number of paintings on the Holocaust, including those dealing with the Warsaw Ghetto. The artist illustrated Holocaust books (see Auerbacher's *I Am a Star*) and devoted himself to presenting slide slows about the Holocaust based on his paintings. (See entry in art section.)

My Brother's Keeper: The Holocaust through the Eyes of an Artist. New York: G. P. Putnam's Sons, 1985. 63 pp. ISBN: 0399212426. Ages 10–13. Memoir.

The author uses his paintings of the Warsaw Ghetto and the Warsaw Uprising as the basis of chapters that tell the story. The work is highly personalized and didactic, addressed as if he were giving his talk to sixth- or seventh-grade children. Bernbaum focuses on Jewish resistance in the ghetto and the Poles' indifference to the horror inside the ghetto. However, he does mention the few Righteous Gentiles who tried to aid Jews. The beginning and closing chapters contain a great deal of historical information on the Third Reich. Bernbaum places his narrative in the context of a moral imperative to care for the persecuted and not be merely a bystander.

BERNSTEIN, SARA TUVEL
(1918–1983)

Bernstein was born in Transylvania, the border region between Hungary and Romania, to poor, nominally Jewish parents who embraced Hungarian culture. She left high school at age 13 to be apprenticed to a seamstress. She experienced anti-Semitism under Romanian rule and continued to face anti-Jewish sentiment when the area was transferred to Hungary in 1940. In spring 1944 the Germans invaded Hungary, and Sara and her sister were sent to the women's concentration camp, Ravensbruck. Her parents disappeared, probably taken by the Nazis. While she was being transferred from Ravensbruck, her train was bombed by Allied planes and, in the course of confusion, its prisoners liberated. Placed in a displaced persons camp, Feldafing in the American zone in occupied Germany, she reunited with her brother Eliezer. Both her brothers made their way to Israel, whereas Esther, her sister, immigrated to the United States. In 1948 Sara married a tailor, and the two immigrated to Canada. From Canada the couple moved to Chicago.

The Seamstress: A Memoir of Survival. New York: Berkley Publishing, 1997. 320 pp. ISBN: 0425166309. Ages 14–up. Memoir.

Sara, called Seren, grows up in a Romanian mountain village in one of those border areas that change hands with political fortunes, Transylvania. Her family is poor and Jewish, but more folkish rather than religiously observant. She accepts a scholarship to a public high school now under Hungarian rule as a result of Hitler's "readjustments" of borders. However, the teacher at the school is so openly anti-Semitic that she leaves school to become an apprentice to a seamstress in Budapest at the tender age of 13. In 1944, with the German invasion of Hungary, Seren is incarcerated for the crime of being Jewish, made to clean streets, and eventually, with her sister and a thousand others, marched out of the city. The sisters are sent to Ravensbruck, a women's concentration camp not far from Berlin. They befriend two other teenagers, and the four survive beatings, SS women, guards' cruelty, frostbite, and starvation. Seren's street smarts enable them to survive. Fearing the Russians closing in, the Nazis place Ravensbruck inmates on a train to Bavaria. The Americans liberate them on April 29, 1945. The autobiography ends with Sara's experience in a displaced persons camp in the American Zone of Occupation, Feldafing.

BETTELHEIM, BRUNO
(1903–1990)

The world-famous psychoanalyst was born in Vienna, Austria, of middle-class Jewish parents. He received his doctorate from the University of Vienna and became a follower of the Freudian school of psychiatry. In 1938, with the German annexation of Austria, Bettelheim was incarcerated in Dachau and later Buchenwald for one year. He was released upon the intervention of First Lady Eleanor Roosevelt and New York's Governor Herbert Lehman. He immediately came to the United States and took up residence in Chicago. The psychiatrist took a position as a professor in the Orthenogenic School, which studies emotionally disturbed children. Bettelheim became an expert on children's emotional disorders and treatment of such diseases. He wrote a major article on his camp experience, "Individual and Mass Behavior in Extreme Situations," which was accepted by the U.S. Army in 1943. *The Informed Heart* and the long essay "Surviving" deal directly with Bettelheim's concentration camp experience and his reflections on the meaning of it. Sickly, in a nursing home in California, he took his own life at age 87.

The Informed Heart: Autonomy in a Mass Age. New York: Avon, 1973. 292 pp. ISBN: 3080018150. Ages 16–up. Memoir.

The psychiatrist-author explores the choice between individualism and the security of mass society. He postulates that social forces are informally eroding the self-realization of the individual. This work reflects much of what Bettelheim wrote in his essay "Individual and Mass Behavior in Extreme Situations." It discusses the daily activities and life in concentration camps, the negative effect of the camps on the inmates, and what behaviors on the part of the inmates contributed to their own suffering. He mentions his own strategies of adjustment. He says that in 1939 the Final Solution was not yet in effect, that later inmates faced more difficult situations. In addition to criticizing the inmates' passivity, Bettelheim indicts European Jewry for docility and compliance, and he attacks Otto Frank, Anne's father, for not joining the Resistance, accusing Frank of having a death wish, passively awaiting his doom. Bettelheim goes on to analyze how National Socialist Germany was organized, how the state was reflected in the concentration camp, and how his own society showed certain tendencies toward acceptance. His appeal is that humans must not be like ants.

Surviving and Other Essays. New York: Random House, 1980. 432 pp. ISBN: 0394743648. Ages 16–up. Memoir.

The key essay in this book analyzes the movie *Seven Beauties*, a spoof on a comic figure in a concentration camp, and the book *The Survivor* by Terrence Des Pres, an examination of why inmates survived in both Soviet and Nazi camps. For Bettelheim, surviving alone was no virtue. Keeping one's moral integrity was. Losing one's dignity, he believes, would be worse than death. Bettelheim rails against *Seven Beauties'* death house comedy. Such works confuse aesthetic discrimination. The observer is induced not to take the murderous situation seriously. The psychiatrist notes that those who had strong religious conviction had a much higher chance of survival. His own experience in the camps informs him that cooperation rather than selfishness was more commonplace in the camps. According to Bettelheim, the situations described in the movie *Seven Beauties* are not credible and the characters are not believable, particularly the female commandant. She understood human nature too well, says the author, to commit such horrible acts. The man who threw himself into a sewer of waste rather than submit to continued indignities is the writer's hero. Bettelheim's critics believe that his views are unrealistic and border on a "blame the victim" psychology.

BITTEN-JACKSON, LIVIA (ELLI)
(1931–   )

Elli's life was dramatically changed by the German invasion of Hungary in March 1944. The 13-year-old Jewish Orthodox girl, her parents, and her brother were forced into a ghetto in April. Her father was placed in a labor camp, never to be heard from again. In May, Elli, her brother, and mother were sent to Auschwitz. Desperately needing labor for the German war machine, the rather fair "Aryan"-looking family was sent to various Auschwitz satellite work camps. Very near war's end, the family was herded onto a transport train, but American forces liberated them. Seeking their missing father, Elli and her brother, along with her mother, returned to their hometown, Samoria. Finding no relatives and the region's Jewish community destroyed, the family entered a displaced persons camp, a makeshift arrangement by Britain and the United States for those survivors unable or unwilling to live in their former homes. There Elli received her high school education. In 1951 she immigrated to New York City, where she received a doctorate in Jewish history from New York University. She became professor of Judaic studies at Herbert H. Lehman College of the City University of New York. In 1977 she married and made her home in Israel. She now teaches at Tel Aviv University.

Elli: Coming of Age in the Holocaust. New York: Times Books, 1980. 248 pp. ISBN: 0812908821. Ages 15–up. Memoir.

In this memoir Elli tells how life changed for her and her family in Hungary in 1944. In that year, when Elli was 13, the Nazis invaded Hungary, Germany's wartime ally, and immediately perpetrated Jewish genocide. The pattern is familiar: ghettoization, deportation, selection at a camp, and, if healthy enough, hard labor. Dr. Josef Mengele, a major examining Nazi physician who decides who will live and who will die in Auschwitz, taken by Elli's and her mother's blonde hair, blue eyes, and perfect German, selects them for life, that is, for slave labor rather than for the gas chambers. Elli and her mother go to the Jewish section of Auschwitz, Birkenau, and are then transshipped to labor camps. Unlike writers of many similar narratives, Elli is very religious, and her strong convictions remain with her in the camps. She explains Jewish traditions to the reader and tries to observe what she can inside the camps. When her mother becomes extremely sick, Elli manages to nurse her back to health. Miraculously, mother, daughter, and brother are placed on a train later liberated by the Americans. The father, also deported, manages to survive until the last two days before liberation, then dies. The family returns to their hometown only to find it decimated of Jews. They recognize that life for Jews with anti-Semitism and communist rule is not for them and they must leave.

I Have Lived a Thousand Years: Growing up in the Holocaust. New York: Simon & Schuster, 1997. 234 pp. ISBN: 0689823959. Ages 11–14. Memoir.

This memoir is basically the same story as *Elli: Coming of Age in the Holocaust,* but it is adapted for middle-school readers. The book tells more about the aftermath of liberation from the concentration camp experience, particularly in the displaced persons camp. Also added are a glossary and a timeline of events both in Elli's life and the Holocaust.

BLUMENTHAL, W. MICHAEL
(1926–1990)

Blumenthal was born in Berlin, Germany, to assimilated middle-class Jewish parents from a distinguished family. He endured the increasing Nazi oppression until 1939, when he and his parents fled to Shanghai, China. Conquered by the Japanese, Shanghai was a city that admitted Jews freely in hope that world Jewry would influence President Franklin Delano Roosevelt to a policy of noninterference in the Far East. Blumenthal stayed in the Honkew Ghetto, outside Shanghai, set up for Jews by the Japanese, from 1939 to 1947; he then immigrated to the United States, where he attended Princeton University, earning a Ph.D. in business. After a successful business career in which he rose to become CEO of the Bendix Corporation, he was chosen by President Jimmy Carter to serve as secretary of the treasury (1977–1979).

The Invisible Wall: The Mystery of the Germans and Jews. New York: Contemporary Press, 1999. 444 pp. ISBN: 1582430128. Ages 16–up. Memoir.

The Invisible Wall reaches into Blumenthal's family tree to spotlight five men and one woman. In nineteenth-century Prussia, with emancipation—the granting of complete civil and economic rights to Jews—Jews became highly assimilated, taking on German identity with a passion. Blumenthal interweaves his family's personal history with German Jewish history and general German history growing out of the characters he describes, two of whom are well known in their own right—Rachel Varnhagen, the hostess of a famous salon, and Giacomo Meyerbeer, the outstanding opera composer. The writer tries to explain why, after such a promising beginning in the mid-nineteenth century, German Jewry experienced such a tragic end. He gives a complicated answer—an authoritarian tradition, the absence of Jews from critical power centers, pervasive social anti-Semitism, and the humiliation of defeat in World War I. In the last part of the book he tells of his father's and his own experience in Nazi Germany and of his flight to Shanghai.

BONHOEFFER, DIETRICH
(1906–1945)

The future theologian was born in Breslau, Prussia (now Wroclaw, Poland), to a religious Protestant family. His father was a distinguished psychiatrist and university professor. He studied theology at the University of Berlin and earned his doctorate at age 21. Soon after, Dietrich became a minister and a pastor in Spain. In 1930 he pursued his studies at New York City's Union Theological Seminary; then in 1931 he returned to Berlin to lecture and with Pastor Martin Niemoeller to create the Pastor's Emergency League, a foil to the increasingly powerful Nazi attempt to make Protestant churches racist. With Hitler's rise to power, he moved to London to work for German churches there. With the establishment of the Confessional Church (a Lutheran evangelical denomination that maintained tradition while the other churches were Nazified), he returned to Germany, where he taught in their seminary, and wrote on religious topics. Admiral Wilhelm Canaris, head of the German army's counterspy agency, Abwehr, recruited Bonhoeffer, who became a courier for Abwehr and stayed under Canaris's protection while acting against the Nazi regime. On April 5 Bonhoeffer was arrested by the Gestapo and placed in prison. After the unsuccessful July 20 plot against Hitler's life in which he was implicated, the pastor was eventually sent to Flossenburg concentration camp. On April 9, 1945, Bonhoeffer, only 39, was executed by hanging on Hitler's orders.

Letters and Papers from Prison. Eberhard Bethge, editor. New York: Simon & Schuster, 1997. 422 pp. ISBN: 0684838273. Ages 16–up. Diary.

This book consists of a series of letters from Dietrich Bonhoeffer while he was imprisoned by the Nazis from April 1943 to April 1945. They deal with mundane family matters and very deep theological concerns. In terms of the latter, the book is most well known for its "religionless" Christianity. He is for a selfless person who seeks no personal gain by being religious, meaning no consideration of a heavenly hereafter, no rewards while living, but who carries out his faith and commitment to the world completely altruistically. He insists that people of faith must stand for truth at all times. Despite his fear and loneliness, he never loses faith in God. As for the former, included in this collection are Bonhoeffer's cheerful love letters to his fiancée Maria von Wedemeyer. Bonhoeffer also describes the life of ordinary civilians under bombardments and the gradual disintegration of life in wartime Germany. His theological thoughts were transmitted to Eberhard Bethge, a colleague, clergyman, and friend. It was he who collected these letters, edited them, and had them published.

BOROWSKI, TADEUSZ
(1922–1951)

Borowski, a poet and a political journalist, was born in Zytomierz, Poland, to Catholic parents. When the border town fell into Soviet hands in 1926, his parents were arrested by the secret police (NKVD) and sent off to a slave labor camp in Siberia. Tadeusz, then only 4 years old, was raised by impoverished strangers. Reunited with his parents in the late 1930s, he moved to Warsaw during the Nazi occupation (1940). He wrote poetry, and in 1942 his collection of poems, *Wherever the Land*, led to his deportation to Auschwitz. He was lucky enough to be assigned a job as a hospital orderly. This gave him a front seat to the maltreatment of prisoners and mass executions of Jews in 1943–1945. Sent to Dachau as the Soviet Red Army approached, he was liberated from that camp by Americans in April 1945. From 1948 to 1951, Borowski served as a Stalinist political journalist and intelligence agent for the East German secret police. Overwhelmed by guilt for having survived the atrocities of that regime, he committed suicide in 1951.

This Way for the Gas, Ladies and Gentlemen. Barbara Vedder, compiler and translator. New York: Penguin Press, 1976. 180 pp. ISBN: 0140186247. Ages 15–up. Fiction.

This anthology of episodic stories covers life in the Auschwitz concentration camp. Although fictional, the tales are based largely on Borowski's personal experiences. The author, taking the persona of Tadek, is part of a work detail (labor kommando) that facilitates the unloading of Jews destined for murder by gassing. He is in the area of the camp where he can see the line of the doomed moving to the gas chambers and crematoria. The stories are filled with antiheroes, individuals who must make choices that result in great injustices. Of course, the SS authorities and the camp system impose these horrible choices to dehumanize the inmates. Like Hannah Arendt, the social and political theorist, Borowski points out the banality of evil—that ordinary men and women merely do their jobs, coolly indifferent to the terrible activities in which they are engaging. Borowski implies that the camp system dehumanizes all those involved in it. The stories' themes reflect the despair and humiliation that characterize life in the camp.

DELBO, CHARLOTTE
(1913–1985)

Writer, poet, and dramatist Charlotte Delbo was born in Vigneux-sur-Seine near Paris. She worked as an assistant to a theater impresario and was on tour when the Germans occupied France in 1940. She returned to Paris in November 1941 to rejoin her husband, Georges Dudach, who was working in the Resistance. In March 1942 the police arrested both and turned them over to the Gestapo. Dudach was executed, whereas Charlotte remained in prisons until she was sent to Auschwitz. She stayed there until January 1944; then she was sent to Ravensbruck, a camp where Gentile women like her were incarcerated. Himmler, head of the SS, negotiated a deal as the Nazi armies were collapsing. In spring 1945, as a result of the efforts of Sweden's Count Folke Bernadette, vice president of the Red Cross, Delbo and a few thousand other Ravensbruck inmates were rescued and sent to Sweden. Delbo then returned to Paris and wrote of her wartime experiences until her death.

Auschwitz and After. Rosette C. Lamont, translator. New Haven, CT: Yale University Press, 1997. 354 pp. ISBN: 0300076578. Ages 15–up. Memoir.

This book is an anthology of Delbo's writings, containing *None of Us Will Return, Useless Knowledge*, and *The Measure of Our Days*. The first, *None of Us Will Return*, written in 1946, is prose poetry using sense memory that expresses unimaginable anguish. It describes extreme cruelty inflicted by Nazi guards on Frenchwomen. The memoir lapses into pure poetry at times, then poetry and prose. The paragraphs are short and simple, with blow by blow descriptions of Delbo's arrival and persecution at Auschwitz.

The second work, *Useless Knowledge*, is straight narrative. It tells of Delbo's arrest and French prison experience. Then it relates events at Auschwitz, a trip as a prisoner through Berlin, and finally the women's camp, Ravensbruck. A Gentile, she describes the fate of fellow Gentile deportees, both men and women. Her release from Ravensbruck, negotiated by Swedish vice president of the Red Cross Count Folke Bernadette, is described. Delbo includes poetry with themes of despair and death.

The third work, a memoir, *The Measure of Our Days*, unlike the first two written soon after the war, was composed near the end of her life in the 1980s. She claims she is two selves, her present one and one with the memory of the camps that she cannot shake. "I died at Auschwitz," she states, "but nobody knows it." Again, Delbo blends sad poetry and prose. "I cannot escape the realm of death." She does not remarry, but her father does. Delbo returns to France and locates the French police officer who arrested her, but she descides not to press charges, learning that the man became a member of the Resistance.

Convoy to Auschwitz: Women in the French Resistance. Carol Cosman, translator. Boston: Northeastern University Press, 1997. 224 pp. ISBN: 1555533132. Ages 15–up. Memoir.

Author Charlotte Delbo was one of 230 women political prisoners deported to Auschwitz on January 24, 1943, who survived. The Resistance prisoners came from all regions of France and from a wide range of social and political backgrounds. In this account Delbo lists the names, numbers, family members, and fates of these 230 women. The life history of each woman from her childhood to her involvement in the Resistance, her arrest, and her experiences in concentration camps is recorded. The writer includes appendices on the relationship between survival and age, profession, and political affiliation. The original work was in French in 1963 entitled *Le convoi du 24 Janvier*. Translation of Delbo's work into English and appreciation of it has come after her death in 1985.

Days and Memory. Rosette C. Lamont, translator. New York: Marlboro Press, 1990. 122 pp. ISBN: 0910395551. Ages 15–up. Memoir.

This memoir, originally published in French soon after the author's death in 1985, is testimony to the atrocities experienced by countless sufferers during World War II. Here Delbo sketches persecuted women and kapo cruelty (kapos were prisoner trustee collaborators). She objectively narrates their tales of woe. She also relates stories of what happened in other countries such as Greece, where in one village the Germans shot all the men, whose mothers, wives, sisters, and daughters then had to find a burial place for 1,300 bodies. Delbo agrees with Holocaust writer Primo Levi, "Prisoners expected the worst, but not the unthinkable."

DRUCKER, OLGA ("OLLIE") LEVY
(1928–   )

"Ollie" was born to an assimilated, wealthy Jewish family in Stuttgart, Germany. Her father was a book publisher; her mother, a homemaker. She spent the first ten years of her childhood under the growing erosion of rights of Jews and persecution by the Nazi regime. During this time she left public school and went to an all-Jewish school. Her father was placed in Dachau concentration camp during Kiystallnacht, the night of widespread attacks on Jews and their property on November 9, 1938. Upon his return in December, all the family's property was confiscated. In 1939 her mother placed her on the Kindertransport, the program for German and Austrian Jewish children to go to England to live in foster care to escape Hitler. In England she was united with her brother, who had escaped earlier. Nethertheless, Ollie had to endure a number of poor situations. Fortunately, she was reunited in America with her parents in 1945. Ollie married Rolf Drucker, an engineer, in 1950 and had three children. The family moved to New York City. After earning an M.A. at Adelphi University, Ollie started the Audio Video Engineering Company in Merrick, New York. She is now a lecturer and author of children's books.

Kindertransport. New York: Henry Holt, 1995. 197 pp. ISBN: 0805042512. Ages 9–12. Memoir.

Ollie just turned 11 when her mother, with the help of the Jewish Refugee Committee, placed her aboard the Kindertransport. This program for 10,000 children escaping the Greater Reich for England would not take adults, so Ollie was all alone. The autobiography starts with the growing persecution of Jews by the Nazis and shows how Ollie's life changed from that of a well-to-do, pampered child to one living in fear. Kristallnacht, that terrible attack on Jews, prompted her mother to send Ollie away. Early in 1939 she traveled to England and moved through a series of foster homes, many not very pleasant. She saw her brother (slightly older than she) only once. He had escaped Germany shortly before Ollie. The writer relates events in wartime England and her interruption of school life. Eventually, she is required to work rather than permitted to be a schoolgirl. The narrative ends happily at war's end, though, with the discovery that her parents had survived and had made their way to the United States. Reunited in New York, father, mother, sister, and brother all live together.

ELIACH, YAFFA
(1935–   )

Eliach was born to Orthodox parents in the village of Eishyshok, Lithuania. With the German invasion all the Jews of this town, or shtetl, were murdered; however, Eliach, her parents, and brother managed to escape and remain hidden during the war. At war's end the family returned to the shtetl only to have Yaffa's father arrested and sent away to Siberia by the Soviet rulers and her mother and brother brutally murdered by the native anti-Semites. Eliach was taken to the safety of Israel by her uncle. In 1954 she immigrated to the United States and earned her Ph.D. in Russian intellectual history. She became a professor of history and literature at Brooklyn College, married David Eliach, a rabbi, and raised three children. She also established the Center for Holocaust Studies in a Brooklyn Yeshiva. Eliach constructed the Tower of Life exhibit at the United States Holocaust Memorial Museum in Washington, D.C., made up of 1,600 photographs from the shtetl. She is the author of a 900-page history book entitled *There Once Was a World: A Nine-Hundred-Year Chronicle of the Shtetl of Eishyshok*.

Hasidic Tales of the Holocaust. New York: Oxford University Press, 1982. 266 pp. ISBN: 0195031997. Ages 15–up. Fiction and nonfiction.

Hasidism, a religious and social movement that spread throughout Jewish communities of Eastern Europe in the mid-eighteenth century, continues even today. It is ultra-Orthodox Judaism based on emotional experiences, prayer through joy, dancing, and fervor with a mixture of mysticism. The followers, Hasidim, revere their Zaddik, righteous man, also called a Rebbe. The disciples believe the Rebbe's unique qualities enable him to come closer to God than can mere humans, and this closeness qualifies him to mediate between the Lord and humanity. He may do this by means of a blessing, a prayer, vows, amulets, and seemingly miracle working. Eliach has conducted eighty-nine interviews with rabbis, wives of rabbis, and Hasidim to hear stories about incidents during the Holocaust in which a Rebbe seemingly wrought a minor miracle that rescued a Jew. Many of the tales revolve around a holiday celebrated under the Nazi heel, whether in a ghetto or a concentration camp or during an Aktion—a Nazi raid against Jews. Some tales relate to a sacred or religious object such as a shofar, Hanukkah lamp, or Seder cup. Others are straight stories of survival. Eliach tells the reader at the conclusion of each very short tale the source of the material and the date of the interview. The notes on the back matching each entry provide the reader with much information about Judaism and Jewish lore. The writer also provides a glossary and an index.

FENELON, FANIA (GOLDSTEIN)
(1918–1983)

Fania Goldstein was born in Paris, France, of a Catholic mother and a Jewish father. Her father died when Fania was a teenager, and her elder brother immigrated to America. During World War II Fania and a younger brother joined the French Resistance after the conquest of France in 1940. The Gestapo arrested Fania in Paris after an informer alerted the secret police in May 1943. After mistreatment in prison she was taken to Drancy, a holding camp, and after nine months transported to Birkenau. At this adjunct camp to Auschwitz she sang a rendition from *Madame Butterfly*, which gained Fania access to the camp's all-girl orchestra. As a singer she survived the Holocaust. Just before the Soviet Red Army closed in on Auschwitz in January 1945, Fania was deported to Bergen-Belsen, the camp from which the British liberated her on April 15, 1945. After this Holocaust experience Fania resumed her career as a singer–entertainer for twenty-five years.

Playing for Time. With Marcelle Router and Judy Landry, translators. Syracuse, NY: Syracuse University Press, 1997. 304 pp. ISBN: 0815604947. Ages 15–up. Memoir.

Singer-survivor Fania Fenelon relates her experiences during 1943–1945 when she was arrested for Resistance activity against the Nazis and incarcerated. The focus of *Playing for Time* is on her activities as a member of an all-female orchestra, the only one of its kind in the vast Nazi concentration camp system. Fannie reveals much of what other eyewitnesses have seen at the infamous Auschwitz complex. New is information on the sadistic Maria Mandel, an SS matron noted for murderous activity against inmates. She basically saved Fannie's life and is seen as a music lover. This memoir also tells about the courageous escapees Mala Zimelbaum and Edele Kalinsky, members of the camp Underground. Fenelon crosses paths several times with SS Commandant Joseph Kramer, whom she meets at both Birkenau and Bergen-Belsen.

Because of her unique position as an orchestra member, Fannie does not detail the most grotesque horrors of the camps but profiles people whom she encounters. However, the reader can surmise how near death she was, for upon liberation by the British on April 15, 1945, Fenelon weighed only 56 pounds and was ill with typhus.

A television program was produced based on the book.

FINK, IDA (LANDAU)
(1921–   )

Ida Landau was born in Zbarezh, Poland, near the Ukrainian border. She was the daughter of highly educated parents: Her father was a physician and her mother a high school teacher. Before World War II interrupted her studies, she attended a high school that specialized in music. When Nazi Germany invaded the Soviet Union in 1941, Jews in the town were put in a ghetto. Ida and her sister were fortunate, for their father had provided a hiding place outside of town and false papers for the two sisters. The two spent the war in hiding. In 1948 Landau married Bruno Fink, an engineer, and the couple had one child, Miriam. Unhappy in communist Ukraine—the region of eastern Poland where they lived had been incorporated into the Soviet Union—the family managed to immigrate to Israel. Ida worked for Yad Vashem, the Holocaust memorial institution in Jerusalem. After being employed there as a librarian, in 1982 she became a freelance writer. She is noted for two collections of short stories, largely semiautobiographical—*A Scrap of Time* and *Traces*—and a novel, *The Journey*, all written in Polish.

> *The Journey*. Joanna Weschler and Francine Prose, translators. New York: Farrar, Straus, Giroux, 1992. 224 pp. ISBN: 0374285411. Ages 14–up. Fiction.

This is Fink's second work, a novel about two sisters who survive World War II with forged Aryan identity papers obtained by their father, which is exactly what happened to Ida and her sister. The girls impersonate impoverished Polish farm workers on their way to volunteer for labor in Germany. This novel describes the poor conditions for foreign workers in German factories. They have many close calls, many narrow escapes, and occasions when they must take on new identities. Suspected of being Jewish, the girls are denounced to authorities. By sheer luck and the help of some kind souls they managed to escape. In spring 1945, French soldiers liberate the region, and the sisters are reunited with their father. The narrator, a sister with the assumed name Katarzyna, tells the girls' harrowing story of survival.

> *A Scrap of Time and Other Stories*. Madeline Levine and Francine Prose, translators. Evanston, IL: Northwestern University Press, 1995. 165 pp. ISBN: 0805045570. Ages 14–up. Fiction.

This work, Fink's first book, a collection of twenty-two stories and a play written in Polish, was published in English in 1987. The title story tells how Nazi atrocities shattered normal life in Poland. The narrator tells of a young boy peering out of the safety of a locked room, watching as the Germans round up and wantonly murder his fellow Jews. In other stories, survivors helplessly look on, unable to save loved ones. Fink relates their great guilt. Other stories illustrate those people who cannot identify with the pain of others. The final piece is a play entitled *The Table*, an interrogation that takes place twenty-five years after the war. Jewish victims are questioned about the identity of a killer who shot Jews. The play illustrates the great gap between legal evidence, cold logic, and emotion, the former demanding evidence that cannot be given well after the fact of war.

Traces. Philip Boehm and Francine Prose, translators. New York: Metropolitan Books, 1997. 210 pp. ISBN: 0805045570. Ages 14–up. Fiction.

Fink deals with events both during and after the Holocaust in this collection of twenty-one short stories. The collection begins in September 1939 with the German invasion of Poland. The first story, "The End," describes the intrusion of marching invaders on the lives of two Polish lovers who pretend they do not hear the rumbling tanks moving down the streets and act as if the invasion is not happening. "Traces," the nineteenth story from which the book's title is taken, takes its title from the scraps of information that remain behind when survivors seek to find out what happened to their loved ones. For example, a woman searching for her sister discovers the sister's initials carved on a windowsill. Fink's survivors are traumatized by Nazi crimes. One woman does nothing but laugh after coming out of confinement in a barn for a year. "Cheerful" is the title of this tale. Fink's stories are anything but cheerful.

FLINKER, MOSHE
(1926–1944)

Moshe was born in the Hague, Holland, one of seven children in a devoutly Jewish family. He attended public school and received private religious and Hebrew lessons. When the Nazis occupied Holland in 1940, the family moved secretly to Brussels, Belgium. There no one knew the Flinkers, so Moshe felt safe for a while. The Gestapo caught up with them, however, and all were sent to Auschwitz on April 7, 1944. Six sisters and one brother survived. He and his parents perished. Moshe's entries start when he was 16 years of age, on November 24, 1942, and end September 6, 1943. Moshe left his copybooks, in which he kept his diary, in the cellar of the house where the family hid. At war's end the sisters rescued his writings.

Young Moshe's Diary: The Spiritual Torment of a Jewish Boy in Nazi Europe. Saul Esh, editor-translator. Jerusalem: Board of Jewish Education and Yad Vashem, 1971. 126 pp. No ISBN. Ages 16–up. Diary.

This, diary, originally in Hebrew, is unusual because it discusses the author's spiritual torment and his grappling with the problems of suffering and divine justice. Unlike many diarists, the writer is very religious, very observant, and thus infuses his entries with a great deal of Jewish religious thought. (A glossary helps the reader.) His diary also contains original short poems and original prayers. In a number of entries the teenager does record the Nazis' activities and his personal experiences. Moshe is aware of the deportations but not fully aware of the ramifications. He believes in a Jewish future and sees one where he is a Jewish diplomat in a Jewish state (Moshe is a strong Zionist). Although like Job in the Bible he questions God while keeping his faith, his last entries show weariness. This is a diary filled with religious philosophizing.

FRANKL, VIKTOR
(1905–1997)

The famous Jewish psychiatrist Viktor Frankl was born in Vienna. Alfred Adler, a disciple of Freud, mentored him. He soon split with Adler to develop his own view of basic motivation, or humans' inner search for meaning in life. He attended the University of Vienna and graduated as a psychiatrist. The young doctor stayed with his family and wife in Vienna when Nazi Germany annexed Austria in March 1938. The Nazis placed Frankl's entire family in concentration camps: His mother, father, brother, and wife all died in them; only he and his sister survived. After World War II and the defeat of Nazi Germany, he returned to Vienna and took a position as a psychiatrist at the University of Vienna Medical School. He visited the United States and became visiting clinical professor at Stanford University and at Harvard University's summer school. He was the leader and originator of the school of logotherapy, also called existential analysis, which treats people with depression by calling attention to a purpose or goal they have in life. The doctor's own suffering and degradation in Auschwitz and Dachau refined his theory of logotherapy. Frankl was the author of over thirty-one books on his theories.

Man's Search for Meaning. Ilse Lash, translator. New York: Simon & Schuster, 1984. 154 pp. ISBN: 0671244221. Ages 15–up. Memoir.

Part 1 of this memoir of three at Auschwitz and Dachau deals with the author's experiences at the camps. It not only tells what happened to him but also explores his and the inmates' mental reactions to these experiences. He came to the conclusion that "he who has a why to live can bear with almost any how." The author was impressed with those inmates who met their sufferings with dignity. To test his theories while in the camps the Viennese existentialist practiced on inmates, giving them a reason to live and not despair, finding something or someone for whom they should survive. He reminded a professor that he should live so he could publish his manuscript on his theories. He persuaded a grandmother that she must survive to raise her grandchild. The second part of this work deals with logotherapy as interpreted by the camp experience. Frankl states that the last human freedom is the ability to choose one's attitude in a given set of circumstances. He sees as the root of neurosis the failure of the sufferer to see meaning and responsibility in his existence. As a foil to the Nazi attempts to dehumanize people, logotherapy attempts to humanize psychiatry.

FRY, VARIAN
(1907–1967)

Varian Fry was born to a wealthy Gentile family in Ridgewood, New Jersey. He attended prep school and went on to Harvard to receive a classical education, mastering a number of languages. He then attended Columbia University, majoring in international affairs and journalism. In 1935 he became editor of a current affairs magazine, then went on to edit educational tracts on conditions in foreign countries for the Foreign Policy Association. After a trip to Nazi Germany, Varian became active in American Friends of German Freedom. The German defeat of France in 1940 put in great danger many artists and intellectuals who had sought refuge in France. Vichy France, the rump state set up after the French defeat, agreed to repatriate to the Nazis German, Austrian, and Czech nationals, most of whom were Jewish and wanted by the Gestapo. Fry became an agent of the Emergency Rescue Committee charged with bringing out these wanted individuals before the Gestapo jailed them. At age 32, for twelve months he rescued 4,000 until he was sent home by the U.S. State Department. After the war he held various writing and editing jobs for left-wing periodicals, but he quit, objecting to their pro-Soviet policies. He died in 1967 of a cerebral hemorrhage, at the time holding a job teaching Latin in a Connecticut high school.

Surrender on Demand. Boulder, CO: Johnson Books, in cooperation with the U.S. Holocaust Memorial Museum, Washington DC, 1997. 273 pp. ISBN: 1555662099. Ages 15–up. Memoir.

President Franklin Delano Roosevelt yielded to his wife, Eleanor, and reluctantly allowed Varian Fry, an editor and journalist, to go to Marseilles, France, with 200 visas. Fry acted as a representative of the Emergency Rescue Committee, an ad hoc agency set up to rescue political, artistic, and intellectual anti-Nazis from the hands of the Gestapo. Fry also worked with the American Friends Service Committee and the Salvation Army. His first-person rescue story is called "Surrender on Demand" because that was a provision of the armistice agreed on by the

defeated French Republic in June 1940 to be carried out by the collaborationist French government, called Vichy, headed by Marshall Petain.
American agent Fry, who had no diplomatic experience and faced ob-
struction by the American consulate in Marseilles, purchased passports,
visas, and entry passes from other consuls. When those sources became
exhausted, Fry smuggled refugees over the Pyrenees to Spain. Although
in Vichy to save only 200 in just a month, Fry is credited with rescuing
4,000 during his stay of fourteen months (1940–1941). Many prominent
writers, artists, scholars, and political leaders, largely Jewish, were rescued before Fry was expelled by the French authorities with the hearty
approval of the U.S. State Department. Varian Fry is the only American
recognized as a Righteous Gentile by Yad Vashem, the Jerusalem-based
Holocaust memorial institution. The award is given only to those who
under the threat of death risked their lives to save Jews.

An easier reading middle-school book that follows the *Surrender on
Demand* narrative put out by the U.S. Holocaust Memorial Museum, *As-
signment Rescue: The Story of Varian Fry and the Emergency Rescue Committee* is available as well as a video with the same title.

GASTFRIEND, EDWARD ("LOLEK")
(1926–   )

"Lolek," as Gastfriend was nicknamed in Polish, was born to a pious
Jewish family, one of eight children in Sosnowiec, Poland. His father was
a tailor and uniform merchant. Lolek attended Jewish religious school
and Polish public school. He was only 12 years old when the German
aggressors occupied his town. The boy endured ghettoization and a
number of concentration camps as well as a death march in his seven
years under Nazi rule. His longest stay was in Blechhammer as a slave
laborer in a chemical factory. Lolek escaped a death march and was
picked up by Soviet Red Army soldiers. Except for two brothers, his
immediate and extended family perished under the Germans. Returning
briefly to his hometown, he saw the world he once knew was lost, so
Gastfriend made his way to the American Zone of Occupation in Germany and resided in a displaced persons camp. In 1947 he immigrated
to Philadelphia in the United States and in 1952 he married Marilyn
Weisman and fathered three children. He earned his living as a pro-
prietor of a men's haberdashery. Now retired, Edward devotes his time
to Holocaust commemoration and education. Chairman of the Association of Holocaust Survivors in Philadelphia, he was a prime mover in
establishing a statue and memorial, the site of annual Yom HaShoah
commemoration, at 16th Street and the Parkway. Gastfriend also spear-
headed the creation of Philadelphia's Interfaith Council, which has an

annual three-day program of the Holocaust at various colleges reaching 2,400 high school students from public and parochial schools. The council encourages youth from Germany to learn and work in Jewish institutions in the Quaker City.

My Father's Testament: Memoir of a Jewish Teenager, 1938–1945. Introduction by David Gastfriend and Afterword by Bjorn Krondorfer. Philadelphia: Temple University Press, 2000. 187 pp. ISBN: 1566397359. Ages 15–up. Memoir.

Gastfriend tells us that the testament is the writer's promise never to denounce God and to maintain his Jewish faith. This promise was the key to his psychic survival throughout the torments of ghetto life, in hiding, as part of the Resistance, in slave labor camps, and on a death march. This is the firm belief of Edward Gastfriend's son David, a psychiatrist who writes the introduction. Eddie keeps his humanity, even protecting a German Gentile, a teenager about to raped. The narrative reveals how industry officials, particularly at the chemical plant at Blechhammer, lost their humanity in cruel and complicit behavior in implementing the Final Solution. It also tells how the Wehrmacht (regular German army) as well as the SS guarded camp inmates. At a number of slave labor sites Gastfriend is surprised by the extent of the hatred and hostility of German civilians who have the opportunity to see the unfortunates. Gastfriend notes the differences among the camps and analyzes the various prisoners and guards he encounters.

In an unusual afterword Bjorn Krondorfer, a teacher of philosophy and religion at St. Mary's College of Maryland, relates how he returns with his father to the Blechhammer region, where the elder was stationed as a teenager during the war. The story juxtaposes Gastfriend, the teenage prisoner, with Krondorfer, the teenage antiaircraft soldier, at the slave labor chemical plant site. The German soldier was just a bystander and rather bemused by the prisoners at the time. The elder Krondorfer has refused to meet with Eddie, although the Wehrmacht soldier has talked to other survivors. Bjorn had come to Philadelphia under the aegis of the Interfaith Council.

Gastfriend decided to write his memoirs after fifty-five years because of an increase in Holocaust deniers and hatemongers and to provide eyewitness testimony to the greatest crime of the century.

GAY, PETER (FREHLICH)
(1923–)

The writer, known in Germany where he was born as Peter Frehlich, spent his formative years in the Berlin of the 1930s. Light-haired, blue-eyed, and culturally assimilated like his parents, he was nominally Jewish. His father was in business with a Gentile partner. With Hitler's advent to power in 1933, the antireligious Frehlichs found they were considered, not Germans, but Jews. Peter attended public schools and was an outstanding student until he was expelled for his religion in 1938. Under increasing threats by the government and neighbors, the family immigrated to Cuba in April 1939, then to New York City. Peter earned degrees at the University of Denver, at Columbia, and at Yale. He also trained as a psychoanalyst. In 1959 he married Ruth Slotkin and cared for his three stepchildren. He became a professor of cultural history at Yale, specializing in Victorian culture and biographies of Sigmund Freud.

My German Question: Growing up in Nazi Berlin. New Haven, CT: Yale University Press, 1999. 256 pp. ISBN: 0300080700. Ages 16–up. Memoir.

This memoir deals with the author's experiences and state of mind in the capital of the Third Reich during 1933–1939. He entitles the work *My German Question* to a parody the Nazi referral to Jews as "The Jewish Question." Jews were no problem to Germany, but Germany became a problem for Jews.

Gay tries to explain why families such as his did not get out of Hitler's Germany right away: They were so assimilated and immersed in German culture that they could not believe their lives could be threatened. They were astounded that their friends and fellow Berliners could become so hostile. The memoir tells of Gay's daily life and his interaction with events such as the Nuremberg laws, which deprived Jews of their German citizenship; the 1936 Olympics; Kristallnacht, the November 9, 1938, riots against Jewish homes, businesses, and institutions; and the refusal of other countries to offer refuge to Jews. Finally, in 1939 the family is able to flee to Cuba. Destitute, Peter's father works at any menial job to survive in Cuba and later New York.

GIES, MIEP
(1909–)

Miep was born in Vienna, Austria, and lived with her poor working-class parents, her two uncles, and her grandmother. After World War I, with the defeat and breakup of the Austro-Hungarian Empire, Miep, sickly and undernourished, was sent to the Netherlands on a special program to be revitalized. A kindly Leiden family "adopted" her. She went to a Dutch high school and became assimilated into Dutch life. Remaining in Holland, at age 24 she answered an ad to be an assistant in a spice import firm run by Otto Frank in Amsterdam. With the German occupation of Holland from 1940 onward, life for Jews in the Netherlands became more and more difficult. In 1942 Otto Frank's daughter Margo, only 16, was summoned to be deported. Frank decided to go into hiding with his family at an annex on top of his place of business. Miep Gies was now a dear friend of the family, as was her husband, Jan. She became the main link of the Frank family to the outside world and provided them with their sustenance. In 1944 the Frank family was discovered by the Gestapo and sent to concentration camps. Only Otto Frank, the father, survived. It was Miep who rescued Anne Frank's diary and gave it to Otto Frank upon his return from Auschwitz. Otto Frank lived with Gies and her husband for seven years after the war. In 1947 she resigned her job at the spice warehouse, and in 1949, at age 40, she had her first child.

Anne Frank Remembered: The Story of the Woman Who Helped to Hide the Frank Family. With Alison Leslie Gold. New York: Simon & Schuster, 1987. 252 pp. ISBN: 067154771. Ages 13–up. Memoir.

This memoir provides the reader with much new information not found in previous sources. It tells about Dutch collaboration with the Nazis as well as Resistance and aid to Jews. It tells more about Margo and about Edith, Anne's mother, than other works and reveals that there were many burglaries of the warehouse while the Franks were in the attic. It relates how Anne and Margo helped with clerical work in the evening downstairs in the warehouse. Miep and her husband, Jan, were in constant danger by their sheltering of Jews. They also sheltered another person elsewhere. Exposure meant death for both of them. The memoir provides details on Jewish life and danger in the former Jewish quarter of Amsterdam and explains how she aided the Franks. The latter part of the book tells about the fate of the diary and how Gies rescued it and gave it to her boarder, Otto Frank, who lived in her apartment for seven years after the war. She reveals how there was little interest by the war-weary Dutch in the Dutch railroad workers' resistance strike against the Germans in anticipation of an Allied advance in the fall and winter of 1944. The suffering made them callous toward Anne's annex problems. Gies does not speculate on who gave the Frank family away. Twenty-two photos, mainly of the Franks, add to the memoir.

GROSSMAN, CHAIKA
(1921–1996)

Resistance fighter Grossman was born in Bialystok, Poland, to parents of modest means. She joined the nonreligious Zionist-Socialist HaShomer

Hatzair and studied at the University of Vilna and later at the University of Tel Aviv. She returned to Vilna and with the German occupation, went underground. Able to procure false identification papers, Grossman could move around as a Polish Gentile woman. Abba Kovner, a leader in the Vilna Ghetto Resistance, chose her to be a delegate, a courier, and an organizer of resistance in Vilna and other ghettos. It was she who was the prime organizer of the Bialystok revolt in 1943. After a bloody battle she managed to escape and continue Resistance activity in the forests as a partisan. In 1948 she immigrated to Israel and worked there with Jewish refugees. In 1963 she was elected to the Israeli Parliament.

The Underground Army: Fighters of the Bialystok Ghetto. Sol Lewis, editor; Shmuel Beeri, translator. New York: Schocken Books, 1977. 426 pp. ISBN: 0896040539. Ages 16–up. Memoir.

This autobiographical narrative deals with the years 1937 to 1944. Chaika Grossman's story begins in Vilna and moves on to other sites— Warsaw, Lublin, Grodno, Volkovysk, and finally Bialystok. The heart of the memoir recalls the Bialystok revolt against the German oppressors. Grossman tells of the bravery of the Resistance fighters, many of whom were women. She speaks much of Abba Kovner, the famous poet and leader in Vilna, as the one who charged her with organizing a Resistance mission. In Bialystok she organized in tandem with Mordecai Anielewicz the revolt in that city. She rallied the dwellers in a desperate attack at the time of deportation. Escaping the enemy cordon in a firefight with SS troops who greatly outgunned and outmanned the ghetto fighters, she continued fighting in the forests as a partisan until the area was liberated by the Soviet Red Army.

GRUNBAUM, IRENE (LEVI)
(1909–1983)

Born Irene Levi in Darmstadt, Germany, she married Bobby Eskenazi, a Jewish merchant. Wishing to escape Nazi persecution, the couple relocated to Belgrade, Yugoslavia. When the Germans invaded Serbia in April 1941, Bobby Eskenazi was captured and deported, never to be heard of again. Irene made her escape to Albania. Sheltered by the Albanians, who opposed both the fascist Italians and the Nazi Germans, she hid out until the end of the war. Early in 1947 she immigrated to Brazil, a country with openings for refugees and a liberal entrance policy. In 1947 Irene married Harry Grunbaum. After he died in 1965, Irene became a social worker for the Hebrew Immigrant Aid Society (HIAS).

Escape through the Balkans: The Autobiography of Irene Grunbaum. Lincoln: University of Nebraska Press, 1996. Katherine Morris, editor and translator. 222 pp. ISBN: 0803221614. Ages 16–up. Memoir.

Grunbaum tells very little of her life under Nazi rule. Her focus is her dodging arrest in Albania. The memoir tells about the Righteous Moslems who aided her. Copious footnotes by the editor as well as a long introduction give a great deal of information about a topic not well known: the fate of Jews in Albania. At war's end when a group of partisans, Russians, British, and Americans liberate the region, Irene goes to Rome. She receives aid in Italy from Jewish agencies. Finding Brazil most amenable to refugees, she departs Italy in December 1946. At that point her narrative ends. Katherine Morris, a friend, came across her 150-page manuscript in Rio de Janeiro, Brazil.

GURDUS, LUBA KRUGMAN
(1919?–   )

Luba Krugman Gurdus was born in Zwierzyniece, Poland, one of four children—one sister and two brothers. She studied art and art history in Lausanne, Berlin, and Warsaw. In Warsaw she married before the war in 1938 and had one child. Her parents were murdered during deportation, but her brothers escaped to freedom. Her sister died from disease during the war. Her husband managed to escape to the Soviet Union and from there to Britain, but she remained in Warsaw and there lost her son. Managing to evade the ghetto by hiding, she set about trying in vain to locate her missing child. She managed to survive until liberation by the Soviet Red Army. Her husband, who had become a British soldier, came to Warsaw in 1946 and took her to the United States. Her artistic impressions of her wartime experiences were exhibited in the United States and Israel, and her portfolio entitled *They Didn't Live to See* is part of a permanent collection housed by Yad Vashem, Jerusalem.

The Death Train: A Personal Account of a Holocaust Survivor. Washington, DC: U.S. Holocaust Memorial Museum Shop Council, 1991. 164 pp. ISBN: 0896040925. Ages 14–up. Memoir.

Gurdus's sketches, on practically every other page, richly illustrate this account. She shows the anguish of the Jewish people. The setting of her memoir is Warsaw, where she manages to escape the Germans and other enemies who happen to be her compatriots, the Poles. Informers and exhorters are everywhere, ready to betray her to the Gestapo. Yet she finds Gentile Poles who shelter her. Living in fear on the so-called Aryan (non-Jewish) side of the ghetto, she is witness to the Warsaw Ghetto Uprising and reveals the falseness of the Polish Underground forces, who do not aid the fighters. She also witnesses the 1944 fight of the Warsaw Poles against the SS in August and early fall. She does not, as do Gentile Poles, indict the Soviets for their delay in aiding the second Warsaw uprising. She reveals that one way the SS discovered Polish Jews was by their knowledge of German. Her title *Death Train* comes from the scenes she describes of Jews deported to the death camps.

HALTER, MAREK
(1936–   )

Marek was born in Warsaw, Poland, one of three children, to highly educated Jewish parents. His mother was a Yiddish poet and his father a printer. With the Nazi invasion, they were incarcerated in the Warsaw Ghetto, but later, with the help of two Polish Catholics, the family escaped to the Soviet-occupied side of Poland. They spent the war years in Uzbekistan in the Soviet Union, then returned to Poland. Marek's brother went to France. Meanwhile, Marek organized self-defense units against the Polish anti-Semites. Soon the family immigrated to France, where Marek studied art. He married Clara, became a human rights activist and became active in peace organizations. He also turned his hand to writing and became a social commentator. His most notable work was *The Book of Abraham*, which gave him the opportunity to review Jewish history and Jewish legends, among which is included the story of the Just—righteous people who exist in every generation. This work led to his return to Warsaw, the site of his birth and his rescue, and to his latest work, *Stories of Deliverance*.

Stories of Deliverance: Speaking with Men and Women Who Rescued Jews from the Holocaust. Michael Bernard, translator. Chicago, IL: Open Court, 1998. 304 pp. ISBN: 0812693647. Ages 14–up. Memoir.

Writer Halter returned to Warsaw, Poland, seeking out and interviewing Gentiles and converted Jews who had risked their lives to save Jews in Nazi-occupied Europe. He called them the "Just," who, according to the Jewish legend of the Thirty-Six Just Men, save the world from destruction (see review of *Last of the Just*). There are thirty-six profiles of rescuers, most containing long quotations from the interviewees explaining how and why they rescued Jews. The short profiles are interspersed with the interviewer's own memories and observations. He includes figures, like Irena Sender, already mentioned by other writers about rescuers. He also reveals new information on Pope John Paul and his friendship with Jews during the Nazi occupation of Poland and tells how he protected them. Halter has a long conversation with Cardinal Lustiger, who as a Jewish boy was converted to Catholicism, and with a Jewish nun who protected her brethren as well as a mischling (part Jew). Most interviewees are not well known in America. Halter relates past genocide to the present by pointing out the connection of the horror of the Holocaust to the tragedy of Rwanda. His conversations with rescuers from fourteen countries form the basis of a film he directed entitled *Tzedek: The Righteous*.

HANDELI, YA'ACOV ("JACKITO")
(1927–)

"Jackito" Handeli was born in Salonica, the largest Jewish settlement in Greece, to well-to-do parents. His father was a building materials dealer and his mother a traditional homemaker. The family on both sides prided itself in tracing its roots back many generations in the port city. Although Jackito's parents were not very observant, he did go to a Jewish religious school before attending a public secondary school. The family, made up of three girls and three boys, lived a happy life until the Germans entered Salonica on April 9, 1941. The pattern of persecution took the usual one—ghettoization and deportation to Auschwitz. Jackito was sent to the Monowitz complex, the inmate of what was also known as Auschwitz III, a concentration camp that serviced the huge I. G. Farben plant. Jackito survived the camp and was transferred to Bergen-Belsen in northern Germany; however, his entire family was murdered. The British liberated him on April 15, 1945, but Handeli wandered away and joined the American army as an interpreter, serving one and one-half years. Unwilling to return to a Greece undergoing civil war, he became a displaced person at age 18 in Bamberg. He made *aliyah* (immigration) to Israel and fought in the Israeli army. Handeli married and fathered a daughter and a son. He worked for the Allied Jewish Appeal as a guide and fundraiser. In 1960 Jackito testified against Adolf Eichmann.

A Greek Jew from Salonica Remembers. Martin Kett, translator. New York: Herzl Press, 1993. 112 pp. ISBN: 0930830000. Ages 16–up. Memoir.

Most memoirs deal with Askenazi Jews from Europe. Little has been written about the Greek Sephardic Jews—Jews who can trace their lineage back to Spain. Although Handeli's story follows the pattern established in Europe—random killing, persecution, ghettoization, deportation, and concentration camp experience—this memoir adds another dimension: background on Greek Jews and Jewish life in Salonica. Sephardic customs differed from those of their Eastern European brothers, and the opening chapters reveal much of a happy childhood and friendly relations with Gentile neighbors. Handeli tells of the persecution under the Nazis and of his experiences in the I. G. Farben plant, his forced march out of the Auschwitz complex (when he meets Elie Wiesel), the V1 and V2 rocket camp called Dora, and finally Bergen-Belsen. The last few chapters are devoted to Jackito's adjustment to living in Israel, his marriage to a female fellow soldier, service to the government, and his devotion to telling his story to young people.

HART, KITTY (FELIX)
(1927–   )

Kitty Felix was born in Bielsko, Poland, to well-educated, middle-class Jewish parents. Her father was a lawyer and her mother a college teacher. She and her brother attended an academy Catholic school. When the Nazis came, the family fled to Lublin and attempted to get to the Soviet Zone of Occupation of Poland but were refused. The family split up when Kitty and her mother pretended to be Gentiles and volunteered for farm work in Germany. Betrayed, mother and daughter were deported to Auschwitz. The brother and father perished. Kitty and her mother were forced on a death march and finally liberated by the Americans. After a very short stay in a displaced persons camp, they immigrated to Birmingham, England, in 1946. In 1949 Kitty married Ralph Hart, with whom she had two sons. Holding a nursing job for a number of years, Kitty saw an opportunity to make a better living as an exporter of Tartan goods.

Return to Auschwitz: The Remarkable Story of a Girl Who Survived the Holocaust. New York: Atheneum, 1982. 178 pp. ISBN: 0689112661. Ages 14–up. Memoir.

Kitty Felix Hart begins her memoir from the perspective of new life in Birmingham, England, where she is a nurse in a nursing home. She tells of the kindness of a Gentile doctor who aids her in her nursing education and in the procurement of the job. Kitty then relates the events that transpired in her hometown in Poland with the advent of the Nazi occupation. Her mother and father are extremely resourceful, but eventually to no avail. She takes the reader through the family's efforts to avoid deportation, yet the inevitable comes with deportation to Birkenau, the adjunct camp of Auschwitz. Kitty is fortunate enough to be sent with her mother, and the two support each other. They are given jobs in Kanada, the clothing-sorting section, which affords them a chance to steal food and warm clothes. Kitty describes the bravery of Mala Zimmerman, an inmate who dies heroically. She also mentions the uprising and destruction of the crematorium by inmates.

After a death march, Nazi guards melt away as the Americans liberate prisoners. She tells of her short stay in an American displaced persons camp. (Survivors know not to enter the Soviet Zone or return to Poland.) The last chapters talk about how she moves to England, where her mother once taught. She mentions her marriage to Ralph Hart and their difficulties in Birmingham. The final chapter reveals a certain cynicism: Kitty sees a resemblance in civilian life to existence in the camps—ruthlessness, greed for power, climbing over others, and manipulation for selfish gain. She is also bitter about the Allied failure to stop Hitler early or to rescue the persecuted victims of Hitler's Final Solution, and she believes another Holocaust could happen. She concludes by agreeing with a British documentary company to make a film where she and her son return to Auschwitz.

HARTZ, RUTH (KAPP)
(1937–   )

Ruth Kapp was born in Mainz, Germany, to a well to-do, traditionally Jewish family. With Hitler's rise to power, her father, Benno, saw the great danger to Jews and immigrated with his family to Palestine. Unhappy there, the family was taken to Paris. With the fall of Republican France in 1940, the family moved to Toulouse in southern France, under the unoccupied independent government of Vichy. Vichy collaborated more and more with Nazi Germany, however, and to avoid deportation the family sought refuge at various peasant homes. Ruth, now called Renee, spent six months as an orphan in a small Catholic convent. With the liberation of France by Allied forces in fall 1944, the family was reunited and returned to Paris. Ruth completed her studies and attended the University of Paris, the Sorbonne, graduating as a biologist. She came to the United States in 1958 and married Harry Hartz, a public relations consultant, soon after. They had two children. For twenty-nine years Ruth Kapp Hartz taught French in a private Philadelphia school and at Bryn Mawr College. Now retired, she devotes her time to lecturing, advising regarding Holocaust education, and counseling in cross-cultural affairs.

Your Name Is Renee: Ruth Kapp Hartz's Story as a Hidden Child in Nazi-occupied France. By Stacy Cretzmeyer. New York: Oxford University Press, 1999. 208 pp. ISBN: 0195132599. Ages 10–16. Memoir.

This autobiography told in the first person through the eyes of a young child begins with a description of Ruth Kapp's life of hiding, which began in 1941 when she was only 4 years old. She is told that she must not reveal her true identity and that her name is not Ruth but Renee Caper. This occurs when her cousin signs her up for kindergarten in Toulouse. By 1942 all of France is occupied by German troops and Jews are being caught and deported by both the French police, called Milice, and the Gestapo. The family cannot stay in the city, and through the French Resistance and kindly peasants, they go into hiding from place to place. Usually Ruth stays with her mother. From age 4 through age 7, the child must always be on her guard and has narrow escapes from detection. She must constantly remember to lie. It becomes necessary to place Ruth in a Catholic convent as an orphan. The mother superior is a member of the French Resistance who shelters Jews. Ruth loses her identity, but after six months France is liberated in the late summer of 1944 and the family is reunited. Ruth's Jewish identity is restored. The three return to Paris. An afterword by Ruth Kapp Hartz relates the immediate postwar experiences of the Kapp family.

The memoir contains twelve photos and a map of southern France. It features a companion *Teaching Guide* written by Hartz and Teresa Morretta, which can be purchased separately. Also available is a companion video that includes interviews with family members who also had to hide from the Nazis, including Ruth's mother, who still lives in Paris, and an uncle, Heinrich.

HEPPNER, ERNEST
(1921–   )

Ernest Heppner was born in Breslau, then a German city, now called Wroclaw, a Polish city. His father owned a matzoh factory and a resort hotel. The family was traditionally religious. When Ernest was 12 years old, he was expelled from school because he was Jewish. With the November 1938 pogrom known as "Kristallnacht" (the Nazi-staged smashing of Jewish property), the Heppners were desperate to leave Germany. Ernest and his mother were able to get papers to escape to Shanghai, a port city under the control of the Japanese that opened its doors to Jewish refugees. Unfortunately, his father, brother, and sister remained in Germany. The Red Cross lost track of them and presumed them deported. Meanwhile, Ernest married in the Jewish ghetto of Shanghai, and he and his mother secured jobs to survive. They were liberated in September 1945 and came to the United States in 1947. Heppner became an independent management consultant.

Shanghai Refuge: A Memoir of a World War II Jewish Ghetto. Lincoln: University of Nebraska Press, 1993. 190 pp. ISBN: 0803223684. Ages 15–up. Memoir.

Part 1 of this memoir tells of the writer's life in Germany in the 1930s. Part 2 relates his experiences in the Shanghai Ghetto, Part 3 deals with life under American occupation, and Part 4 speaks of Heppner's experiences adjusting to life in New York City. The writer details the life of Jews inside the ghetto and tells of the work of Jewish relief agencies. According to Heppner, numerous self-help activities and enterprises sprang up to keep spirits buoyed. Ernest was fortunate enough to work in the Japanese-occupied area of Honkow. His mother became a case-worker for the American Joint Distribution Committee. Heppner was appalled at the poverty in the ghetto and the failure of the Allies to find a refuge for Jews before, during, and after the war. Photos enhance the understanding of the text.

HEYMAN, EVA
(1931–1944)

Eva was born to assimilated, wealthy Jewish parents in Nagyvarad, Hungary, a town close to the Romanian border. She attended a fashionable academic high school. Her mother, Agnes, divorced and remarried, leaving Eva for long periods with her grandparents. The Germans invaded their former ally, Hungary, in 1944 and deported Eva and her grandparents to Auschwitz in June. Dr. Josef Mengele, the infamous physician at Auschwitz, "selected" Eva for the gas chambers in October 1944, ending her thirteen years of life. Her mother and stepfather escaped the Nazis, however. Before deportation Eva entrusted her diary to a family servant, a cook. At war's end the cook gave the diary to Eva's mother, Agnes.

The Diary of Eva Heyman: Child of the Holocaust. Judah Marton and Moshe Kohn, translators. New York: Sure Seller, 1988. 124 pp. ISBN: 0933503644. Ages 15–up. Diary.

Eva's diary starts just a month before the invasion of Hungary by Germany. The beginning of a rather chatty narrative details growing anti-Semitism by the pro-Nazi Hungarian government. It describes life in Nagyvarad and Eva's rather well-off life as a daughter of an architect. Her entries begin February 13, 1944, and conclude May 30, 1944, just before she and her grandparents are deported. Her mother remarries and leaves Eva with her grandparents. Her father is deported, and her stepfather is sent with the Hungarian army as an antitank ditch digger to the Russian front. From March 19 on, Eva comes under the ruthless rule of the Nazis. Her parents' and grandparents' possessions are confiscated. She is taken with other Jews to a ghetto. Eva relates the privations in the ghetto. Her last entry expresses her surprise at the complicity of the Hungarian national police in the liquidation of the ghetto and deportation of the Jews to Auschwitz.

HILLESUM, ETTY
(1914–1943)

Hillesum, a Dutch Jewish intellectual, was born in Middleburg, Netherlands, to assimilated Jewish parents. Her father was a headmaster and professor of classical languages. Etty attended Dutch public schools and then graduated from Amsterdam University with two degrees: one in law, the other in psychology. In her majority, she lived in a communal house with left-wing friends. When Nazi Germany occupied Holland, a Jewish Council was set to self-govern Jewish communal life, but under strict Nazi supervision. Etty was chosen to be a staff member of the Council of Amsterdam. Feeling guilty for working in an office while her coreligionists suffered, Etty volunteered to be a social worker, caring for inmates forced into the nearby concentration camp, Westerbork. After traveling back and forth, she decided to work full time at the camp, particularly with those preparing to make the fatal deportation journey to Auschwitz. Rejecting offers to escape deportation, she boarded the transport with her parents. At age 29 at Auschwitz, Etty was gassed on November 30, 1943, as were her parents and brother.

An Interrupted Life; The Diaries, 1941–1943, and Letters from Westerbork. Arnold J. Pomerans, translator. New York: Henry Holt, 1996. 376 pp. ISBN: 0805050876. Ages 15–up. Diary.

At age 27 Etty Hillesum began a diary of her last three years of life. It extended from March 1941 to September 1943, the last entry being the very day of her deportation to Auschwitz. A friend, Maria Tuinzing, received the diary in the form of eight handwritten notebooks from a member of the Dutch Underground. She turned them over to a Dutch friend, Dr. Klaus Smelik. His son had the diaries published almost forty years later. The entries deal with the Holocaust only obliquely. They move from personal chatter dealing with Etty's lover, many years her senior, to her anguish regarding her own activities and intimate philosophical thoughts that try to make sense of persecution and violence. Although not religious, she wants to share the fate of her Jewish coreligionists at concentration camp Westerbork. She finally decides that rather than be part of the Gestapo's plan for Jews even indirectly, she will stay at Westerbork to become a nurse for the inmates. The second part of this book includes letters to Etty's family from 1942 to 1943. The Dutch Resistance published two long letters replete with details about life and the social structure at Westerbork camp. Klaus Smelik compiled the letters, the last of which was a postcard thrown out of the train window by Etty to a resister friend.

ISAACMAN, CLARA (HELLER)
(1921–)

Clara Heller was born in Borsa, Romania, to observant middle-class Jewish parents. In 1932 she, her parents, and two brothers and a sister moved to Antwerp, Belgium. Her parents opened a soda pop business while her father also engaged in Antwerp's diamond business. Clara attended public school until 1941, when the German occupiers, present since 1940, forced Jewish children out of normal life. Recognizing the great dangers to Jews facing increasing raids and deportations, the Belgian Underground hid the family. Liberated by Canadian and American troops in fall 1944, Clara met an American liberator, Daniel Isaacman, who fell in love with her. While waiting for him to return and marry her at war's end, she located and assisted Jewish refugees. Isaacman returned soon after the war and married Clara and brought her back to Philadelphia. There Clara received a degree in early childhood education. She had one son and served as a youth leader and teacher of Jewish religion, an occupation she still holds.

Clara's Story. With Joan Adess Grossman. Philadelphia: Jewish Publication Society, 1984. 120 pp. ISBN: 082760243-X. Ages 9–14. Memoir.

This memoir told in the first person is essentially about a child in hiding. It starts in 1938 and concludes just at liberation day in 1944. Isaacman makes sure the reader learns about the history of the times and about some of the Jewish customs practiced by her family. She explains how the noose of Nazi oppression slowly tightened about Antwerp's Jews, until the family realized they must hide. On the last day of school, her teacher put her in touch with the Belgian Underground, which had among its activities hiding Jews in safe houses. Clara relates how the constant fear of detection brings about her father's suicide and how her brother Heshie was caught and deported to doom. The narrative tells how she, her mother, her other brother, and her sister used their wits to survive as well as details the generosity of the Righteous Gentiles who aided them.

Pathways through the Holocaust: An Oral History by Eye-witnesses. Hoboken, NJ: Ktav Publishing House, 1988. 109 pp. ISBN: 0881252689. Ages 9–12. Memoirs.

Essentially this anthology of narratives is a textbook for middle-school students. It has eleven chapters. The first two are overviews—one on the history of the Jewish people, the other on the rise of Hitler and the Nazis. The last chapter deals with an African American soldier who was witness to the liberation of Buchenwald. One narrative in the first person relates the seduction and disillusionment of a member of Hitler Youth. The rest are brief autobiographies of survivors who experienced different aspects of the Holocaust. Two chapters are on well-known resisters: ghetto fighter Zivia Lubetkin and partisan Abba Kovner. The rest are testimonies of survivors who related their stories to the Holocaust Archive at Gratz College in Elkins Park, Pennsylvania. Isaacman includes a number of relevant photos and rather simple sketches. At the conclusion of each chapter she includes quotations about morality from great rabbis and thought questions.

JAGENDORF, SIEGFRIED ("SAMI") (1885–1970)

The rescuer of thousands of Jews in the Ukraine, Siegfried Jagendorf was born in the Austro-Hungarian province of Bukovina, in a village, Zviniace, to wealthy Orthodox Jewish parents. Siegfried and his three sisters lived on their parents' farm with its profitable flourmill. As a teenager he abandoned this life and went to Vienna, where he attended high school and technical college, majoring in mechanics and engineering. "Sami" married in 1909 and led a conventional bourgeois life as an Austrian citizen until 1914. He served as a first lieutenant in the Austro-Hungarian army. After World War I he worked as an electrical engineer for a number of German concerns. He changed his residence to his hometown in Bukovina, which now became a province of Romania. A German ally joined in battle against the Soviet Union, Romania received a huge slice of the captured Ukraine. The fascist country and its dictator decided to deport its Jews to this captured region under Romanian control. As a result, Jagendorf and many thousands of Jews were forced to march into the Ukraine, which temporarily stopped at Moghilev. Using his wiles and vast engineering skills, he persuaded the Romanian authorities to permit him to repair the city's power supply and then reconstruct a damaged iron foundry. These projects provided work for Jews, who remained alive by working until liberation by the Soviet Red Army in spring 1944. He sought emigration and finally was able to immigrate to California in 1946, where his wife and daughters joined him.

Jagendorf's Foundry: Memoir of the Romanian Holocaust, 1941–1944. Introduction and commentary by Aron Hirt-Manheimer. New York: HarperCollins, 1991. 209 pp. ISBN: 006016106X. Ages 16–up. Memoir.

This memoir is divided into six parts: fall 1941, winter 1941–1942, spring–summer 1942, fall 1942, winter 1942–1943, spring–summer 1943, and the years 1944–1946. Aron Hirt-Manheimer, editor-in-chief of the Holocaust Library Publishers, has a long historical introduction and interjects often into Jagendorf's manuscript. The editor dug into the memoirs in 1984, fourteen years after the author's death. The narrative is basically a defense of Jagendorf's actions to save himself and 15,000 Jews in Moghilev, a large city in the Ukraine. The author persuaded the Romanian prefect to permit him to repair the war-damaged electrical works in the city. Jagendorf found other vital tasks to aid the Romanian masters, such as repairing and operating a foundry. Across the Bug River from Moghilev stood the murderous SS mobile killing squads bent on the Final Solution. Jagendorf, as chief engineer and head of the Jewish Council, which helped govern the region, held the fate of the Moghilev Ghetto in his hands. Unlike other ghetto council elders, however, Jagendorf was successful in using productive work to save Jewish lives.

KAPLAN, CHAIM A.
(1880–1942)

Chaim A. Kaplan was born in Baranovici, Belorussia, to observant Jewish middle-class parents. He received an intensive Talmudic education as well as a secular one. He became a Hebrew teacher, then founded a Hebrew school in Warsaw. Kaplan authored several Hebrew textbooks and was a frequent writer for Yiddish and Hebrew periodicals. Trapped in Warsaw with the Nazi invasion, he was deported in August 1942 during the first great Aktion there in the ghetto. The educator continued to teach Jewish tradition despite the Nazi penalty of death against it. He died in Treblinka, but before deportation Kaplan hid his diary, written in Hebrew, in the earth in a kerosene can on a farm where it was found after the war.

Scroll of Agony: The Warsaw Diary of Chaim A. Kaplan. Abraham I. Katsh, translator. Bloomington: Indiana University Press, 1999. 410 pp. ISBN: 253212936. Ages 16–up. Diary.

Kaplan's entries take place from September 1, 1939, the day of the German invasion of Poland, to August 4, 1942, the height of mass deportation from the Warsaw Ghetto. Two days after his last entry Kaplan was deported. His manuscript, written by hand in Hebrew, records Nazi oppression, cruelty, and destructiveness. It deplores the politics of the occupation and the complicity of the Jewish Council. It extols the Jewish capacity for survival, for expressing religiosity, and for preserving communal life in defiance of Nazi dehumanization. He admires the children's desire to learn about Jewish tradition despite the great dangers involved and how services and holiday observances continue by their outwitting the German overlords. He believes in the Jewish people's "hidden power" and the ultimate victory of the Jewish worldview over Nazi paganism.

KATZENELSON, YITZCHAK
(1886–1944)

Yiddish and Hebrew poet Katzenelson was born in a small town near the Bylorussian city of Minsk. His father was a rabbi who ran a modernized religious school, which moved near Lodz. Until 1919 there was no Poland; large regions in the north belonged to the Tzarist Empire. Yitzchak became a teacher in that school and later formed a secular Hebrew school which he ran. When the Nazis captured Lodz in 1939, Katzenelson moved with his family, consisting of a wife and three sons, to Warsaw. There he joined the Zionist-Socialist underground organization, *Dror* (Freedom). This ghetto period, 1940–1944, was his most productive, and he was considered a foremost playwright of the time. Unfortunately, his wife and two younger boys were caught by the Germans and sent to their deaths in Auschwitz. He and his older son, also in the Warsaw resistance, hid out, and were given Honduran passports, with exchange in mind, their freedom in Honduras for a German subject. The father and son came out of hiding, but the Germans who interned them at Vittel, a holding camp in France, did not keep their bargain and shipped the two to death at Auschwitz. It was at Vittel, from May 1943 to April 1944, that Katzenelson wrote *Vittel Diary* and his classic poem, "The Song of the Murdered Jewish Nation."

Vittal Diary. Translated by Myer Cohen. Israel: Ghetto Fighters' House, Kibbutz Hameuchad Publishing House, 1972. 276 pp. No ISBN. Ages 16–up.

The *Diary* is one of Katzenelson's experiences in the Warsaw Ghetto although it begins with his life at the internment camp, Vittel. It is a lament for the death of his wife, children and the Jewish people. The writer describes the horrible conditions inside the ghetto itself and the anguish the writer feels as freight trains take the residents to their deaths. Katzenelson condemns the activities of the Jewish police assigned to the Jewish Council who help the Nazis in their murderous task of round-ups and deportation. He judges all the German people harshly and the rest of the world for their silence in the face of mass murder. The one bright note is his praise of the Zionist fighters, his own son, Zvi, included, who fight back in the face of overwhelming odds.

"The Song of the Murdered Jewish People." Translated by Noah Rosenbloom. Israel: Ghetto Fighter's House, Kibbutz Hameuchad Publishing House, 1980. 135 pp. No ISBN. Ages 16–up.

This book length poem, written originally in Yiddish, was penned at Vittel, the German run internment camp in France, between October 1943 and January 1944. It is dedicated to the memory of Katzenelson's wife, Channah, and his brother, Berl, both of whom perished at Auschwitz. The poet, steeped in Jewish learning, was alluding to the biblical Book of Lamentation. At certain points he compares himself to the Hebrew Prophets. He cries out against the senseless torture and murder like Job. This was a dirge to the Jews who perished during the Holocaust. The poem is composed of 15 sections, each with 15 stanzas with 4 long lines. Katzenelson is very pessimistic about the survival of European Jews. The work relates the everyday agony of Warsaw's Jews, the suffering of children, particularly the orphans, the deportations, and finally the bravery of the ghetto fighters in the April 1943 Uprising.

KLEIN, GERDA WEISSMANN
(1924–)

Gerda was the daughter of an assimilated, wealthy Jewish family who lived in Bielitz, Poland. Her father was part owner of a fur-processing plant; her mother, a homemaker. The Weissmann family wanted a private academic education for Gerda, so their daughter attended an exclusive Catholic high school until she was 15. In fall 1939 she came under the heel of the Nazi occupiers. She endured separation from her parents and brother, ghetto life, and the torture of labor and concentration camps. After a death-dealing forced march of 1,000 miles, an event few survived, she was liberated by the Fifth U.S. Infantry Division in May 1945. The commander, Lieutenant Klein, took great interest in

Gerda, facilitating her hospitalization. The two married in June 1946, and in September 1946 they immigrated to Buffalo, New York. The couple opened a printing business and had three children. Gerda Klein took to writing her memoirs, lecturing, and actively engaging in Holocaust and Zionist organizations.

All But My Life. New York: Hill and Wang, 1995. 264 pp. ISBN: 0809024608. Ages 13–up. Memoir.

The first part of Klein's memoir deals with her life under Nazi occupation in Bielitz and how she, her parents, and her brother coped with privation and persecution. In 1942 the family was separated and deported. Gerda never heard from them again. She tells much of incarceration at Sosnowitz, a transit camp. Then Gerda is transferred to labor camps and is lucky enough to come under the rule of a kindly woman leader and have the help of a fellow inmate, Ilse. In January 1945 she is forced with 4,000 other slave women on a 1,000-mile trek from East Germany to Czechoslovakia. Her liberator, Lieutenant Klein, commander of an American infantry group, falls in love with her and helps nurse her back to health as she convalesces in a hospital. The narration ends with their plans for marriage.

Promise of a New Spring: The Holocaust and Renewal. Chappaqua, NY: Rossel, 1981. 64 pp. ISBN: 094064651X (pbk.). Ages 6–9. Fiction.

This picture book for young children explains the Holocaust to them without delving into the events in Europe. Klein uses the allegory of a forest fire that destroys most of the lush vegetation and creatures before it, leaving very few survivors. There are black and white photographs, subdued nonthreatening drawings, and for the forest rich colors that include the fire. The book attempts to show that despite the devastation life continues, but those who survive seek to remember.

KLEMPERER, VICTOR
(1881–1960)

Victor Klemperer was the youngest of nine children born to the wife of Rabbi Wilhelm Klemperer in Lansberg, Germany. His father was an ultra-Reform rabbi, so Victor had no Bar Mitzvah. He attended Berlin public schools, for the family had moved to Berlin when Wilhelm Klemperer became a preacher at a large Reform temple. Victor did not finish high school until age 21. In 1906 he married a Gentile German woman, Eva Schlernmer, and converted to the Protestant faith. He joined the

German army and served as a frontline soldier in World War I. The couple had no children. Klemperer received his doctorate in romance philosophy and was given a teaching job as a full professor in a technical academy in Dresden. He lost his job two years after Hitler came to power in 1935. Because of his "Aryan" wife and sheer luck, he survived the war years. His brother George helped to sustain him. The other brothers lived abroad and survived. Klemperer, a German patriot, had chosen not to join them.

After the war Victor Klemperer lived and taught in East Germany and became a communist.

I Will Bear Witness: A Diary of the Nazi Years, 1933–1941. Martin Chalmers, translator. New York: Random House, 1998. 519 pp. ISBN: 0679456961. Ages 16–up. Diary.

This diary details Victor's daily life under the Nazis. He documents the many restrictions placed upon him as a Jew, even though he does not identify as one. He has to give up his job, radio, bike, and apartment and suffer many indignities. His rations are reduced, his movements restricted. The Germans living around him come off quite well: They do not persecute him, and they show no outward anti-Semitism. He remains an avid Protestant and anti-Zionist. Mixed in the entries are his comparisons between the French Revolution and the Nazi period. Klemperer, who posed as a Gentile, a cultural aristocrat, was shocked to have to wear the yellow star in 1941 and suffer the indignities meted out to Jews by the Third Reich. The diary, though recording what it was like living in the heart of Germany, also records this astute man's everyday thoughts on the events that unfold before him.

I Will Bear Witness, 1941–1945: A Diary of the Nazi Years, Vol. 2. Diary.

This second volume covers the worst years of World War II. The diaries remained out of sight when Klemperer lived in communist East Germany. After his death in 1960, his wife placed them in the Dresden archives. The writer tells us much about his feelings: how he felt about wearing the yellow star, facing interrogations by the Gestapo, arbitrary arrests, house searches, very scarce rations, and going on forced labor. Here is a man 60 years old, very learned, a former professor who jettisoned his Jewish heritage, faced with numerous humiliations in civilian life under the Nazi regime in the Germany he loves because he was born Jewish. Klemperer's insights into wartime Germany include an amusing analysis of the Nazi use of language, which he entitles "Lingua Tertii Imperii." After being told how the Russians were annihilated, he says, sardonically, they are a "tremendous and quite inexhaustible opponent."

The diarist describes the Allied bombing of Dresden and his escape with his wife to the countryside. He paints a picture of the chaos of German defeat in the last days of the war and the immediate aftermath.

KOESTLER, ARTHUR
(1905–1983)

Writer-journalist Arthur Koestler was born in Budapest to assimilated Jewish parents of modest means. He studied technical engineering at the University of Vienna, but he left before receiving a degree. He became a militant Zionist and immigrated to the Jewish settlement in Palestine in 1926. There he became a journalist, but he left the Holy Land for the Soviet Union in 1931. Koestler became a communist; then after viewing Stalin's purge trials in 1936, he quit the party in 1938. As a war correspondent for the London *News Chronicle*, he sympathized with the Loyalists during the Spanish Civil War (1936–1939). Arrested by the victorious Franco fascists, he was released only to be incarcerated by collaborationist Vichy France in 1939–1940 in the concentration camp Le Vernet. Koestler was able to escape to Britain and serve in the British Pioneer Corps throughout World War II. During the war he wrote about his outrage at the apathy toward the murder of Europe's Jews. After the war he continued his journalistic work, but by the early 1950s he turned to writing on the arts, science, and religion. On March 3, 1983, he and his third wife committed suicide.

The Scum of the Earth. Daphne Hardy, translator. London: Victor Gollancz, 1941. 255 pp. ISBN: 0090872800. Ages 15–up. Diary.

This was Arthur Koestler's first book in English and was written soon after his incarceration in Le Vernet, then escape to England. It is a diary of his experiences in the camp. The entries give details of life at the camp—the unsanitary conditions and the lack of basic amenities of life such as light, heat, blankets, furniture, replaceable clothes, soap, or eating utensils. He describes manual labor performed by detainees. Le Vernet held 2,000 prisoners, mainly antifascist refugees, with 200 to a dirty hut. Koestler pens a number of portraits of his fellow internees and the French guards and officers. He cites maltreatment and inhumanity. With the defeat of Republican France and its ideals of liberty, equality, and fraternity, the rump state Vichy France became a Nazi Germany collaborator. Cynically, the perceptive journalist writes: "A few years ago we antifacists were called martyrs of fascist barbarism and defenders of liberty. Now we are the scum of the earth."

KOSINSKI, JERZY
(1933–1991)

The novelist was born in Lodz, Poland, to well-to-do, assimilated Jewish parents. His father was a textile merchant and his mother a concert pianist. With the coming of the Nazi occupiers, Jerzy and his parents moved from Lodz and hid out in the countryside. They pretended they were Christians and found refuge in two villages. After liberation by the Soviet Red Army, the family moved back to Lodz, where Jerzy completed high school. Jerzy went to the Soviet Union for college studies in history and political science. In 1955 he completed a second master's degree in Poland in history. In 1957 he traveled to America as a Ford Foundation fellow and remained here. Mary Weir, a wealthy woman, married him in 1962; however, she died in 1968. He held various blue-collar jobs until he became a resident fellow in English at Wesleyan University in 1967. From then on he was a college professor at Ivy League institutions and a recognized photographer. Kosinski was best known for his novels and social commentary. *The Painted Bird*, based on wartime experiences, made him famous as a writer. He remarried in 1987, but four years later he took his own life.

The Painted Bird. New York: Bantam, 1983. 320 pp. ISBN: 9992223677. Ages 14–up. Fiction.

Originally published in 1965, this novel has been reissued a number of times and published in thirty languages. The narrative is a horrifying story of the adventures of an innocent 10-year-old boy in Poland during World War II. Abandoned by his parents, he drifts from village to village seeking a haven, only to be eventually rejected by cruel and primitive peasants. This transforms the protagonist into a cynical savage caring little for morality, seeking only self-preservation. For a large part of the story because of physical attacks, he is struck dumb. The novel gets its title from an incident observed by the boy: Peasants paint a raven's feathers different colors and send the bird back into flight; the other ravens cruelly and murderously attack the painted bird until it dies. This little story parallels Kosinski's story of the boy out of place and different from the peasants he meets and explains their cruelty. The episodes in the novel emphasize Kosinski's cynical view of humanity. The boy kills a tormentor who sought to murder him. At the end of the novel the main character is reunited with his parents, but this does not bring happiness. To regain his health, he goes skiing, has an accident, but regains his speech. Although the boy is now able to communicate, he remains dissatisfied with humanity.

KOVNER, ABBA
(1918–1987)

Abba Kovner, Resistance fighter and poet, was born in the city of Se-
vastopol in what is today the Ukraine, but once was Russia. His family
moved to Vilna, Lithuania, where he attended public schools. As a youth
Abba joined the Zionist-Socialist HaShomer Hatzair. In July 1940 the
organization went underground, for the Soviets were anti-Zionist. The
Nazis entered Lithuania in summer 1941 and in the fall began to murder
Jews, shooting them in a nearby ravine called Ponary. Abba was a major
force in starting the Lithuanian Resistance by revealing the true nature
of the Nazi menace. He then organized messengers to other Jewish communities, warning them that they faced extermination. After an unsuccessful Vilna Ghetto fight, he took the resisters to a nearby forest and
continued guerrilla warfare until the Soviet Red Army liberated the area
in 1944. He and his Vilna partisan group then organized escape routes
to the Jewish settlement in Palestine known as Bricha. Immigrating to
Palestine in 1947, he fought in its War of Independence in 1948, which
established the State of Israel. His wife, Vitka, whom he met in the Resistance, joined him on the kibbutz (collective farm) Ein HaHoresh.

My Little Sister and Selected Poems, 1965–1985. Shirley Kaufman,
translator. Oberlin, OH: Oberlin College Press, 1986. 159 pp. ISBN:
0932440207. Ages 15–up. Fiction.

"My Little Sister" is a poem that deals directly with the Holocaust and
Kovner's pain in losing his mother, whom he abandoned in the city of
Vilna. The sister is an archetype for all the women who were brutally
murdered by the Nazis. There is a hint of guilt in not being able to save
them. It is also a testament to the little girl who alerted Kovner that mass
murder was occurring in the Ponary ravine outside Vilna.

This is a book-length poem with forty-six passages and five sections.
The first section tells of a little girl who seeks safety in a convent, but
receives just temporary shelter and must face death. Here and throughout the poem Kovner notes the world's indifference to the plight of the
Jews. The little sister also alludes to the Bible's Song of Songs, where the
sister is really the Jewish people, God's bride. Parts 3, 4, and 5 dwell on
death, focusing on the great numbers of Jewish dead. The poet tries to
speak for them, to mourn for them, particularly for all the little sisters
whose lives were so horribly cut short.

KUPER, JACK
(1932–)

Jakob Kuperblum was born in Lyraidow, Poland, to a poor family. His father was a shoemaker and irreligious; his mother a housewife and traditionally Jewish. With the invasion of Poland in 1939 by both the Soviet Union and Germany, his father opted for the Soviet Red Army, since he was in sympathy with Stalinist communism. However, with the German attack on the Soviet Union in 1941, his mother, Jakob, and his brother, after leaving Warsaw for Kulik in the Soviet sector to avoid the Nazis, found themselves in German hands. Upon returning from a short stay out of town, Jakob discovered his family had been deported and Jews ghettoized. His struggle to avoid capture and survive under trying conditions is the subject of his first book, a memoir, *Child of the Holocaust*. Jakob survived the war and at age 15, in 1947, his whole family murdered, he immigrated to Toronto, Canada. He graduated from Central Technical School in 1953, and in 1955 he married. After a career in advertising and broadcasting, Kuper established his own motion picture company

Child of the Holocaust. Garden City, NY: Berkley Publishing Co., 1999. 288 pp. ISBN: 0425165949. Ages 16–up. Memoir.

This memoir of Jack Kuper's childhood experience is about hiding to avoid destruction. A boy of 8 returns to his hometown to find his mother, brother, and relatives as well as the Jews in his town rounded up and taken away by the Nazis. He never sees them again except for an uncle just three years his senior. Jakob disguises himself as a Gentile in a desperate search for safety and goes from town to town. Kindly families, although anti-Semitic, take pity on him and provide him with temporary food and shelter. However, the fear of detection by the dreaded Gestapo forces his hosts to send him off for fear that they would be executed for harboring a Jew. Jakob has to impersonate a Christian so often that he takes on a Christian persona and has great qualms about being Jewish. The fact that at that time in Poland only Jews were circumcised placed the writer in constant danger of discovery. Much of the memoir deals with Jakob's identity problem and discovery by local peasants, who are anti-Semitic. The narrative does not come to a developed end. The Russians "liberate" Poland, and Jakob is united for a short while with a Jewish cousin and family. The memoir is punctuated with little songs Jakob sings to entertain his hosts and with discussions he has with himself as if he were two different people.

LASKA, VERA
(1923–   )

Vera Laska was born in Prague, Czechoslovakia. She joined the Czech Resistance and traveled underground to Kosice, then under Hungarian occupation (1940). A Gentile, she smuggled refugees escaping Nazi persecution across the Slovak-Hungarian border. (Hungary and Slovakia were allies of Nazi Germany.) Laska was captured and deported to Auschwitz, then to Gross Rosen concentration camp, and lastly to Nordhausen-Dora, the rocket V1 and V2 site. In spring 1945, near World War II's end, she liberated herself by hiding. Returning to her homeland, a reconstituted Czechoslovakia, she became the executive secretary of the Czechoslovakian War Crimes Investigation Commission. In 1947 Laska immigrated to Chicago. She received a Ph.D. from the University of Chicago and became a writer, often on World War II topics and the camps.

Women in the Resistance and in the Holocaust: Voices of Eyewitnesses. Westport, CT: Greenwood Press, 1983. 330 pp. ISBN: 03134674. Ages 16–up. Memoir.

This book is an anthology of memoirs, including two eyewitness accounts by Vera Laska herself. The entries have been translated from other works. The writer provides the reader with a scholarly introduction as well as an informative overview including time, place, and setting for each entry. This gives the reader a framework for understanding female resisters and concentration camp deportees. All testimonies are graphic and detailed. Laska and her fellow authors explain very well the methods used by Nazi authorities to degrade inmates. Readers gain insight into the fate of non-Jews as well as Jews in the camps and clearly see the role of women in the Resistance. A short final section of the anthology concerns the survivors' reentry into "normal" life.

LEVI, PRIMO
(1919–1987)

Chemist, survivor, and writer Primo Levi was born in Turin, Italy, of middle-class, assimilated Jewish parents. He matriculated through Italy's public schools and graduated college in 1941 as a chemist. After the downfall of Benito Mussolini and the subsequent Nazi German occupation of Italy, Levi founded an Italian partisan antifacist resistance movement entitled "Justice and Liberty." At age 24 he was captured by fascist militia and sent to Auschwitz. Levi survived because of his chemistry training, for he was attached to Monowitz, the part of the Auschwitz complex at the I. G. Farben chemical firm that made artificial rubber. His technical knowledge, wits, and good luck and the support of a non-inmate Italian worker enabled him to survive. Levi took sick in January 1945 and was left behind in the infirmary when the death march of inmates occurred as the Soviet Red Army closed in. Free, he journeyed about Europe, then returned to his hometown, Turin, and resumed his old job as a chemist in a paint factory. In 1977 he retired to devote his full time to writing. In 1987 Levi is alleged to have committed suicide.

The Drowned and the Saved. Raymond Rosenthal, translator. New York: Vintage International, 1989. 203 pp. ISBN: 067972186X. Ages 16–up. Memoir.

Published after his death, this was Primo Levi's last book. The survivor recalls the concentration camp Auschwitz and reflects upon his experiences once again. He bemoans the useless cruelty and endless irrationality he witnessed there. In fact, the writer sees all violence as useless. He points out not only the depravity of the murderers but also the extremity of circumstances that drove victims to violate their better natures and commit acts unthinkable in their normal environments. Deportees were forced into "choiceless choices" that eradicated their innocence. Levi understood how the camp experience poisoned the mind of his friend at the camp, Jean Amery, the intellectual and fellow writer who committed suicide. The memoir concludes with correspondence between Levi and Germans who responded to his earlier memoir, *Survival at Auschwitz*.

If Not Now, When? William Weaver, translator. New York: Viking Penguin, 1995. 356 pp. ISBN: 0140188932. Ages 15–up. Fiction.

Although Levi himself was a charter member of an Italian partisan unit, this is a novel, an imaginative depiction of a Jewish band fighting the Nazis. Levi was very impressed with the fighting spirit of Jews he met at Auschwitz and later on in his travels in Eastern Europe. In this nonautobiographical novel he reveals much about the daily life of resisters in the forests. Characters and landscapes are detailed, with characters talking back at the world, a world in which Nazis and others brutalized them. The partisans hold on to their humanity, however, and we learn much about the daily life of resisters in the forests.

Moments of Reprieve. Ruth Feldman, translator. New York: Viking, Penguin, 1995. 128 pp. ISBN: 0140188959. Ages 16–up. Memoir.

This work consists of fifteen portraits of Jews from many areas of Europe, from many occupations, and from diverse religious beliefs. The tone is upbeat and positive. Primo Levi, an Italian Jew from a Sephardic background—descended from Spain—is surprised to discover at Auschwitz Yiddish-speaking Jews from central and Eastern Europe. These Askenazi Jews (Jews from Germanic states) fascinate him, and he learns Yiddish to communicate with them. In the course of these portrayals the writer illustrates falseness of the stereotyped weak Jew who is unable to resist persecution.

The Periodic Table. Raymond Rosenthal, translator. New York: Schocken Books, 1985. 233 pp. ISBN: 0805210415. Ages 16–up. Memoir.

A lifelong chemist, Primo Levi bases this memoir of twenty-one prose pieces around the elements of the Periodic Table, which is a list of the chemical elements of all matter. Each element serves as a reminder of an incident or period in Levi's Holocaust life. For example, the element gold reminds him of the holding cell in Italy after his capture by fascist militia. Cerium recalls his slave labor at the I. G. Farben chemical plant. In Argon he draws an analogy between the nonreactive nature of this element and the nonassimilation of the Jews in the Piedmont region, where Levi grew up. The work also includes two fables he remembered from Piedmont.

The Reawakening. Stuart Woolf, translator. New York: Simon & Schuster, 1996. 240 pp. ISBN: 0684826356. Ages 16–up. Memoir.

This is a memoir of Levi's postwar experiences with reflections back to Holocaust occurrences. Liberated by the Soviet Red Army in January 1945, the author is placed in a transit camp in Poland, then shipped to a Russian village near Minsk. Hoping to find his way back to his former life, he boards a train that takes him on a circuitous journey through Eastern Europe. After a month he travels through Austria, over the Brenner Pass, and on to his old home in Turin, Italy. In this work Levi is more descriptive of personalities he meets than in previous works. Here we meet former inmates of the camps as well as Russian soldiers. Levi's odyssey is a search for his own physical and spiritual recuperation.

Survival at Auschwitz: The Nazi Assault on Humanity. Stuart Woolf, translator. New York: Collier Books, 1993. 189 pp. ISBN: 0020291922. Ages 15–up. Memoir.

In his first book, Levi tells of his arrest and imprisonment at Auschwitz. The memoir describes the horrible world of the *lager* as Germans called the concentration camp. This was the ultimate in dehumanization, the reduction of humans to beastlike behavior. Offering many philosophical and psychological insights, Levi notes the complicity of the chemical industrial giant I. G. Farben in the gross exploitation of slave labor. He explains the factors that enabled him to survive: friendships, a righteous Italian worker, and the exchange of goods for food.

The last chapter, "Story of Ten Days," is a diary recorded between January 18 and January 27, his day of liberation by the Soviet Red Army.

LUBETKIN (ZUCKERMAN), ZIVIA
(1914–1976)

The brave founder and leader of the Warsaw Ghetto Uprising, Zivia was born in Byten, a border area between Poland and Russia. She was one of five daughters and one brother in a traditionally Jewish family. She attended a Polish state-run public school. Her father was a religious Zionist, one who believed that Jews should settle in the Holy Land and create a state according to the Bible. However, Zivia joined a nonreligious Zionist-Socialist movement called Dror (Freedom). The movement prepared young people to live in Palestine as farmers but sharing ownership in a collective. Her devotion to the movement and her work on the training farm earned Zivia the title of director of training farms, an activity that took her throughout Poland and to the group's headquarters in Warsaw. Caught in the Soviet sector of Poland when the Soviet Union and Germany invaded Poland in 1939, she went to Warsaw to organize Dror groups there. In January 1943 she participated as a fighter in the first armed resistance against the Germans; then on April 19, as a leader, she was a major figure in the great Warsaw Ghetto Uprising of April–May 1943, along with her husband-to-be, Yitzhak Zuckerman, another major resister. On May 10, 1943, the last days of the uprising, Zuckerman led Zivia and others out of the ghetto to the "Aryan" (Gentile) side of Warsaw. In August 1944 she fought with remnants of ghetto fighters in the general Warsaw uprising that was crushed by the SS. Liberated by the Soviet Red Army, she and her husband organized a secret escape route to the then-British-controlled Jewish settlement in Palestine. In 1946 the Zuckermans formed the Ghetto Fighters' Kibbutz and Museum in the Galilee.

In the Days of Destruction and Revolt. Ishai Tubbin, translator. Israel: Ghetto Fighters' House. 275 pp. No ISBN. Ages 14–up. Memoir.

The heart of the book is Lubetkin's narrative concerning her observations on the fight against the Germans in Warsaw. She gives no figures on German losses, but she indicates that the Germans suffered many casualties and describes the battles in a number of places in the ghetto. Cynically, she notes the carnival right outside the burning ghetto walls as Poles watch in amusement. She tells how brave fighters continued their battles despite terrible odds, starvation, and the conflagration of crumbling buildings.

Yitzhak Zuckerman is able to use the services of a Gentile Pole who has a map of the sewers under Warsaw. When Zivia returns to the command post and sees the death of the gallant fighters, she agrees to go underground through the sewers to questionable safety on the so-called Aryan side. A number of civilians and fellow warriors make their way. They form a fighting group aiding Polish forces against the SS in August 1944. Her troupe luckily avoids capture as the SS crushes resistance. They are finally liberated from Nazi oppression by the Soviet Red Army.

LUSTIG, ARNOST
(1926–   )

The prolific Czech writer was born in Prague, the son of Emil and Therese Lustig. His mother was a distant relative of Sigmund Freud. In 1939, when Arnost was 13, he was forced out of public school by the German conquerors because of his Jewish birth. He became an apprentice tailor and leather worker. At age 15 he was interned at Theresienstadt, later at Buchenwald and Auschwitz. In April 1945, taking advantage of a strafing by an Allied plane of the freight train transporting him to Dachau, he escaped to Prague and joined the Czech resistance there. Liberated in 1945, he married Vera Weisly and fathered two children. He graduated from a university in Prague with two degrees, one in political science, the other in journalism. A communist party member, he went on to produce radio plays, screenplays, and documentaries. With the Soviet invasion of Czechoslovakia in 1968, however, he was declared "an enemy of the state." He then came to the United States, where his works were translated into English, and began writing particularly on Holocaust themes. Currently Lustig teaches English and the history of film at American University and resides in Washington, D.C.

Children of the Holocaust. Jeanne Nemcova and George Theiner, translators. Evanston, IL: Northwestern University Press, 1995. 516 pp. ISBN: 0810112795. Ages 15–up. Fiction.

This anthology consists of Lustig's three earlier works: *Night and Hope*, *Diamonds in the Night*, and *Darkness Casts No Shadow*. This first work consists of seven short stories. In "The Return" a 40-year-old bachelor hides in Prague to avoid deportation. He cannot take the restraints, so he leaves his hiding place only to fall into Nazi hands. "Rose Street" relates how a noncommissioned German soldier befriends an elderly Jewish women in Theresienstadt. "Hope" and "Blue Flame" deal with elderly people trying to cope in Theresienstadt, whereas "The Children and Moral Education" describes how young people adjust in the Czech ghetto.

Diamonds in the Night contains nine short stories dealing with moral behavior in the face of cruelty; in particular, with ethical behavior, which shines like "diamonds in the night." In "The Lemon" a son takes the gold teeth out of his dead father's mouth and strips him of his trousers in order to barter for a lemon to help his sick sister. In "White Rabbit" a boy goes to great lengths to obtain a white rabbit to cheer up a fellow Theresienstadt resident, a sick girl. Another boy working on the railroad risks death in order to obtain precious bread for starving fellow inmate workers.

The third work, *Darkness Casts No Shadow*, is a single novel, the most autobiographical of Lustig's writings. It relates the story of two young men bonded by their suffering at Auschwitz, now on a freight train to Dachau. A strafing by an Allied plane gives them a chance to escape, and they try to make it across Germany to Prague, their hometown. Starving and ravaged by dysentery, they enter a German town. The citizens see them as dangerous. When contact with the Gestapo cannot be made, the townspeople decide to murder the young men. Taken to the woods, the fugitives face death bravely.

Dita Saxova. Evanston, IL: Northwestern University Press, 1993. 358 pp. ISBN: 0810111314. Adult. Fiction.

In this biographical novel Dita is a young woman survivor of the concentration camps who tries to cope with postwar living. The story is set in 1947 Prague. Dita lives with other survivors, all orphaned teenagers rostered at an art school. They are at an in-between age, too old to be considered children, yet too young to be considered adult. They must nonetheless cope with adulthood. Their emotional strategy is nonattachment, for their previous hard, brutal life has made them mistrustful. All are lonely and enmeshed in a mass of contradictions. Dita expounds many ideas and philosophizes, but before she reaches any conclusions she meets death on a Swiss mountainside.

Indecent Dreams. Paul Wilson and Iris Urwin-Levit, translators. Evanston, IL: Northwestern University Press, 1990. 159 pp. ISBN: 0810109933. Ages 16–up. Fiction.

Lustig wrote three novellas to explore the lives of three characters, all females and Gentile living under the yoke of national socialism. The first fictional biography narrates the problems of a German prostitute assigned to occupied Prague. The second reveals the mind of a girl in a Nazi home for orphans, and the third examines the life of a young woman working as a cashier in a movie theater. All characters teeter on the edge of chaos, on the brink of death, and are faced with the brutality of a dehumanizing Nazi power.

The Unloved: From the Diary of Perla S. Evanston, IL: Northwestern University Press, 1996. 196 pp. ISBN: 0810113473. Ages 16–up. Fiction.

Set in Theresienstadt in 1943, this novel in diary form focuses on a 17-year-old girl, Perla. She offers sexual favors for advantages in the bitter ghetto. Perla avoids transports to Auschwitz by sleeping with the chairman of the Jewish Council of Elders. In this quasidocumentary, Lustig paints a picture of the ghetto's attempt at normalcy while each resident is faced with the prospect of deportation to doom. The Nazis permit such things as cafes, art, and soccer games to deceive the Red Cross about the true nature of ghettos and concentration camps. The diary records five months of Perla's life and includes her thoughts on the meaning of love, hate, sex, and generational relationships. It also documents increasing Nazi brutalization.

MEED, VLADKA (FEIGELE PELTEL MREDZYZECKI) (1922–)

Feigele Peltel Mredzyzecki was 17 years old when the Germans conquered Poland in 1939. In 1942, when it became apparent that the Nazis sought to destroy the Jews, she joined the Jewish Underground. Her blonde hair, fair complexion, and false papers gave her cover to act as a courier on both sides of the Warsaw Ghetto wall. Vladka, as she was known in the underground, helped Jews get out of the ghetto to the so-called Aryan side and smuggled weapons to the Jewish fighting groups inside. She played a vital part in the Warsaw Ghetto Uprising. When the Jewish revolt was put down, Vladka escaped through the sewers and joined the general Polish uprising in Warsaw in August 1944. Eventually, the Soviet Red Army liberated her and her fellow resisters. However, her parents, left behind in the ghetto, died at the annihilation camp Treblinka. Faced with postwar Polish anti-Semitism, she immigrated to New York City, married Benjamin Meed, and became very active in Holocaust education.

On Both Sides of the Wall. Steven Meed, translator. New York: Holocaust Library, 1979. 270 pp. ISBN: 0896040135. Ages 16–up. Memoir.

In her firsthand account the writer tells of the many enemies of the Jews and shows the Jews' isolation, victimization, and abandonment. The memoir relates the activities of the murderous Germans and their collaborators in the Final Solution. It bemoans the lack of support among the Poles and their many betrayals, such as the activities of the *szmalcownicy*, Polish civilian blackmailers who threatened to betray to the Gestapo Jews hiding outside the ghetto if they did not receive money. Vladka becomes a member of the Jewish Bund, a group that believes in Jewish cultural autonomy and socialism, but her idealism is seriously challenged by the indifferent, sometimes hostile performance of Gentiles, whose conscience she thought would be activated. The narrator tells of Jewish self-help in the ghetto: soup kitchens, schools, and nurseries. She describes the Jewish resisters, their preparations for armed revolt, and the two Jewish revolts (January 1943 and April 1943). Vladka describes her activities as a courier, not only outside the Warsaw Ghetto but in Czestochowa and Radom, two other Polish cities. Other chapters relate the deeds of righteous Polish friends and the bravery of Jewish partisans. She and a band of Warsaw fighters joined with Gentile Poles in their August 1944 uprising. The last two chapters focus on her return to Warsaw years later and her reactions to her wartime experiences.

NYISZLI, MIKLOS
(1919?–)

Miklos Nyiszli was a mature man, a physician, with a wife and daughter when the German army invaded his hometown, Orade-Nagyvarad, Hungary, in March 1944. Soon after, he and his family were deported to Auschwitz. Dr. Josef Mengele, the infamous Nazi doctor who performed inhuman experiments, took a liking to him, and thus Miklos became the chief physician in charge of the Sonderkommando, the workforce of 860 males whose task was cleaning out the gas chambers; removing hair, gold teeth, and valuables from the corpses; and taking the bodies to the furnaces to be burned. Nyiszli survived the camp, endured a death march in 1945, and was reunited after the war with his wife and daughter.

Auschwitz: A Doctor's Eyewitness Account. Tibere Kremer and Richard Seaver, translators. New York: Arcade Publishing, 1993. 222 pp. ISBN: 1559702028. Ages 14–up. Memoir.

Nyiszli's memoir, first published in 1960, reveals much about the infamous Dr. Josef Mengele. It exposes the the SS doctor's terrible experiments and the nature of the "selections" prisoners underwent, which most often led to their execution by gas. The text reveals Nyiszli's complicity in the experiments, particularly on twins and gypsies, a complicity severely condemned in the long introduction by Bruno Bettelheim, the famous psychoanalyst. Nyiszli also details the Sonderkommando revolt in Crematorium Number 3, which killed seventy SS guards. The physician inmate describes the death march from Auschwitz to Mathausen, then his further incarceration at Ebensee, and the site of his liberation by the Americans. The autobiography concludes with the doctor's surprise that his daughter and wife survived. He and his family return to their home in Hungary, where Nyiszli resumes his practice.

OPDYKE, IRENE GUT
(1922–)

Irene Gut, a Polish Catholic, eldest of four sisters, was born in Kozienice in eastern Poland, an area bordering Russia. Her father, an architect and chemist, and mother, a homemaker, moved about in Poland and settled in Radom. There Irene went to high school as well as nursing school. In September 1939 the Soviet army conquered the region, and Irene, only 17, went to work as a nurse in nearby Ternopol. She and her family were maltreated by the Soviets. Her father was reduced to making carpet slippers; she was raped.

With the Nazi invasion of the Soviet Union in 1941, worse treatment was in store for Irene Gut, her family, and the Polish people. Irene came under the protection of a German army major. As a housekeeper in Radom, she witnessed the persecution and murder of Jews. Soon she found a way of rescuing a number of them. The Germans murdered her father. "Liberated" by the Soviet Red Army in 1944, again she was mistreated, this time by the Soviets, who arrested and imprisoned her mother for a time. Escaping their grasp and impersonating a Jewess, she fled to the American Zone of Occupation in Germany to a displaced persons camp. In 1949 she immigrated to Brooklyn and later married a UN worker whom she had met in the displaced persons camp. A winner of the Righteous Gentile Award from the Holocaust memorial institution Yad Vashem, she lectures, writes, and speaks on her wartime experiences.

In My Hands: Memories of a Holocaust Rescuer. Irene Gut Opdyke with Jennifer Armstrong. New York: Alfred A. Knopf, 1999. 276 pp. ISBN: 0679891811. Ages 13–17. Memoir.

Irene is only 17 in 1939 when the maelstrom of war separates her from her family—her parents and three sisters. For a while she is part of a remnant of Polish soldiers; then she is in the hands of the Soviet Red Army, which has taken over eastern Poland. She serves as a nurse for them. In 1941 the invading Germans conquer Poland's Soviet-occupied area. She is made to work for her new masters by serving German officers in a hotel in Radom. Her blonde hair and fair looks are an advantage with the "Aryan"-loving Nazis. The hotel is next to the newly created Jewish ghetto. Irene is sickened by the murder of a Jewish baby killed by German soldiers after being thrown up and shot in the air. She notes the suffering inflicted upon Jews and schemes to help them. At first came small steps: slipping food into the ghetto; providing information on Nazi plans overheard at the officers' table; and then came the task of smuggling Jews from a forced labor group into a hiding place in the forest.

A German army major who takes a liking to Irene employs her as housekeeper for his nearby villa. Irene now shields Jewish slave laborers working at the hotel where she formerly waitressed by hiding them in the basement of the villa. When the major discovers the twelve Jews, Irene becomes his mistress to protect them. With the approach of the Soviet Red Army and the German retreat from Poland, Irene, a patriot, joins a partisan band. When the Soviets take over again, she manages to elude them and get to the American Zone of Occupation of Germany.

Children's writer Jennifer Armstrong translates this first-person Polish narrative into an English memoir. Its straightforward style tells much about Polish life under both the Nazis and the communists during World War II. The postscript tells in pictures and words the fate of Irene Gut's family and of those whom she rescued.

ORENSTEIN, HENRY
(1923–)

Henry Orenstein was born in Hrubrieszow, Poland, a town very close to the White Russian border. His father was a well-to-do commodities broker; his mother, as usual in those days, a homemaker caring for five children. Henry attended Polish public schools until he was 16 in 1939, when German and Soviet aggressors dismembered Poland. The family lived a short while under the communists; but when Germany attacked the Soviet Union in June 1941, the Final Solution was unleashed. Henry's parents were immediately murdered and his siblings transported to concentration camps. Brothers Henry, Sam, and Fred survived, but Felix and a sister, Hanka, perished. Upon liberation the brothers went to a displaced persons camp in the American Zone of Occupation. In 1947 an uncle in New York helped the brothers immigrate to the United States, where Henry Orenstein became a partner with his uncle and manufactured toys. He married and devoted a great deal of his fortune to charitable work among the elderly poor.

I Shall Live: Surviving against All Odds, 1939–1948. New York: Simon & Schuster, 1987. 272 pp. ISBN: 0825304415. Ages 14–up. Memoir.

In this autobiography Henry Orenstein presents his life in a town in Poland before World War I, then under the communists, and then under the Nazi boot. He was an inmate in five concentration camps and a participant in a death march. What is unusual about his narrative is that Orenstein volunteered for an ultrasecret "Chemical Commando" (work squad) of inmate chemists, engineers, and mathematicians (most of whom were impersonators). The purpose of this group was to create a gas that would paralyze the Allies' armed forces engines, including tanks, planes, and motorized vehicles. Orenstein's membership enabled him to avoid the worst conditions of the camps, which could have meant death. The commando unit was phony from the start, according to Orenstein, a ruse by certain SS officers and professors to avoid Russian front duty. The equipment and assignments had no relationship to the task. Orenstein hypothesizes that the SS kept prisoners alive, guarded them, and moved them about in the face of collapsing German resistance in order to stay away from the dangerous front lines. Since the author wrote this memoir forty years after the events, he had to verify his recollections by conversing with inmates who had been with him. Another author, George Topas, was in the same chemical work squad but came to a different conclusion regarding the Chemical Commando. (See Topas's *The Iron Furnace*, reviewed in this volume.)

ORGEL, DORIS (ADELBERG)
(1929–)

Doris Adelberg was born in Vienna, Austria, to middle-class Jewish parents. She endured the growing Nazification of her country, then the final annexation in 1938. She attended a private girls school. Her parents, after much difficulty, obtained visas to immigrate to the United States in 1940. There Adelberg attended Radcliffe College, 1946–1948, and then Barnard College, graduating in 1950. She married Shelly Orgel, a psychiatrist, in 1949 and became the mother of three children. Orgel worked in the magazine and book-publishing fields to 1955; she then devoted herself to full-time writing. She lives in Scarsdale, New York.

The Devil in Vienna. New York: Puffin, 1988. 246 pp. ISBN: 014032500X. Ages 9–12. Fiction.

In this autobiographical novel written as a diary, a Jewish girl, Inge Dornenwald, and a Christian daughter of a Nazi, Lieselotte Vessely, have been "blood friends" since they started school in 1931. However, the Nazi Party is growing more powerful in Austria, and the friendship is becoming more and more difficult to maintain. In 1938 Nazi Germany annexes Austria, and a flood of anti-Jewish laws comes forth. The novel relates violent scenes in Vienna's streets, with attacks on Jews and the Dornenwald family's difficulty in gaining exit from a dangerous situation.

Lieselotte faces punishment and rancor for her friendship with Inge. She is forced to join the League of German Girls (Hitler Youth), yet the friends continue to meet secretly. The devil in Vienna is the Nazis. The girls manage to elude the devil to maintain their friendship.

ORLEV, URI (JERZY HENRY ORLOWSKI) (1931–)

Jerzy Henry Orlowski was born in Warsaw, Poland, in 1931, the son of upper-middle-class assimilated Jewish parents. His father, a physician for the Polish army, was captured at the outbreak of the war in 1939 fighting the Soviet Red Army, which invaded Poland from the east; he perished as a result of the Soviets' policy of killing Polish army officers. The Germans occupied the western half of Poland, including Warsaw. The Nazis eventually trapped Jerzy, his mother, and his brother in the Warsaw Ghetto. His mother was killed during the uprising, and upon the defeat of the ghetto fighters, the brothers were sent to Bergen-Belsen. After liberation by the British in 1945, Orlowski immigrated to Palestine, where he changed his name to a more Hebrew one. He worked on a kibbutz in the Lower Galilee from 1950 to 1957. He also served in the Israeli army. He left the kibbutz and now lives in Jerusalem with his second wife and four children, earning a living as a writer.

Island on Bird Street. Hillel Halkin, translator. Boston: Houghton Mifflin, 1984. 176 pp. ISBN: 0395338875. Ages 11–14. Fiction.

Published in Hebrew in 1981, the novel revolves around Alexander, a Jewish boy living under siege in a ruined house in Nazi-occupied Warsaw. Because the enemy captured his father and mother, Alex is alone and must survive by his wits. This third-person account in matter-of-fact novel form views the Warsaw Ghetto through the peephole of an abandoned building at 78 Bird Street. However, on occasion Alex does lower a rope and forage for food and fuel. Later in the novel he meets up with his father, who takes him to the so-called Aryan (non-Jewish) side of Warsaw and then to a forest to become a partisan. Alex gets the chance to shoot a German soldier. As in his other novels, Orlev draws upon his personal childhood experiences, particularly in the Warsaw Ghetto.

The Lead Soldiers: A Novel. Hillel Halkin, translator. New York: Tap-linger, 1980. 234 pp. ISBN: 0800845765. Ages 13–16. Fiction.

This is Orlev's first novel based largely on personal experiences from his shattered childhood in Nazi-occupied Poland. It is told in the first person through the eyes of a child. Two brothers, Yurik and Kazid, are Polish Jews who are unaware of their Jewish origins. Their highly assim-ilated parents send them to Catholic schools. With the German invasion of Poland, the brothers' parents are murdered and the boys come under the care of an aunt. Very resourceful, she hides them in attics and cellars in the Warsaw Ghetto. To smash the uprising, the ghetto is set afire. Captured, the family is sent to Bergen-Belsen. Despite the terrible events crashing upon them, as a means of escape the brothers create an imag-inary world that includes stories about lead soldiers (hence the title). The brothers, like Orlev himself, survive Bergen-Belsen. The novel also con-tains commentary on the Holocaust in Poland.

Lydia, Queen of Palestine. Hillel Halkin, translator. Boston: Houghton Mifflin, 1993. 176 pp. ISBN: 0395656605. Ages 9–12. Fiction.

Lydia, a novel told in the third person, is a book for middle-school children. Lydia is 11 years old residing in prewar Bucharest, Romania, with her mother, recently divorced from her father, who now lives on a kibbutz (collective farm) in the Jewish settlement in Palestine. Her fan-tasy is to marry Prince Michael of Romania and become queen. She faces growing anti-Semitic hostility as her country aligns with Nazi Germany. Sensing great danger, Lydia's mother smuggles her out of the country to a kibbutz. The narrative describes a tense train ride out of Romania. When Lydia arrives in Palestine, she has great difficulty adjusting to communal life. Finding her father married, she greatly resents her step-mother. Her fantasies now move to being the Queen of Palestine. When Lydia's mother comes to Palestine, remarried, Lydia resents her stepfa-ther. Finally, she reconciles herself to her stepparents and to her new life, but not fully. Her experiences as narrated by Orlev are at the pe-riphery of Jewish life during World War II.

Man from the Other Side. Hillel Halkin, translator. New York: Pen-guin, 1994. 186 pp. ISBN: 0140370689. Ages 10–14. Fiction.

Marek believes he is a Gentile Pole. He lives with his mother, stepfather, and grandparents just outside the Warsaw Ghetto. The family helps the entrapped Jews by smuggling goods for profit though the foul sewers. Marek has very negative feelings toward Jews, and he and two buddies mug an escaping ghetto Jew, taking away his valuables. Marek's mother explains to him that, in effect, the escapee has been given a death sentence. She also reveals that Marek's father was Jewish and murdered in prison by the Nazis. Changed by this news, the boy resolves to help Jews. The family aids Jozek, another escapee, taking him into their home, though the stepfather and grandparents still dislike Jews. Based on true events as told by a 14-year-old boy, Marek, the story reveals much about the uprising in the Warsaw Ghetto.

PEREL, SOLOMON
(1925–)

Solomon Perel was born in Peine, a town near Brunswick, Germany, and was the youngest of four children. The family was supported by a shoe store. When Hitler came to power, Solomon's father decided to move his family to relatives in Lodz, Poland. Nazi Germany caught up with them with the invasion of Poland in September 1939, but Sol and his older brother escaped to the Soviet Zone of Occupation in eastern Poland. Sol was sent to an orphanage run by the communists. The Germans caught him again with their invasion of the Soviet Union in 1941. Pretending he was of German descent, Perel attended an elite Hitler Youth school, then fought against the Soviet Red Army. The Reds captured him, but by a fluke, identified by his brother, Sol was liberated. He immigrated to Israel in 1948 and fought in its War of Independence.

Europa, Europa. Margot Bettauer Dembo, translator. New York: John Wiley & Sons, 1997. 217 pp. ISBN: 0471172189. Ages 14–up. Memoir.

Solomon Perel wrote this memoir in 1988, forty-three years after the events of his life during the war. He gives us a glimpse of the persecution Jews faced when Hitler came to power, but only just past 1935. Then the scene switches to Lodz, Poland, first under Polish rule, then as a German-installed ghetto. Perel escapes to the Soviet-controlled section and to a communist-run orphanage, where he is exposed to antireligious indoctrination. Here Perel reveals the persecution and repression of peoples under Soviet rule in the Soviet sector of Poland. With the German invasion of the Soviet Union in 1941, Perel falls into the German army's hands and is mistaken for an Aryan German. The reader learns about the war against the Russians. A long section ensues about Perel's induction into an elite Hitler Youth school. Sol is returned to the German army and falls into Russian hands after a fight. Finally, liberation comes: Sol meets his brother, a concentration camp survivor, now a Soviet soldier, the only one left of his family. Finding freedom, the author leaves Europe and ends up in Israel. His stated motive in writing the memoir is to oppose neo-Nazism and to keep alive the memory of the evils of Nazism and communism.

A full-length movie was made of Perel's narrative.

PERL, GISELLA
(1925–   )

Gisella Perl was a native of Maramaros Sziget in Transylvania, a province sandwiched between Romania and Hungary. She was born to rather well-to-do, assimilated Jewish parents, attended Hungarian public schools, then the universities, and graduated as a medical doctor. Germans occupied the region in March 1944 and created a ghetto for Jews. Perl was permitted to run a clinic for women started by her and her physician husband in the ghetto. Her husband became head of the Judenrat (Jewish Council), which helped govern the ghetto. After a few months she and her husband and son were deported to Auschwitz and separated. Her husband and son were murdered, but Dr. Josef Mengele, the chief Nazi physician at the camp, chose her to serve as a gynecologist, her specialty. In 1945 she was transferred to Bergen-Belsen concentration camp in northern Germany, where she contracted typhus. Liberated by the British, she spent a short time recuperating in a convent. She soon immigrated to New York and became an American citizen. In 1970 Perl immigrated to Israel and assumed a position at Shaari Zedek Medical Center, where she now makes special efforts to care for the children of former survivors.

I Was a Doctor in Auschwitz. North Stratford, NH: Ayer Company Publishers, 1998. 1989 pp. ISBN: 0881432008. Ages 14–up. Memoir.

Dr. Perl's first-person memoir relates how as a Jewish gynecologist, with practically no medical supplies or equipment, she tried to relieve the suffering and save the lives of hundreds of women exposed to extreme and brutal depravity at Auschwitz and Bergen-Belsen. She describes the horror of both camps, giving intimate details about the daily life of inmate deportees. Gisella Perl has to perform abortions and infanticide in order to save the lives of women, since discovery of the pregnant women or Dr. Perl's clandestine activity would send them all to the gas chambers. Dr. Perl's memoir illuminates the depraved psyche of the female Nazi guards, the doctors, and the prisoner trustees, called kapos, as well as the dehumanization of the inmates. She exposes the SS matron Irma Grese, the sadistic guard over female prisoners, and the infamous Dr. Josef Mengele, who conducted painful experiments on children. Upon liberation by the British in April 1945, Perl seeks her husband and son, only to find they had been murdered. Very depressed, she attempts suicide. The narrative ends with the efforts of a kindly Catholic priest who restores her health and will to live.

REDLICH, EGON (GONDA)
(1916–1944)

Egon Redlich (Gonda) was born in the Czechoslovakian city of Olmutz, the youngest of five children. His legal studies after high school were interrupted by the Nazi occupation of Czechoslovakia in 1939. He then became a teacher in a Zionist-oriented Jewish school. In December 1941 he was deported to the ghetto–concentration camp in the city of Terezin, called Theresienstadt by the Germans. His work as an educator impressed the "elders" (leaders of the Jewish Council of the ghetto), and Gonda was appointed to this governing body, which was under the control of the Nazis. In January 1942 he began a diary that concluded in October 1944 just before his deportation to Auschwitz-Birkenau, where he perished.

The Terezin Diary of Gonda Redlich. Saul Friedman, editor; Laurence Kutler, translator. Lexington: University Press of Kentucky, 1992. 177 pp. ISBN: 081311842. Ages 16–up. Diary.

Gonda's diary begins in January 1942 and ends in October 1944. It is actually two diaries, one in general and the other written for his son, Dan, started in March 1944. The first diary contains very short entries that tell about the daily life in the ghetto—the social breakdown; the inhumane conditions; and the cultural, class, and individual conflicts. Whereas the diary entries are brief, the editor's footnotes are long, rich with historical information about Terezin and the Holocaust in general. Gonda deals with the massive preparations for the Red Cross visit in June 1944, revealing how the Nazis tried to create the false impression of a humane camp. One terrible responsibility of the elders was to choose inmates for deportation. Gonda struggles with his conscience in having to be involved with selections for such deportations, which he knows go to Auschwitz, the death camp. The second diary is a chronicle of a lover and a father and is directed to his son, Dan, who is born in the ghetto. Both diaries were smuggled out by friends who survived.

REESE, JOANNA
(1932–)

Joanna Reese was born and raised in Wunterswijh, Holland, to an assimilated Jewish family. Her father, Mr. de Leeuw, was a wealthy cattle dealer; her mother, a housewife, was sickly. With the conquest of the Netherlands by Germany in 1940, her father went to Rotterdam with Joanna's older sister Rachel to care for his wife, who died shortly after. Annie and her sister Sini, three years her senior, were provided with a hiding place by a friendly Gentile farm family in an out-of-the-way rural area, Usselo. The girls spent two and one-half years in an upstairs room, sometimes with German officers quartered in the dining room below. Liberated in 1945 by Canadian forces and reunited with her sister Rachel and her father, Annie completed her education and in 1948 immigrated to New York City. She attended college, graduated as an elementary teacher, married, and had two children. She taught elementary school and later in life turned to writing and became an editor.

The Journey Back. New York: Crowell, 1976. 212 pp. ISBN: 0054470423. Ages 10–13. Memoir.

It is spring 1945, and Annie is now 13. She and her sister Sini, 16, say goodbye to their protectors, the Oostervelds. They return home and reunite with their father and sister Rachel, 21. Their mother had died in 1942, the year they went into hiding. Rachel has converted to Christianity. Sini enjoys dancing every night with Allied soldiers. Annie must adjust to her new stepmother. The memoir describes the aftermath of war in Holland, which included revenge upon traitors and the confusion of returning Jews who had lost all or part of their families. From time to time the narrative reverts to memories of occupied World War II Holland.

The bulk of the memoir, however, deals with Annie's adjustment to "normal" life—adjusting to school, making friends, and rediscovering her Jewish identity.

The Upstairs Room. New York: Thomas Crowell, 1972. 196 pp. ISBN: 0690851278. Ages 10–13. Memoir.

The upstairs room was where Annie and her sister Sini hid for over two and one-half years during the German occupation of Holland in

World War II. Their father, trying to care for their sick mother along with their older sister Rachel, was in Rotterdam. The story, written from a first-person perspective, was thirty years in the writing. The Oostervelds, a kindly Dutch family, tried to entertain the girls by bringing them books. Meanwhile, the girls had to be very cautious, for German officers often occupied the living room downstairs. The situation was fraught with danger both for the girls and for their protectors, for if discovered, all of them would be executed. The narrative contains very little about Jewish tradition or practices. It does relate the difficulties Jews had in Holland, particularly in trying to escape the Nazi noose. It also shows the gradual Nazi restrictions, including forced labor raids, prior to implementation of the Final Solution.

RINGELBLUM, EMMANUEL
(1900–1944)

The historian–archivist was born in Buczucy, Poland, to middle-class Jewish parents. He attended Polish public schools and then graduated with a Ph.D. from a Polish university, specializing in medieval Warsaw Jewry. He married in Warsaw and had a son, Uri. From 1930 on he represented the American Joint Distribution Committee, a welfare organization. He also was attached as a historian to the Institute for Jewish Research (YIVO). Ringelblum was in Geneva when the Germans attacked Poland; however, he returned to Warsaw. Enclosed in the ghetto, Ringelblum organized self-help committees and soup kitchens. As a member of the Resistance, he gathered a group of historians around him and formed an archive known as the "Oneg Shabbat" (Sabbath Joy), since they met on Saturdays. They recorded information on daily life in the ghetto, stored much of it, and gave details of the Final Solution in Warsaw to the Polish Underground, who in turn passed the news on to the Polish government-in-exile in London. Ringelblum was captured and placed in a slave labor camp, from which he escaped. However, he was recaptured with his wife and 12-year-old son, and the Gestapo shot them all.

Notes from the Warsaw Ghetto: The Journal of Emmanuel Ringelblum. Jacob Sloan, editor and translator. New York: Schocken Books, 1986. 389 pp. ISBN: 080204601. Ages 16–up. Diary.

This book, a diary comprising two years in the Warsaw Ghetto, is taken from Ringelblum's personal notes found in a milkcan. Three cans filled with notes and data compiled by the archivists of the Oneg Shabbat were hidden in the ghetto. Two were retrieved after the war. Ringelblum's notes reveal a man trying to record events objectively but moved deeply by the plight of children who are hungry and often orphaned. He notes how they beg for food and alms and how they cry at night, often under his window. He admires the children who wish to learn about their Jewish heritage despite severe Nazi penalties against such instruction. He relates the random shootings by the Nazis and the capricious withdrawal from time to time of vital services such as electricity. He records the growing desperation of ghetto residents, a desperation that led some to blackmail fellow Jews and even to extract teeth from dead bodies. He and ghetto residents know what deportation really means, and he writes of the horror, but also humanitarianism, of those selected for doom. His most critical remarks are reserved for the Jewish police and their leaders, members of the Jewish Council, whom he believes are wrong in carrying out the terrible decrees of their Nazi overlords. Ringelblum hoped that by recording the evil deeds of the Nazis and the sufferings of the Jews, the perpetrators would be brought to the door of justice.

ROTH-HANO, RENEE
(1931–)

Renee Roth-Hano was born in Muloune, Alsace, which at the time belonged to France. She lived with her assimilated middle-class Jewish parents and two sisters until 1940, the year of the defeat of France by German armed forces. Her mother escaped with the family to Paris. When the Germans passed more and more oppressive decrees against French Jews, Renee's mother arranged for the three sisters to live as Catholics in a Catholic women's residence in Flers, Normandy. Only a few nuns knew the girls were Jewish and kept the secret. The family was reunited after the liberation in August 1944. Renee completed her high school education in Paris, then traveled to the United States as an au pair for a New York Jewish 10-year-old. She had become a Catholic in Flers, but returned to Judaism in New York. Attending college, she graduated with a master's degree in social work and became a psychotherapist.

Touch Wood: A Girlhood in Occupied France. New York: Four Winds Press, 1988. 297 pp. ISBN: 003777340X. Ages 13–16. Fiction.

This autobiographical novel, told in diary form, is set in occupied France during 1940–1944. The storyline closely follows Renee's personal experiences. In the beginning of 1942, the Nazis began to institute their so-called Final Solution to the Jewish problem. Mrs. Roth finds shelter for Renee and her sister in a Catholic women's residence in Normandy.

The story reveals the kindness, sympathy, and heroism of the mother superior and two nuns who shelter the sisters. Only they know the girls are Jewish. Discovery by the German authorities would mean disaster for the institution and its residents. The girls suffer from illness, hunger, Allied bombings, and narrow escapes until liberation by British soldiers in 1944 after the Allied victories in Normandy. The family is reunited in September 1944 in Paris. All come through alive.

RUBINSTEIN, ERNA (FERBER)
(1922–   )

Erna Ferber was born in Krakow, Poland, the daughter of Arnold Ferber, a businessman, and Eleanor Ferber. The Jewish Orthodox family had five siblings: four girls, of whom Erna was the eldest, and a boy. After the German occupation in fall 1939, the family went through life in a ghetto. In 1942 the family was deported to Auschwitz, where Erna's parents and brother perished. Supporting each other, the four sisters survived the rigors of the concentration camp. After surviving a death march liberated by American soldiers in Czechoslovakia, Erna served the army as an interpreter for a while. She became a child welfare worker for the UN Relief and Rehabilitation Administration (UNRRA) in Germany. She married Dr. Henry Rubinstein, an American soldier, in 1946. In 1949 the couple immigrated to the United States, where the sisters were reunited. In Syracuse, New York, Erna graduated from the State University of New York and then taught at that institution. The couple has two children.

After the Holocaust: The Long Road to Freedom. New York: Shoe String Press, 1995. 192 pp. ISBN: 0208024202. Ages 14–up. Memoir.

Erna Rubinstein picks up her autobiography near the end of the death march described in her first book. She describes the prisoners' fear of the Germans as they realize they are losing the war and the end is near. At the surrender she is in American hands and serves the American army as an interpreter, for Erna speaks six languages. She is soon sent to a displaced persons camp because she does not wish to return to Krakow, the scene of murder and anti-Semitism. Serving as a child welfare worker for UNRRA, Erna recounts the frustrations felt by stateless and homeless displaced persons. She recounts a number of stories of war survivors, how some survived in bunkers, how others were sheltered by righteous Christians, and how yet others escaped to Russia. She tells how her hus-

band, Henry Rubinstein, a physician, liberated Dachau and concludes
with her immigrating to America and the reunion with her three sisters.

The Survivor in Us All: Four Young Sisters in the Holocaust. New York:
Shoe String Press, 1986. 185 pp. ISBN: 0208021280. Ages 14–up.
Memoir.

This autobiography by Erna Ferber Rubinstein delineates the horrors
of war, in particular the atrocities committed during the Holocaust. The
four sisters, supported by their religious faith and loyalty to each other,
survive the ghetto ordeal and life in Auschwitz. The most graphic part
of the narrative is the death march in March 1945 when the sisters trudge
many, many miles without proper food, clothing, or shelter and endure
the brutality of sadistic guards. They are in constant hunger and in pain
from bleeding feet and freezing cold, and they fear mindless, random
execution. In the chaos of the closing days of the war against Germany,
the sisters escape their captors until the final surrender by Nazi Germany
to the Allies in early May 1945.

SCHLOSS, EVA (GIERLANGER)
(1929–   )

Eva Gierlanger was born in Vienna to a wealthy, nonobservant Jewish
family. Her father was a shoe manufacturer; her mother (as was common
seventy years ago) was a homemaker. The family, which included an
older brother, left for Holland soon after Hitler came to power in 1933.
They were friends of the Frank family, and Eva went to school with
Anne in Amsterdam. With the conquest of the Netherlands by Germany,
the family went into hiding. Discovered in 1944, they were sent to
Auschwitz-Birkenau. Eva and her mother survived, but her father and
her brother perished. Liberated by the Soviet Red Army, they eventually
returned to Amsterdam. Eva's mother, Fritzi, later married Otto Frank
and resided in Switzerland. In 1952 Eva, who immigrated to England,
married an Israeli, and today the couple dwell in England earning a
living in the antiques business.

Eva's Story: A Survivor's Tale by the Step-Sister of Anne Frank. With
Evelyn Julia Kent. New York: St. Martin's Press, 1989. 224 pp. ISBN:
0312029136. Ages 12–up. Memoir.

This memoir reads very much like the diary of Anne Frank, but where
the Frank story ends, Eva's picks up. Fortunately, Eva survives with her
mother through Birkenau. The two rely on each other through SS tor-

ments. However, her father and brother perish. Part 3 deals with liberation by the Russians and the aftermath of World War II. Eva includes much about her mother, Fritzi, who later marries Otto Frank, Anne's father. (Fritzi has a chapter of her own.) Unlike Polish Jews who return home to find themselves dispossessed and facing murderous anti-Semitism, Eva and her mother find a friendly and helpful Dutch people and a return to "normal" life. Living in Holland is painful, however, reminding Eva of the past, and so she immigrates to England. Eva includes a number of photos of her former life as a refugee in Holland, where Eva and her family were welcomed and aided in hiding by Dutch resisters. She dates her memoir using headlines from events in the European theater during World War II.

SCHNEIDER, GERTRUDE
(1929–   )

Historian Gertrude Schneider was born in Vienna to a highly educated, assimilated Jewish family. In November 1941 she, her parents, and younger sister were deported, along with 20,000 other Austrian Jews, to a ghetto in Riga, Latvia. When the ghetto was dismantled in late fall 1943, her father took sick and died, and Gertrude, now an adolescent, her younger sister, and her mother were taken to the nearby Kaiserwald concentration camp. In August 1944, as the Soviet Red Army began to close in on the Germans in Latvia, they were transported by barge to the Stutthof concentration camp near Danzig (Gdansk). The three of them participated in a death march through freezing weather and snow in Pomerania, Germany, until liberated by the Red Army. Soon after the war Gertrude moved to New York City, completing her education and eventually receiving a doctorate in history. Dr. Schneider heads a survivor group of ex-Latvian prisoners; she collects and edits their stories and has them published.

Exile and Destruction: The Fate of Austrian Jews, 1938–1948. Westport, CT: Greenwood Publishing Group, 1995. 256 pp. ISBN: 0275951301. Ages 17–up. Memoir.

Schneider provides an overview of the events that overtook Austria's 180,000 Jews. She covers the annexation by Nazi Germany, Kristallnacht, and then the transports to Litzmannstadt, Riga, and Minsk as well as other ghettos and camps in Poland, Russia, and Latvia. The Holocaust historian follows the transports to their destinations and personalizes the events, for she was one of those Austrian Jews. Included are stories not only of these ghetto and camp experiences but also of the homecoming of the survivors. A chapter gives an accounting of each camp survivor and the statistics of the victims who perished. The work is permeated with biographies and personal experiences.

Muted Voices: Jewish Survivors of Latvia Remember. New York: Philosophical Library, 1987. 276 pp. ISBN: 0802225365. Ages 15–up. Memoir.

The organization Jewish Survivors of Latvia commissioned this anthology of memoirs. The centerpiece story by Semyon Peyros tells about five human guinea pigs who underwent ghastly so-called scientific experiments for their Nazi captors. Other voices speak of children in the ghetto, of the music, and of the weapons obtained and hidden there. Powerful is the narrative by David Packer, a resister, aided in his escape by the righteous Roman Catholic priest Father Kaisers. All entries are edited by Schneider, a survivor of the ghetto, whose introductions have the authenticity of firsthand knowledge. The anthology reveals the uncommon courage of inmates.

The Unfinished Road: Jewish Survivors of Latvia Look Back. New York: Praeger, 1991. 232 pp. ISBN: 0275940934. Ages 15–up. Memoir.

This book is an anthology of firsthand eyewitness accounts (including Gertrude Schneider's) of Jews in captivity in the Riga Ghetto and in the Kaiserwald and Stutthof concentration camps. Some of the accounts were written in Russian and not discovered until 1967 in New York. They reveal the unhappy fate of children in Camp Kaiserwald. The writer tells her own harrowing journey on a barge from Kaiserwald to Danzig on the way to Stutthof, a punishment camp. Schneider reveals how prisoners were treated according to Hitler's racial theories: Nordic "Aryan" Danish prisoners received far better treatment than did Jews. The writer graphically relates the cruel death march from Stutthof until liberation.

SCHULMAN, FAYE (LAZEBRICK)
(1923–)

Faye Lazebrick was born in Lenin, Poland, close to the White Russian border. Her parents, observant Jews, were middle class, for her father, Yakov, was a fabric merchant. Faye was one of three girls and four boys. After the Soviet invasion of eastern Poland in 1939, the family lived under communist rule. In June 1941 the Nazis attacked the Soviet Union and occupied Lenin. In August 1942 the occupiers instituted their genocidal policies, and only Faye and her brother, Kopel, survived. Brother and sister joined Soviet partisans in nearby woods and fought with them for two years. In July 1944, the Soviet Red Army liberated the Pinsk region in which the Molotavia partisans, Faye's group, operated. Faye married a fellow Jewish partisan, Morris Schulman. Unwilling to live under capricious communist rule, they made their way to the American Zone of Occupation in Germany and to the Landsberg displaced persons camp. A baby girl was born to the couple, who in 1946 immigrated to Toronto, Canada. Currently, Faye Schulman lectures on her experiences as a partisan.

A Partisan's Memoir: Woman of the Holocaust. With Sarah Silberstein Swartz. Toronto, Canada: Second Story Press, 1995. 224 pp. ISBN: 0929005767. Ages 14–up. Memoir.

The heart of this memoir is Faye Schulman's story of two years with Soviet partisans, August 1942 to July 1944. Faye, only 19 in 1942, acted as a soldier, nurse, and photographer to the partisans. She was the only female in the Molotavia Brigade, made up of former Russian POWs. The brigade started with ninety members and grew to 2,000 fighters. There was no deference to her as a female; Faye relates the difficulties of keeping up with hardy soldiers. Because many of the partisans were anti-Semitic, she did not reveal that she was Jewish. Her brother, a photographer, had taught her his trade, and a Jewish doctor they met early in the woods taught Faye elements of nursing. The partisans were crude, suspicious, and unpredictable, and Faye had to use all her wits to avoid murder by her comrades. Later she met up with Kopal, her brother, who had joined another partisan group. Upon liberation she became romantically involved with Morris Schulman, a partisan commander whom Faye soon married. The goodwill generated by their soldiering enabled them to get out of Soviet hands in Pinsk and make their way to the Americans. Her memoir is augmented by Faye's photos and reveals the extent of activities of Soviet partisans and the role of Jews who fought with them.

SCHWARZ-BART, ANDRE
(1928–   )

The historical novelist Andre Schwarz-Bart was the son of Polish Jews who migrated to France in 1924. Andre was born in Metz. In 1941, when he was only 15, his parents were brutally murdered by the Nazis. Andre joined the French Resistance. He was captured once, but escaped. Upon the liberation of France in World War II, he joined the regular Free French army. Afterward he worked in a factory as a simple blue-collar worker. *The Last of the Just*, published in 1959, was his first novel. Schwarz-Bart then took an interest in blacks and black slavery, most notably in his novel *La Multatresse Solitude*. He wrote novels in French exploring this subject, showing parallels with the incarceration of Jews during World War II.

> *The Last of the Just*. Stephen Becker, translator. New York: Fine Communication, 1996. 374 pp. ISBN: 1567311407. Ages 14–up. Fiction.

This historical novel spans 1185 to 1943. It deals with Jewish martyrdom in European Christian society. Schwarz-Bart changes the legend of the "Righteous Thirty-Six Just Men" to the story of the Levy family. The original legend states that the thirty-six mortals, based on a passage from the prophet Isaiah, "are the hearts of the world multiplied and into them, as one receptacle, pour all our griefs." The Just Men accept the suffering of humanity, enabling humankind to survive because with the knowledge of man's inhumanity against man it could not do so. *The Last of the Just* traces Rabbi Yom Tov Levy's family and descendants. The rabbi is martyred at York, England, in 1185. The story moves from Levy's martyrdom to Levy experiences in the Spanish Inquisition, expulsions in the Middle Ages, and various pogroms. However, the crux of the novel is Ernest Levy's story and his death at Auschwitz. To Schwarz-Bart, Ernest Levy is the last of the just (although the legend contends there are thirty-six all the time at random). Persecution drives Ernest and his family from Germany to France, which then falls to German arms. Ernest tries to conceal his identity. Having married Golda Engelbaum, a cripple, he cannot remain free, so he presents himself for capture as a Jew at Drancy, the transit concentration camp near Paris. The narrative relates his horrible ride in a cattle car to Auschwitz and then his last moments inside the gas chamber. Schwarz-Bart has chronicled the sufferings of the Jewish people, which he believes are the distinctive feature of Jewish history. He also implies there is no Jewish existence independent of the Jewish religion.

SENDER, RUTH ("RIVA") MINSKY
(1926–   )

"Riva" was born in Lodz, Poland, to a traditional Jewish family of modest means. In September 1939 she faced the German occupiers with her widowed mother and three younger brothers, one quite sickly. Her mother was deported in 1942, leaving Riva to care for the brothers. She endured the ghetto life in hiding until she was deported and sent to

Auschwitz. In dire need of labor, the Nazis sent her to labor camps. As the Soviet Red Army closed in on the Polish camps, inmates were marched into Germany's interior. So many inmates died during the walk, it was dubbed a death march. Liberated by the Red Army, Riva returned to Lodz only to be met with rampant anti-Semitism. In 1945 she made her way to the American zone in Berlin into a displaced persons camp. There she married and had two children with Moneck Sender. Aided by Jewish overseas agencies, the Senders immigrated to the United States, where Riva was reunited with a brother. In New York, after attending college, she became a teacher of Jewish history and a lecturer specializing in Holocaust studies.

The Cage. Ruth Minsky Sender with Jim Coon. New York: Aladdin Paperbacks, 1997. 264 pp. ISBN: 06898132X. Ages 13–16. Memoir.

This autobiographical memoir relates Ruth Sender's experiences as a teenager in Poland during the Holocaust. The first and last chapter are in the form of an explanation by the writer to her young daughter. The first section of the narrative tells of her widowed mother's deportation and the author's attempts to hide and survive with her two brothers, plagued by privation and persecution in the Lodz Ghetto. Starving and hunted like an animal, Riva decides to surrender to the Gestapo in order to get shelter and food. The second half of the autobiography deals with Riva's experiences in Auschwitz, then in two labor camps. The narration concludes with a terrible death march that ends in liberation by the Red Army early in 1945.

To Life. New York: Puffin (Penguin), 1990. 229 pp. ISBN: 0027818314. Ages 13–16. Memoir.

Here the author continues where she left off in her memoir, *The Cage.* She begins with May 3, 1945, in southern Germany by describing the final days in the death march. A number of flashbacks recall the horrors Nazi guards perpetrated on inmates. Finally the Red Army liberates Riva, and she returns to her birthplace, Lodz. In her hometown she is greeted by hostility and anti-Semitism, particularly by vigilante Polish Gentiles. Deciding life in Lodz is untenable, she leaves the city for the American Zone of Occupation in Germany, where she believes she will be safe. She makes her way to the American section in Berlin and to a displaced persons camp. There she meets and marries Moneck Sender, who was a partisan during the war. Together they make their way to the United States.

SIEGAL, ARANKA ("PIRI") DAVIDOWITZ
(1930–   )

Aranka Davidowitz, known as "Piri," was born in Beregszasy, a town
on the border of Hungary and the Ukraine. Hungary became an ally of
Nazi Germany in 1940 and joined in Germany's aggressive wars. Piri
endured growing anti-Semitism along with her mother and grandparents
as the fascistic Hungarian government became more and more repressive. Piri's father was drafted into the Hungarian army's special labor
battalions for Jews and sent to the Russian front to perform menial and
dangerous tasks. As the war dragged on and the Nazis suffered defeat
after defeat, Hungary appeared to wish to bolt the alliance. Germany
invaded her former ally in spring 1944 and instituted the Final Solution.
As a result, Piri and her family were placed in a ghetto, then deported
to Auschwitz. She survived because she was selected for factory work
not far from the Bergen-Belsen camp in Germany. Liberated on April 15,
1945, by the British, she went to Geneva, Switzerland, to recuperate.
There she met her future husband, married, and immigrated to America.
A mother of two daughters, she currently lives in Tarrytown, New York,
and works as a social anthropologist.

Grace in the Wilderness. New York: Puffin, 1994. 224 pp. ISBN:
0140309678. Ages 9–14. Memoir.

The story of Piri starts with her liberation from Bergen-Belsen concentration camp where she was transferred from Auschwitz. Her parents
and family lost to Nazi murder, only she and her sister Iboya survive.
Piri is placed in a Red Cross hospital and recuperates. Then she and her
sister are sent to Sweden, where Piri attends a refugee school. A friendly
couple "adopt" her. This memoir flashes back to her Holocaust experiences, but it is basically one of the difficult adjustment to so-called normal life after her traumatic uprooting. The horrible events are only
hinted at, not fully described. The narrative, about a displaced person
struggling with identity problems in a foreign country, concludes with
Iboya, her strong supporter, and Piri immigrating to America.

Upon the Head of a Goat: Childhood in Hungary, 1939–1944. New York:
Penguin, 1994. 214 pp. ISBN: 014036966X. Ages 9–14. Memoir.

This children's book is an autobiographical account of the author's
childhood in Hungary in the face of growing anti-Semitism and the disintegration of the family's way of life. The book consists of a number of
personal vignettes of small-town Jewish life and Germany's occupation

and the complicity of the Hungarian gendarmerie (state police) in confining the Jews to ghettos. Almost the entire memoir takes place in Hungary. Piri describes happy times with the family despite growing repression. The narrative ends when the family boards a transport headed for Auschwitz. A one-page epilogue gives a nongraphic account of what happened at Auschwitz.

SLIWOWSKA, WIKTORIA
(COMPILER AND EDITOR)

The Last Eyewitnesses: Children of the Holocaust Speak. Julian and Fay Bussgang, translators. Evanston, IL: Northwestern University Press, 1998. 334 pp. ISBN: 0810115107. Ages 14–up. Memoir.

This anthology is a compilation of short testimonies of sixty-five survivors of the Holocaust in Poland. The book is divided into sections of stories of children from central Poland and prewar eastern Poland. All the Jewish children were very young at the time of the Nazi occupation of Poland in 1939, with most contributors born between 1928 and 1935. They submitted their testimonies in the course of joining the Association of the Children of the Holocaust, a group created in Warsaw, Poland, in 1991. All the contributors except two remained in Poland after the war, mainly at the locales where their experiences took place. Their accounts, rather short and fragmentary, document lives of Jewish children in cities, towns, and rural areas; in ghettos, concentration camps, and partisan camps. Many of these children spent six years of their childhood hiding their Jewish identity; they had to change their names several times, change their mother tongue (Yiddish), and in many cases learn Catholic prayers and rituals. Some never quite recovered their identities as Jews; one even became a Catholic priest. The children represented a wide range of former religious observance and socioeconomic backgrounds. Quite a few came from highly educated families, some with mothers who were professionals.

Although the work includes a number of testimonies of heroic Gentiles who risked their own and their families' lives to aid Jews, the narratives reveal a great deal of Gentile anti-Semitism. The children faced persecution not only from Poles but also from Belorussian, Lithuanian, and Ukrainian collaborators. These included denunciations to the Nazi authorities, betrayals, and the killing of innocent people. In contrast, Polish nuns are portrayed as reliable rescuers. Heroic Jewish parents went to great extremes to protect and save their children. Often fathers were killed or taken away, so mothers showed great resourcefulness and resolve.

A number of accounts include the postwar dangers and anti-Semitism encountered by survivors. Jews were often treated as unwanted aliens in their homeland. Whereas a few remained permanently traumatized by their war and postwar experiences, a remarkable number of others went on with their lives—they married, had children, went to universities, and became professionals. One account chronicles the compiler herself, the Polish-born survivor Wiktoria Sliwowska. The translators, Julian and Fay Bussgang, were also born in Poland, but they managed to get out in 1939. Because members of their large families were murdered, the complier and translators have empathy for the eyewitnesses.

SWIERAKOWIAK, DAVID
(1924–1943)

David lived with his assimilated Jewish parents of modest means in Lodz, Poland. He received a good education in Polish public schools, majoring in languages. David had just turned 15 in 1939, three months before the Nazi invasion of Poland, when he began his diary. After mountain climbing in southern Poland, he returned to his home when the Nazis overran his town, and he and his family were placed with 200,000 Jews in the Lodz Ghetto. Two collaborationist Czech doctors selected his mother for deportation and death, and soon after, David's father died of malnutrition. David managed to survive by tutoring and working in the ghetto Underground finding food for Jewish schoolchildren. Swierakowiak succumbed to tuberculosis on August 18, 1943, at age 19. A Gentile Pole returning home after the war found David's diary in notebooks placed in a stove.

The Diary of David Swierakowiak: Five Notebooks from the Lodz Ghetto. Alan Adelson, editor; Kamil Tuorski, translator. New York: Oxford University Press, 1998. 550 pp. ISBN: 0966044037. Ages 16–up. Diary.

The five notebooks from a seven-notebook diary written between June 28, 1939, and April 15, 1943, reveal a tale of horror and resentment. David, though only a teenager of 15, is an avid Marxist, a believer in Stalin and the Soviet system. He writes of the caste and class system within the Jewish ghetto, and he deeply resents the gross inequalities he sees—those who live comfortably while the great majority waste away. David feels great contempt for Chaim Rumkowsky, chairman of the Nazi-controlled Jewish Council, for council members, and for their families. He also regards his father unfavorably, noting his parent's moral breakdown while pining over his mother, who is betrayed and deported to doom. David paints a careful picture of the starvation, diseases, deprivations, and death within the ghetto. He documents the slave labor and the Nazi methods of deceit and control. One reads of his growing despair. Stark photos augment the diary.

TEC, NECHAMA BAWNIK
(1931–)

Nechama Bawnik was born to upper-class parents in Lublin, Poland. Her father was irreligious, whereas her mother kept certain traditional Jewish practices. Her father owned a chemical factory and could afford to send Nechama and her sister, four years her senior, to a private academic school. Caught up in the occupation of Poland by Nazi Germany, the Bawniks passed as Polish Christians by using the money Mr. Bawnik received by selling his gold and jewelry on the black market. They hid, used forged papers, or bribed Christian families in Lublin, Otwick, Warsaw, and Kielce. Returning to their home after liberation by the Soviet Red Army, the father faced death threats from hostile Polish Christians. They escaped to a displaced persons camp in the American Zone. There she married Mr. Tec and the couple immigrated to America, where Nechama received her doctorate. She is currently an associate professor of sociology at the University of Connecticut in Stamford, where she resides. Nechama Bawnik Tec has penned six nonfiction books on Holocaust themes.

Dry Tears: The Story of a Lost Childhood. New York: Oxford University Press, 1984. 242 pp. ISBN: 0195035003. Ages 14–up. Memoir.

Dry Tears is the Nechama Bawnik Tec memoir covering the years 1939 to 1945. It includes the period just before the Nazi occupation of Poland and persecution of the Jews, liberation by the Soviet Red Army, and the escape to the American Zone of Occupation of Germany. The story is told in the first person through the eyes of a preteen. Nechama reveals all the dangers she and her sister, four years her senior, endured and shows the resourcefulness of her mother and father in finding places to hide and escaping the Nazi net. She describes the virulent anti-Semitism of Polish Christians, but she also tells of Righteous Gentiles—the non-Jews who risked their lives to shelter the family—and of a kind German commissioner in Lublin who protected them from deportation. Her father, an owner of a chemical factory, had his property restored after liberation by the communist authorities, only to face death threats from resentful Polish Christians. The writer's narrative also provides insight into Gentile Polish life during the German occupation and the immediate postwar period under communist occupation.

TEN BOOM, CORNELIA (CORRIE)
(1892–1983)

Corrie Ten Boom was born in Haarlem, Holland, to a middle-class, very devout Dutch Reform family. She attended local public school and became a watchmaker like her father. She lived a rather uneventful life with her sister, a few years older than she, and her parents in a large home with the watchmaking shop attached. Both women were spinsters. When Corrie Ten Boom was 50 years old, in 1942, the family joined the Dutch Underground against the Nazis, who had occupied their country since 1940. They created a hiding place where they sheltered Jews. In February 1944 the Ten Boom sisters and their father were arrested by the Gestapo and placed in prisons in Holland. Their father died in prison. In spring 1944 Betsy and Corrie were placed in Ravensbruck, the infamous women's concentration camp. Betsy died, but as a result of a clerical fluke, Corrie was released. She returned to Haarlem and courageously continued underground work, this time sheltering feebleminded people also slated for murder by the Nazis. Upon liberation in spring 1945, this very religious woman went on a lecture tour recounting her wartime experiences and evangelizing. She also wrote religious books.

The Hiding Place: The Triumphant True Story of Corrie Ten Boom. With John and Elizabeth Sherrill. New York: Bantam Books, 1974. 256 pp. ISBN: 0553256696. Ages 14–up. Memoir.

This autobiography focuses on World War II and its immediate aftermath, 1940–1947. Corrie Ten Boom, in midlife, and her sister and father become involved in underground work in Holland that leads them to construct a secret hiding place for Jews. Saving the lives of Jews slated for genocide by the Nazi occupiers of Holland was part of Dutch Resistance. In her memoir Ten Boom tells about both Dutch collaborators and Dutch resisters. Just reaching age 50, Corrie, along with her sister, Betsy, and her father, is arrested by the Gestapo. The Ten Booms endure three months of prison in nearby towns, but poor conditions lead to the death of the father. The last quarter of the memoir explains what happened to the two sisters at Ravensbruck concentration camp, a women's camp near Berlin that claimed 96,000 women. Even under these extreme conditions the sisters keep their faith; they preach and pray and uplift other inmates. Betsy dies in the winter of 1944. However, because of an administrative clerical error, Corrie is released. In Haarlem she continues sheltering people, mentally challenged souls slated for murder by the Nazis. Near the end of the narrative Corrie sets up two homes for people broken by war, one inside Germany at Darmstadt. Throughout the work Corrie expounds her strong Christian faith.

TOLL, NELLY
(1935–   )

The painter-diarist Nelly Toll was born in Lwow, Poland, to upper-class, moderately religious Jewish parents. Her father, Zygmunt Mieses, a manufacturer, recognizing the dangers of both Stalin and Hitler, alerted Gentile friends to hide the family. When the Soviets took over the eastern half of Poland, which included Lwow, Mieses was caught and arrested as a "capitalist"; he disappeared behind the Gulag (slave labor camp in Siberia set up by communists). In June 1941 the German army invaded Soviet-held territory and occupied Lwow. Nelly's 4-year-old brother was caught and murdered by Nazis. Rose Mieses, Nelly's mother, escaped the Jewish ghetto in a dash for Hungary, but failed. She and her daughter did manage to find a Christian couple who hid them for thirteen months. Nelly's diary and her watercolors were created in this time period. In July 1944 they were liberated by the Soviet Red Army, and in 1951 mother and daughter immigrated to America. Nelly eventually settled in Cherry Hill in southern New Jersey. She received degrees from Rowan College and Rutgers and is now completing a doctorate from the University of Pennsylvania.

Nelly married Erv Toll, and they have two grown children, Sharon and Jeffrey.

Behind the Secret Window: A Memoir of a Hidden Childhood during World War II. New York: Penguin, 1993. 161 pp. ISBN: 0803713622. Ages 11–14. Memoir.

This first-person memoir begins in June 1941 when the Germans overran Lwow. A Jewish ghetto was set up, and during this time Nelly's brother was taken away, never to be seen again. The writer describes her sad adventures with her neighbors and the Germans who persecuted her and her mother. She tells of her shrinking world from a cramped ghetto to even more confining quarters in a small room behind a secret window in the Gentile part of the city. The neighbor, a psychotic Gentile who abused his wife, found a boarded-up window area in his apartment, where they could hide. Here Nelly wrote a diary for thirteen months and painted twenty-nine watercolor pictures. These pictures are fantasies of what the preteen dreamed life would be like if she were living in freedom. The cheerful watercolors are based on stories her mother told her about what normal children do living a normal life. The diary records the tedium of waiting behind a bricked-up bay window, the tension between her mother and the host couple sheltering them, the fear of discovery, and the narrow escapes from discovery. Nelly's small black journal tells of the persecution she and her family endured prior to hiding, her hopes for the future, and some insights into their predicament.

When Memory Speaks: The Holocaust in Art. Westport, CT: Praeger, 1998. 125 pp. ISBN: 0275955346. Ages 16–up. Memoir.

Nelly Toll has compiled a diverse collection of paintings, sculptures, and sketches of camp life drawn at great personal risk by those who suffered during the Holocaust. This book presents retrospective commentary by Toll herself and by some of the artists. In addition to color pictures are black-and-white reproductions and poetry. There is a long section on historical perspective and a concluding section on living memorials and educational institutions. Also included are illustrations by nonsurvivors such as the sculptor George Segal. Nelly Toll includes herself under N. Mieses, her maiden name. Samuel Bok and Mia Fendler-Immerman are also represented.

TOPAS, GEORGE ("JUREK")
(1924–)

George Topas was born in Warsaw, the eldest of three sons. His parents were not very observant Jews of modest means; his father operated his grandfather's shoe store. His mother was highly educated for her times, for she attended an agricultural school in 1931. George attended Polish public schools and then a Zionist-oriented agricultural school. He was 15 when the Germans occupied Warsaw. "Jurek," as he was commonly known in Poland, spent five years under the Nazi boot. He lived through the privations of the Warsaw Ghetto, the famous uprising, and then a number of labor and concentration camps. The Nazis murdered his parents, a sister, and a brother. Along with two brothers he survived the terrible camps of Budzyn (a satellite of Majdnek), Plaszow, and Flossenbuerg. On a death march, he was liberated by the Americans, then volunteered to serve in the U.S. Army's Twenty-sixth Infantry Division. For five months he was in counterintelligence ferreting out former SS officers. He had a grandmother who had wisely immigrated to New York City before the war, so he also immigrated. However, wishing to take advantage of the GI Bill of Rights, which would afford him a college education, he enlisted in the army for eighteen months in April 1947. Returning to the United States, he married Bella, whose parents also came from Warsaw, and he became a contractor in Philadelphia. Later he attended Rutgers University and earned a master's degree in European history. Currently he and his wife live in Lakewood, New Jersey, where he gives occasional courses in local colleges and lectures widely on the Holocaust.

The Iron Furnace: A Holocaust Survivor's Story. Lexington: University Press of Kentucky, 1990. 286 pp. ISBN: 0813116988. Ages 15–up. Memoir.

George Topas's story begins with his testimony at a war crimes trial in Kiel in 1967. This deposition prompted Topas to recall and record his memoir of events during World War II. He tells of his parents and grandparents and their family life before the Nazi storm broke. In the narrative he reveals the false assumptions Jews had prior to the war. A trained historian, Topas provides the reader in his narrative with historical asides and explanations. He takes us through the ghettoization, the uprising, a number of concentration camps, a death march, and finally liberation. Toward war's end, desperate for secret weapons to turn the tide of Allied advance, some professors and high-ranking Wehrmacht members assemble about sixty Jewish prisoners, supposedly scientists who could create a gas that would immobilize gasoline engines. (A similar story is told in Henry Orenstein's book *I Shall Live.*) The group Jurek volunteered for was closely watched, however, and when an experimental model they constructed did not work, the prisoner-foreman was executed. The time wasted on the secret weapon afforded Jurek freedom from the murderous SS and reasonable shelter from late 1944 to early 1945. Topas provides the reader with a long epilogue telling what happened in the aftermath to him and characters he introduces in the book. He also includes documents from German and American army sources.

TORY, AVRAHAM
(1909–)

The diarist was born in Lazdyai, Lithuania, the youngest in a family of six siblings. His parents, moderately religious Jewish farmers, sent him to Jewish parochial elementary school and a religious high school. At age 19 he took up law at Kovno University, and for a year he also studied in Pittsburgh, Pennsylvania. In Kovno he became very active in the Zionist movement, including its sports arm, Maccabi. When the Soviets took over Lithuania in 1940, he eluded the communists and maintained his Zionist activity. When the Germans took over Kovno after their attack on the Soviet Union in 1941, Tory, now a lawyer and active in Jewish affairs, was selected to serve on the Jewish Council, a self-governing body under the Nazi thumb. As deputy secretary he kept a diary of the events in Kovno during the German occupation. In March 1944, with the approach of the Soviet Red Army, he escaped with his future wife, Penina, and her child, Shulamit. After brushes with the Soviet occupiers, he joined the Bricha movement, an organization that arranged secret escape to Palestine). After great difficulty, including a stay in Italy, he and his wife and stepdaughter reached the Jewish settlement in Palestine in October 1947. Tory continued his activities in Maccabi and in 1952 set up his law practice in Tel Aviv, a practice that lasted twenty-seven years.

Surviving the Holocaust: The Kovno Ghetto Diary. Martin Gilbert, editor; Jerzy Michalowicz, translator. Cambridge, MA: Harvard University Press, 1990. 554 pp. ISBN: 0674858107. Ages 16–up. Diary.

This diary was published in Israel in Yiddish in 1988, forty-four years after it was written. It covers October 28, 1941, to January 3, 1944. It also contains an epilogue and historical notes throughout by the Israeli historian Dina Porat. The diary is augmented by an historical introduction by the prolific Holocaust historian Martin Gilbert, as well as by photos, maps, and German decrees and announcements. The manuscript served as evidence against Nazi war criminals living in the United States and Canada who were under investigation by immigration authorities. Tory recounts the Lithuanians' anti-Semitism before, during, and after the war and shows their complicity in the Final Solution, though he does note righteous individuals who aided Jews. Although touching on the abuses of Soviet occupation in 1940–1941 and 1944–1946, the book's major thrust is the Nazi occupation. As a deputy secretary of the Jewish Council, Tory was in a position to chronicle the perpetrators' activities in mass murder. Tory is sympathetic to the attempts of the Jewish Council to soften the decrees of the Nazi masters, to save as many Jews as possible, and to do this by making the Kovno Jews useful through light manufacturing for the German war effort. He does mention the Jewish Underground there, Jews who harassed Germans in the woods. The latter part of the diary tells of his escape from ruthless Soviet occupation and about the Bricha movement, the secret underground cadre that shepherded Jews by stages to Palestine. Tory recovered his diaries, but not all pages, from a hiding place in the foundation of a ghetto building. The Bricha transported it later to his home in Tel Aviv.

TROLLER, NORBERT
(1896–1981)

Norbert Troller was born in Brno, Czechoslovakia, to well-to-do Jewish parents. He attended public schools in the Austro-Hungarian Empire, then architectural school in Prague. He was married briefly. Troller practiced his architectural craft until the German invasion in 1939. In 1942 he was taken to Theresienstadt, a ghetto–concentration camp in Czechoslovakia. In 1944 he was transferred to the Little Fortress prison at Theresienstadt, and from there to Auschwitz. He managed to survive despite special torments because he smuggled realistic critical paintings to Switzerland. After the war he returned to Prague and found that his family had perished at the hands of the Germans. He resumed his trade as an architect in Prague, but in 1948, with the communist takeover of Czechoslovakia, Troller immigrated to the United States, where he was commissioned for many years to design synagogues for the Jewish Welfare Board.

Theresienstadt: Hitler's Gift to the Jews. Joel Shatzky, editor; Susan E. Cernyak-Spatz, translator. Chapel Hill: University of North Carolina Press, 1991. 182 pp. ISBN: 0807819654. Ages 15–up. Memoir.

Troller recounts his two years in the so-called model ghetto of Theresienstadt until he was deported from the horrors of the "Little Fortress," a prison next to the ghetto, in September 1944. His narrative ends with his leaving his two prison tormentors as he heads for Auschwitz. Troller reveals much about the "painters' affair," when he and other artists were discovered smuggling out drawings that revealed the true horrible conditions at the camp. He explains how they did it and how his own drawings were retrieved. This work includes Troller's drawings in watercolor and in black and white published for the first time. In them he depicts various scenes of the physical surroundings and the forlornness of the inmates. The memoir contains copious endnotes revealing much about other painters.

VELMANS, EDITH VAN HESSEN
(1925–   )

Edith Van Hessen was born to a secular middle-class family in Amsterdam, Holland. Her tie with Judaism was through her grandmother. Her mother was irreligious and her father a Gentile. When the Germans occupied Holland and it became evident Jews were in grave danger, Edith was sent away to a Protestant family to impersonate a Christian. Her father died in a hospital, and her mother and grandmother and brother were deported and murdered in concentration camps. At liberation she was reunited with her remaining family member, her brother. Edith became a psychologist in Amsterdam and married. She eventually immigrated with her family to Sheffield, Massachusetts, where she gave birth to three daughters and where she lives today.

Edith's Story. New York: Soho Press, 1999. 240 pp. ISBN: 1569471789. Ages 14–up. Memoir.

Edith Van Hessen went into hiding in Amsterdam about the same time as Anne Frank. Unlike Anne, however, she survived the war and began her diary as early as 1938 at age 13. When the Nazis occupied Holland in 1940, her life began to disintegrate. Never recognizing herself as a Jew, German restrictions made her see herself as one. She was forbidden to attend public school, had to wear a yellow star, could not ride her bike, and was not permitted to use public transportation or enter public accommodations. Her parents, recognizing the mortal danger to Jews, arranged for Edith to impersonate a Gentile and live with a Protestant family in another town. The zur Kleinmiedes family was billeting a Nazi officer in their home, and Edith was asked to do chores for him, a perfect cover. The teenager kept a diary. It was not until forty years after the war, however, that Edith Velmans put together her diary notes and the letters she wrote, along with her adult comments, to produce this book.

VOS, IDA GUDEMA
(1931–)

Ida Gudema was born in Groningen, Netherlands, to a middle-class, traditional Jewish family. Her father was a commercial agent. The Gudema family moved to Rotterdam, where in 1940 they experienced heavy bombing by Nazi invaders. The family moved again, this time to Ryswik, a town near the Hague. Ida had to leave public school and was forced to go to an all-Jewish one by German authorities. Early in 1943, after many of the family's relatives and friends were deported to concentration camps, including Ida's maternal grandparents, the Gudemas fled. The local Underground found hiding places for the Gudemas. Ida, 12, and her sister, a few years younger, moved from house to house, hiding for three years. Liberation came in May 1945 with the Canadian army, and the family was reunited. Ida returned to public school and then went on to teachers college and received a graduate degree. In 1956 she married Henrk Vos, an insurance broker, and had three children. While teaching in 1973, upon hearing about Holocaust deniers, she decided to write poetry and prose about the Holocaust and her wartime experiences. She now devotes full time to writing and lecturing, particularly to schools, about the war and the Holocaust.

Anna Is Still Here. Terese Edelstein and Inez Smidt, translators. New York: Puffin Books, 1995 (reissued). 141 pp. ISBN: 0140369090. Ages 9–12. Fiction.

Anna Markus, the heroine of the novel, is 13 years old and reunited with her parents after liberation from the Nazis. She had been hidden in Holland in an attic during the occupation. Now she and her parents face postwar adjustment. She cannot understand why her parents will not talk about their wartime experiences or what happened to relatives. Anna, on her part, cannot talk above a whisper and relates better to a German neighbor, a Mrs. Neumann, than to her parents. The neighbor had lost her daughter in the maelstrom of war, but she lives in hope of the daughter's return. The vignettes are told in the third person from Anna's perspective. Much is revealed about the difficulties of reverting to peacetime life. Anna and the Jews still face a great deal of native prejudice and are surprised at the lack of sympathy for survivors. Anna cannot understand such callousness. A subplot emerges with the return of Mrs. Neumann's daughter, for Anna must now relate to her parents.

Hide and Seek. Terese Edelstein and Inez Smidt, translators. New York: Puffin Books, 1995. 132 pp. ISBN: 0190369082. Ages 9–11. Fiction.

This preteen book was originally published in Dutch in the Netherlands in 1981. Although a novel, it has many autobiographical elements. Short chapters relate the experiences of a Jewish girl—Rachel Hartog—living in Rotterdam with her sister and parents when the Nazis invade. The 8-year-old then undergoes many humiliating experiences as she and her family's lives are circumscribed by increasingly restrictive decrees directed against Jews. When the protagonist's grandparents are deported to a concentration camp, the family decides to go into hiding. At the last house where they hide, Rachel and her younger sister find much kindness and consideration by their hosts, to whom Vos dedicates the novel. The last few chapters deal with liberation in May 1945 and the immediate aftermath. Rachel and her sister, Esther, are reunited not only with their parents but also with their grandparents, who managed to survive Theresienstadt. The last chapter tells what happened to Hartog relatives.

VRBA, RUDOLF (WALTER ROSENBERG)
(1924–)

Rudolf Vrba was born in Topolcany, Czechoslovakia, to middle-class Jewish parents, and he attended Czech primary and secondary schools. At 18 he was arrested by the Nazis and deported to Majdanek and Auschwitz death camps, where he remained from 1942 to 1944. Rudolf worked as a registrar to the Property Department of Auschwitz, a position that gave him a front seat to the arrival of deportees and the data about the camp. He and a fellow inmate, Alfred Wetzler, successfully escaped on April 7, 1944. They made their way to Bratislava and the safety of an underground Jewish group there. Rudolf's detailed report on Auschwitz found its way to Switzerland and to the War Refugee Board in the United States. The report contained a map of the gas chambers, the crematoria, and railway lines leading to the camp. Its recommendation to bomb railroad hubs and crematoria to slow up or stop the trainloads of Jews being transported to doom was not acted upon, however. Vrba joined the partisans of western Slovakia and upon liberation was highly decorated by the Czech government. In 1949 he graduated from Czech Technical University in Prague; then he received a doctorate in neurochemistry. He served in various Czech ministries before immigrating to England. Dr. Vrba has held various posts in academia as a professor of pharmacology. He lectures and writes often about the Holocaust.

I Cannot Forgive. With Alan Bestic and Afterword by J. S. Conway. New York: Regent College, 1997. 431 pp. ISBN: 1573830968. Ages 14–up. Memoir.

This memoir recalls the high adventure of an 18-year-old's defiance of a pro-Nazi fascistic regime and his determination to fight oppressors. The work is crammed with historical information about what happened to Jews in Slovakia and Hungary. Vrba appears to be an escape artist, escaping from various internment centers and life-threatening tight spots. A good portion of the narrative deals with his incarceration at Birkenau, the part of the Auschwitz complex set aside for Jews. He becomes a member of the underground network at the camp, a position that enables him eventually to escape. The method of escape described is ingenious: He and his fellow escapee naively believe that with detailed information about the mass murder center, the Western Allies will bomb the camps and will do all humanly possible to stop the deportations and rescue the Jews. Sadly disappointed at the failure to rescue or arouse the conscience of the free world, Vrba declares, "I cannot forgive."

WELLS, LEON
(1925–)

Physicist Leon Wells was the second of seven children born to an Orthodox Jewish family in Stojanov, Poland, a town near Lvov. He attended Polish public schools during the day and Jewish religious schools in the late afternoon. He also attended public high school and a Hebrew academy. After a brief period, 1939–1941, under Soviet communist rule, when religion was suppressed, he and his family came under Nazi German rule. The Germans imprisoned Wells in a camp located on Janowska Road in Lvov. After his first escape, he was assigned to a notorious brigade whose function was to exhume murdered Jews and burn their bodies, a brigade entitled Sonderkommando 1005. Wells escaped from his captors a second time and remained in hiding until liberation by the Soviet Red Army. Russian prosecutors at the Nuremberg Trials (1946) used Wells's testimony several times against Nazi defendants on trial for crimes against humanity. Disgusted by the heavy inhumane hand of communism, Wells found refuge in the American Zone of Occupation in Germany. He continued his academic studies and received a Ph.D. in physics, and in 1949 he immigrated to the United States. He married Frieda Weiss in 1955 and is the father of three children. Since 1962 he has been a director of research in the field of optics.

The Death Brigade (also known as *Janowska Road*). New York: Holocaust Library, 1963, 1978. 306 pp. ISBN: 7789008. Ages 15–up. Memoir.

This memoir originated as early as 1946 as testimony growing out of the Central Jewish Historical Commission in Poland. It covers the period 1939 to 1946, starting with Wells's Jewish life in Lvov before the communist invasion. At the heart of the work is the Nazi German occupation, the Nazis' murderous policies, and in particular their plan to try to wipe out evidence of mass murder. The Death Brigade exhumed and burned bodies beyond recognition. Wells details not only the inhumanity of the SS at the camp but also the cruel complicity of the collaborators, the non-German volunteers such as Russian ex-soldiers and Ukrainian militiamen. The communists' corruption and repression in 1939–1941 and in postwar Poland are revealed. Wells comments on Jewish life after the war, the displaced persons camps, the Nuremberg Trials, the fate of his Janowska inmate companions, and some murderous SS officers. Wells states that his purpose in writing is to alert the world to the terrible events of those war days.

Shattered Faith: A Holocaust Legacy. Lexington: University Press of Kentucky, 1995. 175 pp. ISBN: 0813119316. Ages 16–up. Memoir.

In this contemplative memoir Wells recalls the daily life in the village of Stojamor, focusing on the Jewish holy days. He recalls the vanquished way of life, of family and community, of the very gentle and devout people who worship God with great love and emotion. His memory recounts the High Holy Day, Yom Kippur, which he celebrated while imprisoned and while hiding from his tormentors. He bemoans his loss of dear ones, members of his immediate family—mother, father, four sisters, and two brothers—as well as his extended family, which numbered seventy. This wartime shattering of his life and the hardships he experienced lead him to question his religious beliefs and start a quarrel with God. Wells shares his disillusionment with the reader and provides intellectual insight into the mind of this Holocaust survivor.

WERNER, HERSCHEL
(1917–1989)

Herschel was born in Gorzkow, eastern Poland, where he attended Polish public schools. He left his family in Gorzkow to go into business with a friend at age 20 in the capital city, Warsaw. The Germans occupied Poland, and in the winter of 1942, faced with the increasing brutality of the invaders, Herschel joined a Jewish partisan group operating in the Polish forests near the old Soviet borders. The resisters, headed by a Jewish man, were backed by the Soviet-supported Polish partisan movement. By 1944, the fighting group was made up of 400 partisans and 400 noncombatants. They engaged in attacks on German troops and supplies and in humanitarian operations to save Jews. Meanwhile, the Nazis murdered Werner's parents and siblings. In 1944, his band was directly aided by a Soviet-sponsored Polish partisan group and earned their gratitude. When the Soviet Red Army liberated Poland, Werner stayed a little while in his native land but felt he had to leave because of anti-Semitism. He met his wife, Dorothy, in the United States, and they raised their three sons in Vineland, New Jersey. Werner saw the publication of these memoirs as an answer to questions by his children.

Fighting Back: A Memoir of Jewish Resistance in World War II. New York: Columbia University Press, 1992. 236 pp. ISBN: 023187882X. Ages 15–up. Memoir.

This personal narrative related by Werner to his wife shortly before his death in December 1989 was edited and published through the efforts of their son Mark. The writer relates that his purpose in telling his story was to answer the falsely premised question, "Why did the Jews go so easily to their slaughter?" Werner provides the reader with vignettes of his life in a Jewish village prior to World War II. He gives a romantic version of a religious and ethnic way of life now extinct. His narrative chronicles the growing anti-Semitism of Werner's neighbors during the prewar years. When the German conquerors came, very few of the Gentile Polish neighbors offered help. Indeed, according to the writer, many turned against the Jews. Later, as the war turned against the Nazi forces, aid did come from the population. Werner gives credit to the Soviet-backed Polish Armia Ludowa (People's Army) and condemns the murder of Jews by some elements of the Polish nationalist Armia Krajowa (Home Army). The narrative deals with the many military actions of the Jewish partisan band until their liberation by the Soviet Red Army in 1944. Werner's return to his native areas of Poland resulted in disillusionment when he confronted vicious anti-Semitism. Happily, he found that two brothers had survived the war. In 1947 Werner took a troopship for the United States.

WIESEL, ELIE
(1928–   )

The prolific Holocaust writer Elie Wiesel was born in Sighet, Romania, to very religious parents of modest means. His father and mother operated a grocery store. Elie received intensive religious training; he was a student of the Talmud and Kabbalah, the Jewish mystical tradition. In spring 1944, when he was 15 years old, the Nazis occupied his town and deported him and his parents and three sisters to Auschwitz. Only Elie and an older sister survived the camps. At war's end he traveled with 400 orphans to Paris. There he finished his schooling from a French orphanage and attended the University of Paris, the Sorbonne (1948–1951). After graduation he became a writer–reporter. He worked for an Israeli newspaper until persuaded by a famous French writer, François Mauriac, to write about his experiences in the Nazi concentration camps. Wiesel's novel, *Night*, brought him fame. He immigrated to the United States in 1956 and taught Jewish studies at the City College of New York. In 1969 he married Marion Rose and had one child. In 1972 Wiesel became a professor of humanities at Boston University, a position he still holds. The author of forty books, he speaks and writes widely on Holocaust-related topics.

All the Rivers Run to the Sea. New York: Schocken Books, 1996. 432 pp. ISBN: 0805210288. Ages 15–up. Memoir.

Volume 1 of a two-part memoir of Elie Wiesel's life starts with a well-known mystic rabbi foretelling of Elie's greatness upon his birth in Romania. In this volume of reminiscences and anecdotes, the writer revisits his village life and then devotes only twenty pages to his concentration camp experiences, the shadow of which continues to have a profound influence on him. He continues into the postwar period—orphanages, education in Paris, and journalist years. He covers the Jewish struggle for independence from British rule in Palestine and relates how he was involved in the underground struggle for independence. Later, when he testifies about the Holocaust for the Israelis, Wiesel is moved to write about the Holocaust years. In 1958 his autobiographical novel *Night* catapults him to fame. Wiesel drops anecdotes on famous people he came to know—Golda Meir, David Ben Gurion, Abraham Heschel, and Gershon Scholom. He concludes with a trip back to his hometown of Sighet in Romania.

And the Sea Is Never Full. Marion Wiesel, translator. New York: Alfred A. Knopf, 1999. 384 pp. ISBN: 0805210288. Ages 15–up. Memoir.

Volume 2, the concluding book of Elie Wiesel's memoirs, begins when the author is 40 years old. The writer becomes involved in the pressing issues of the day, particularly those involving human rights. He defends persecuted Soviet Jews; he supports the South African dissidents against apartheid. While receiving an award from President Reagan, Wiesel scolds him for preparing to visit a German military cemetery where members of the SS are buried. The writer confronts French premier François Mitterrand for misleading statements about his role in France's collaborationist regime the Vichy government, during World War II. He does battle with Holocaust deniers. As President Clinton's emissary, he supports the president's use of troops to prevent further atrocities in Bosnia and Kosovo. Throughout Wiesel supports Israel's struggle to survive and laments the religious internal dissention in the Jewish state.

The Fifth Son. New York: Schocken Books, 1998. 220 pp. ISBN: 0805210830. Ages 15–up. Fiction.

A first-person narrative told by the protagonist, this novel is about a son trying to carry out a mission for his father. The father, the elder Tamirof, is brooding regarding the failure to murder a brutal SS officer known as the Angel of Davarowski—the Nazi who oversaw the destruction of a Jewish village during World War II. A friend of Tamirof reveals that the officer did not die in the assassination attempt but is living peacefully as a respected businessman. The son goes to the site of the Jewish village. Letters flow back and forth between father and son, and the narrative switches back and forth between the present and past as the Holocaust is reconstructed. Both father and son wish to become closer through this venture. The story is complicated because the elder Tamirof was president of the Jewish Council, the so-called self-governing body of the ghetto operating under Gestapo orders. The title is a reference to the Passover prayerbook section on the four sons who have to be told by the father about the Exodus.

The Forgotten. Stephan Becker, translator. New York: Schocken, 1995. 256 pp. ISBN: 0805210199. Ages 15–up. Fiction.

Like *The Fifth Son*, this novel centers around a son sent on a mission by his father to recapture the past. Elchanan Rosenbaum is suffering from Alzheimer's disease and wants to remember as much as he can about his Holocaust experiences. He recalls escaping the mass killing and deportation in his native village in Romania and joining the partisans. He survives the war and falls in love with Talia, whom he meets in a displaced persons camp. The young woman convinces Elchanan to make *aliyah* (permanent immigration to Palestine), and aboard the refugee ship to the Holy Land, they marry. She dies giving birth to Malkiel.

Malkiel is charged by his father to recapture the past. He goes to the small Romanian village, and the only Jew there is a gravedigger. The deformed old man relates that Elchanan had committed a crime in the village, which partially explains why the father is haunted by the past. The gravedigger conjures up tales of demons and buried rabbinical judges. He advises Malkiel to leave the dead and the past. Malkiel then meets an old woman who had befriended Elchanan in his youth; she reveals the Holocaust past. Finally, the son resolves to leave well enough alone and accept the ambiguities of life.

Night. Stella Rodway, translator. New York: Bantam Doubleday, Dell, 1982. 109 pp. ISBN: 0553272535. Ages 13–up. Fiction.

Elie Wiesel's first novel is a highly autobiographical account of a young Jewish boy who is taken to Auschwitz. The boy is shocked at the insane cruelty of the Nazis who come into his home town and murder babies as well as women and children. The youngster describes a cattle train ride without proper food, water, sanitation, or clothing. Arrival at the infamous Auschwitz brings new tortures. He bears witness to horrifying scenes, including the death of his family. First, he is separated from his mother and sisters. Then, he accompanies his father to camp barracks. He faces all kinds of hardships and privations. He watches the death of innocents, an oblique reference to the suffering of Christ on the cross. He loses his innocence, his faith in humanity, even his faith in God. The writer's first book, and the first one translated into English,

Night is augmented by a foreword by François Mauriac and preface by Robert McAfee Brown.

Twilight. Marion Wiesel, translator. New York: Schocken Books, 1995. 224 pp. ISBN: 080521058X. Ages 15–up. Fiction.

In *Twilight* Wiesel brings to bear his mystical Kabbalahistic training. Raphael Lipkin is a professor of mystical tradition who is in search of a friend and hero named Pedro. Pedro had rescued Raphael as a 15-year-old boy during the Holocaust, brought him from postwar Poland to Paris, and served as a surrogate father. Unfortunately Pedro was caught by the Stalinists and disappeared behind the Iron Curtain. Lipkin goes to a mountain clinic to study the relationship between madness and prophecy. The madmen he encounters are Cain, Abraham, Joseph, and the Messiah, all characters from the Bible. Raphael is searching for a hint about the Holocaust, his own survival, and the role of God during the period and perhaps a clue about Pedro in this upstate New York psychiatric hospital.

WIESENTHAL, SIMON
(1908–   )

The famous Nazi hunter Simon Wiesenthal was born in Buczacz to middle-class Jewish parents. His father was a sugar trader. His mother and younger brother struggled to survive when his father died on the Russian front as a Polish soldier. However, his mother married again in 1925; her second husband was a tile manufacturer. Simon attended public schools and the universities of Prague and Lvov, graduating as an architect and engineer. In 1936 he married Syla Muller, a childhood sweetheart. Incarcerated by the Nazis in 1941, Wiesenthal survived a number of concentration camps, including Plaszow, Gross Rosen, Buchenwald, and Mauthausen. His parents and eighty-nine relatives died at the hands of the Germans. Liberated from Mauthausen in 1945, he recognized the victorious Allies' lack of interest in apprehending Nazi murderers, so he started his own research center in Vienna devoted to tracking down and calling to the attention of authorities escaped Nazi war criminals. Wiesenthal has maintained the Jewish Documentation Center in Austria with few funds; however, the Museum of Tolerance and well-funded (mainly from Hollywood donors) Wiesenthal Center continues his work in Los Angeles.

The Murderers among Us. Joseph Wechsberg, editor. New York: Mc-
Graw Hill, 1967. 340 pp. ISBN: 67–13204. Ages 15–up. Memoir.

Joseph Wechsberg provides a profile of Wiesenthal in chapters 1, 2,
11, and 18. The remaining twenty-two chapters comprise Wiesenthal's
autobiography. The Nazi hunter tells about a number of cases and criminals he has brought to justice. He spells out the difficulties he has had
in apprehending war criminals. Actually, he believes those who stayed
behind the front lines in ghettos and in camps as SS were not soldiers
but merely vicious criminals, mass murderers. He explains how on numerous occasions he acted as a friend of the court when a criminal was
tried, providing vital evidence for conviction. Wiesenthal speaks of the
complicity of many types of people—among the Germans, Austrians and
Ukrainians—and of the apathy of many, including the Allies and even
survivors. He explains how secret international SS organizations helped
Nazi big shots to escape, whereas the "small fry" was tried in the courts.
Revealing is the description of the righteous who aided Jews and the
euthanasia administered at Hartheim Castle near Linz, Austria.

The Sunflower: On the Possibilities and Limits of Forgiveness. Bonny V.
Fetterman, editor. New York: Schocken Books, 1998. 216 pp. ISBN:
0805210601. Ages 15–up. Memoir.

This memoir has two parts. The first 100 pages narrate Wiesenthal's
experiences in a concentration camp near Lvov next to the ghetto set up
for Jews. He relates his school years and the many anti-Semitic activities
of the Poles. Wiesenthal describes the Russian deserters who aided the
Nazis, the Askari, and tells how they were used to guard Jewish prisoners. He also provides detail of torments and means of murder used
by the SS. The central theme of this autobiography is revealed in Wiesenthal's encounter with a young German soldier: When Simon is near
a makeshift army hospital, located in a graduate school the author attended, a nurse leads him to the bedside of a dying SS soldier swathed
in bandages. The Nazi confesses to a number of murders of Jews, including burning them alive. Recognizing he is dying, the soldier asks
forgiveness from Wiesenthal, as if the Jew is a priest and can give him
absolution. Wiesenthal does take some of the Nazi's personal effects, but
he walks out without answering. He returns the effects to the Nazi's
mother and finds out that the 21-year-old was just an ordinary boy
caught up in the maelstrom of war.

Part 2 of the book is a forum of responses to Wiesenthal's question,
Was ignoring the request for forgiveness right or moral? Many promi-
nent people give their opinions, including theologians such as Martin
Marty, Abraham Heschel, Jacob Kaplan, and Edward Flannery.

WILLENBERG, SAMUEL
(1923–   )

Samuel Willenberg was born to middle-class, assimilated Jewish parents. His father was an artist. He attended Polish public schools in Opatow, Poland. In 1942 the young man was deported from the Opatow Ghetto separately from his family and taken to the infamous death camp Treblinka. Friendly inmates there advised him to pretend to be a construction worker. In this way, he would avoid selection for execution as an "unproductive." Willenberg joined the camp underground and participated in the famous uprising and breakout in August 1943. He escaped and managed to reach Warsaw, where he joined the general Polish revolt in August 1944. Liberated by the Soviet Red Army, he discovered that the Soviets also saved his mother and father, who had managed to survive under the Nazi heel. Soon after, the Soviets allowed former Polish citizens to leave, so Samuel made *aliyah* (immigration) to what is now Israel. He worked as chief surveyor in a development company in Jerusalem.

> *Surviving Treblinka*. With Wladyslaw Bartoszewski. Naftali Greenwood, translator. Oxford, New York: Basil Blackwell, 1989. 250 pp. ISBN: 0685253050. Ages 15–up. Memoir.

This personal narrative relates the story of one of the few inmates who survived the Treblinka death camp, in which 880,000 people were murdered. The memoir gives a detailed description of the camp and of the brave uprising of August 2, 1943. The account gives much information about the political-military Polish cliques, anti-Semitic Poles, and sympathetic Righteous Gentiles who supported Jews. After escaping to Warsaw, he fights as a member of the pro-Soviet, left-wing Polish People's Army, a political party and military organization that welcomed Jews to its ranks. Assimilated, sophisticated, although only 20 years old when he is incarcerated, he is able to mingle freely with Polish Christians and other nationalities, even befriending them, all of which is helpful in escaping death. Wladyslaw Bartoszewski, a survivor-fighter and a Righteous Christian, member of the Polish Home Army's special section to aid Jews, Zegota, wrote a long historical introduction to this work and is Willenberg's editor.

WOLFF, MARION FREYER
(1925–   )

Marion Freyer was born in Berlin to traditionally Jewish middle-class parents. Her father was a button manufacturer, her mother a housewife.

The family, made up of Marion, the two parents, and a sister, Ulla, was very close-knit and loving. Marion attended public school until forced by Nazi law to attend Jewish school in 1936. She witnessed the impoverishment of her father, hostility, Kristallnacht (the November 9, 1938 pogrom in Greater Germany), and the deportation of relatives and friends. Finally, the family was able to procure the proper documents in December 1938 and after much red tape came to America in 1939 and settled in Baltimore. Marion married Manny Wolff in June 1950. The couple had one child. Marion attended Johns Hopkins University and graduated with a degree in mathematics, a subject she later taught. Now retired, she relates her Berlin experiences to young people.

The Shrinking Circle: Memories of Nazi Berlin, 1933–1939. New York: Union of American Hebrew Congregations, 1989. 133 pp. ISBN: 0807404195. Ages 12–14. Memoir.

Marion Freyer Wolff's autobiography begins with her entrance to public school in 1933 and ends in December 1939 when she reaches America. Twenty-two chapters chronicle her encounter with Nazi rule. Nazi persecution shrinks her circle of friends and relatives, who either die or disappear. Marion's narrative offers the perspective of a girl from the ages of 8 through 14 trying to survive and maintain the semblance of normalcy as hatred and anti-Semitism is unleashed. She details the economic and psychological strangulation of her parents by Nazi law and acts. She also shows the difficulties in emigration, in particular the many permits and procedures needed to get out of Germany and to the United States. Even the train ride out of the Third Reich was harrowing.

WYSZOGRAD, MORRIS
(1920–)

Morris Wyszograd was born in Warsaw, Poland, one of four children. He attended Polish public schools and was a 19-year-old graphic arts student in Warsaw when the Nazis took over the city. He spent time in various concentration camps and survived largely through his great drawing skills. He painted for the SS and survived, but his family perished. After spending two years at Budzyn, Poland, he was deported to Theresienstadt, where he was liberated by the Soviet Red Army in May 1945. He counterfeited a visa and passport to France and stayed there until he was able to immigrate to New York. He married and had a son and a daughter. Wyszograd earned a living by running a very successful design studio.

A Brush with Death: An Artist in the Death Camps. New York: State University of New York Press, 1999. 192 pp. ISBN: 0791443132. Ages 15–up. Memoir.

Wyszograd provides the reader in this memoir with a look at prewar Poland before the Nazi assault. He is taken for slave labor at an airplane factory. The air officers note his artistic talents, particularly his gothic calligraphy. Later they have him do all kinds of paintings. This gives him bread and less grief. Sent to Budzyn, he is placed under the SS. At Budzyn he decorates SS barracks and other facilities, but he is exposed to the gross inhumanity as he witnesses SS atrocities against prisoners. Wyszograd's work is augmented with five sketches that illustrate the horror: They include whippings; officers on horses using reins to choke prisoners; also officers with their sons in uniforms and whips; a prisoner eating his soup with his hands from a bowl. Morris Wyszograd was called upon to dig up dead bodies and pile them for burning. He continues today relating his experiences about those terrible times.

ZUCKERMAN, YITZHAK ("ANTEK")
(1915–1981)

Yitzhak Zuckerman, the leader of the Warsaw Jewish Fighting Group, was born to a middle-class Jewish family in Vilna, a city that was part of either Russia, Poland, or Lithuania, depending on the politics of the time. He attended the local Hebrew high school and then joined the city's Socialist-Zionist youth group, Dror. With the Nazi invasion of Poland, Yitzhak went to Warsaw, where he urged all Zionist factions and non-Zionists such as the Jewish Union (Bund) to unite against the German masters of the Warsaw Ghetto. He became the first commander of the Jewish Fighting Organization, which used the Polish initials ZOB. Later he yielded his position to Mordechai Anelievitz and served as deputy commander. Moving back and forth through the Warsaw sewers from the Warsaw Ghetto to the Gentile side, he negotiated military supplies for the ZOB. "Antek," his code name, became the editor of the clandestine newspaper *The Fighting Ghetto*. When resistance was crushed in May 1943, he led a group, including his wife, Zivia Lubetkin, also a ZOB commander, through the sewers to the Gentile side. In August 1944 the small group fought with Polish Gentiles in the general Warsaw uprising. Liberated by the Soviet Red Army, Zivia, Antek, and other fighters helped Jews to get out of Poland to Palestine, a movement known as Bricha. In 1947 husband and wife started the Ghetto Fighters' Museum and Kibbutz in Israel. Antek died of a heart attack at the kibbutz on June 17, 1981.

Surplus of Memory: A Chronicle of the Warsaw Ghetto Uprising. Barbara Harshav, editor. Berkeley: University of California Press, 1993. 702 pp. ISBN: 0520078411. Ages 16–up. Memoir.

This personal, emotional memoir by a pivotal leader of the Warsaw Ghetto Uprising reveals much about the greatest crime in human history. The autobiographical narrative covers the period from the German invasion of Poland in 1939 to the pogroms (riots) against Jews after World War II in 1946. Zuckerman explains much about Jewish resistance to both the Nazis and their collaborators, including Jewish traitors. The author is bitter, believing that had the Jewish Fighting Organization (ZOB) focused on deterring Jewish collaboration and had the Polish Underground military been more forthcoming, many, many more Jews might have been saved. Zuckerman is particularly contemptuous of the Jewish police who aided in the deportations to the death camp Treblinka. He also resents both the Allies and the Jewish settlement in Palestine (called Yishuv) for their lack of support of the Jewish uprising. Antek, as Zuckerman is known during the war, tormented himself for not acting sooner, particularly during July–September 1942, the period of mass deportations. He does praise ordinary residents of the ghetto who showed moral dignity and courage during the revolt, and he has great admiration for the resisters fighting impossible odds under extreme circumstances. Much of Zuckerman's narrative can be found in sixty hours of recorded testimony taped in 1974 and published in Hebrew as "Those Seven Years: 1939–1946."

2

Poetry of the Holocaust

INTRODUCTION

Poets who wrote about the Holocaust composed in the tradition of Jeremiah, the author of the biblical book Lamentations. Indeed, the Holocaust itself, in terms of its destruction, fits the events of Tisha B'av, the day of mourning for the destruction of the two temples. Their stanzas are mournful, full of grief and woe, condemning the guilt of their contemporaries and either implicitly or explicitly referred to a higher ethical and moral law.

The poetry selected in this chapter may be found in the works listed and is reasonably available to the reader. The poets selected are those most often included in anthologies and are well known for writing on Holocaust themes. Some poets included here are also well-known writers such as Charlotte Delbo and Primo Levi. Other poets were also artists or musicians, like Hersh Glik, author of a rousing march, and Luba Krugman Gurdus, the painter. An attempt has been made to include well-known poets such as Czeslaw Milosz, Paul Celan, Nelly Sachs, and Abraham Sutzkever. Two of the poets were famous Protestant religious leaders from Germany, Pastor Martin Niemoller and Dietrich Bonhoeffer.

In general, the poets tended to write short pieces, always free verse and often prose poetry, based on their experiences in prewar Germany as well as on their dealings with the Nazi regime in the ghetto and the concentration camp, on the death march, with partisans, in making an escape, and in hiding. Bertolt Brecht, who had to flee, was shocked at the Nazis' mass burning of books by Jews and other intellectuals. Pastor

Niemoller declared, "First they came for the Jews." Karen Gershon wrote about her agony of separation from her parents as she boarded the Kindertransport. Jerzy Ficowski, a Polish Gentile, focused on the suffering of Gypsies and Jews in the Warsaw Ghetto. Abba Kovner wrote about tribulations in the Vilna Ghetto. Pavel Friedman found solace in a butterfly at the Theresienstadt Ghetto. In the belly of the beast, the death and concentration camps, Tadeusz Borowski, Primo Levi, Dan Pagis, and Charlotte Delbo described the unspeakable and unthinkable lack of humanity of their oppressors. Miklos Radnoti wrote about his "forced march" of September 15, 1944, while Abraham Sutzkever, Abba Kovner, and Hannah Senesh were resisters and allude to their resistance in their poetry.

The style and themes of the poets of the Holocaust vary from individual to individual. Paul Celan, Nelly Sachs, and Elie Wiesel use a great deal of biblical and traditional Jewish symbolism. Wiesel, for example, entitles his poem, a rather long one with many stanzas, "Ani Maamin," meaning "I Believe" from the Jewish morning prayer. Paul Celan entitles his poem "Psalm." Nelly Sachs's "O the Chimneys" refers to the biblical books Job and Jeremiah.

Some poets have dedicated their works to the memory of an individual or a group. Nelly Sachs and Tadeusz Rozewicz wrote a great deal about the transgressions against children. Abba Kovner wrote a very long poem entitled "My Little Sister." Jerzy Ficowski wrote "In the Memory of Janusz Korczak." Yitzhak Katzenelson's "The Song of the Murdered Jewish People" is a shout against genocide.

Some poets are sentimental about the past that is lost and the future that might be once the Holocaust nightmare is over. Boris Slutsky remembers his aunt and cousins in the poem "Burnt." Abraham Sutzkever returns to a land he knew and also dedicates a poem, "1980," to his rescuer.

Many poets do not mention a person, place, or term specifically related to the Holocaust but allude to it in their lines. For example, Tadeusz Rozewicz in his "What Luck" writes, "Trees I thought no longer gave shade." Yala Korwin in "They Had a System" fails to mention the word German or Nazis, yet she describes how a young girl just disappeared.

The overwhelming imagery of Holocaust poets is dark. Paul Celan's "Death Fugue" is perhaps a good example, in which he starts out by saying, "Black milk of daybreak." Anne Ranasinghe writes in her "Holocaust 1944," "and did you think of me/that frost-blue December morning/snow heavy and bitter." Karen Gershon writes in "Race," "and found in every German face behind the mask the mark of Cain."

The poets' works, in summary, are a cry, a lament, sometimes shrill, sometimes soft, sometimes saying to the world, "You are guilty for letting this happen." And perhaps in their heart of hearts the poets believe that the message of their poems will somehow, in some way, reduce man's inhumanity to man.

AMICHAI, YEHUDA (1924–2000). Born in Germany, Amichai immigrated to the Jewish settlement in Palestine in 1936. Amichai reflects upon his own safety in Palestine contrasted to the horrors of the Holocaust. The poet saw military action both before and after the Israeli War of Independence. He became a teacher, published many volumes of poetry, and received many prestigious awards, including the Bialik Prize (1975) and the Israel Prize (1981).

"Almost a Love Poem." In Hilda Schiff, *Holocaust Poetry*, p. 131. New York: St. Martin's Press, 1995. ISBN: 031243575, 234 pages.

The Early Books of Yehuda Amichai. Hanover, NH: Sheep Meadow Press, 1988. ISBN: 0935296751, 265 pages.

The Great Tranquility: Questions and Answers. Translated by Glenda Abramson and Tudor Parfitt. Hanover, NH: Sheep Meadow Press, 1997. ISBN: 1878818686, 80 pages.

A Life of Poetry, 1948–1994. Translated by Barbara and Benjamin Harshem. New York: HarperCollins, 1994. ISBN: 006092666X, 476 pages.

Open Closed Open: Poems. Translated by Chana Bloch and Chana Kronfeld; edited by Drenka Willen. New York: Harcourt, 2000. ISBN: 0151003785, 184 pages.

Poems of Jerusalem and Love Poems/English and Hebrew. Hanover, NH: Sheep Meadow Press, 1992. ISBN: 1878818198, 265 pages.

AUERBACHER, INGE (1934–). See entry on Auerbacher under Memoirs, Diaries, and Fiction. Inge describes the situations in which Jews found themselves in each stage of the Nazi onslaught. Much of her story about life at Theresienstadt is told in poetry form.

Beyond the Yellow Star to America. Unionville, NY: Royal Fireworks Press, 1994. ISBN: 0880922524, 200 pages.

I Am a Star: Child of the Holocaust. New York: Prentice-Hall Books for Young Readers, 1986. ISBN: 0140364013, 87 pages.

BIRENBAUM, HALINA (1929–). Born in Warsaw, Birenbaum was trapped in the ghetto and deported to four concentration camps—Majdanek, Auschwitz, Ravensbruck, and Neustadt-Glewe. She survived these experiences and wrote a memoir entitled *Hope Is the Last to Die: A Coming of Age under Nazi Terror.* Her poems reflect her experiences in the Holocaust and the world's lack of response to the slaughter of the Jews.

Sounds of Guilty Silence: Selected Poems. Translated by Joan Friedman. Krakow: Centrum Dialogy, 1997. 61 pages.

BONHOEFFER, DIETRICH (1906–1945). See entry on Bonhoeffer under Memoirs, Diaries, and Fiction. His poetry, like his prose, reflects his experiences in jail and his thoughts about religion.

Patten, Thomas, E. *The Twisted Cross and Dietrich Bonhoeffer.* Lima, OH: CSS Publishing Company, 1992. ISBN: 1556734751.

"Who Am I?" In Hilda Schiff, *Holocaust Poetry*, p. 182. New York: St. Martin's Press, 1995. ISBN: 0312143575, 234 pages.

BOROWSKI, TADEUSZ (1922–1951). See entry on Borowski under Memoirs, Diaries, and Fiction. He describes the most grotesque horrors with a detachment that makes the abnormal seem almost normal.

"Farewell to Maria," "Night over Birkenau," and "The Sun of Auschwitz." In Hilda Schiff, *Holocaust Poetry*, pp. 120, 55, and 119. New York: St. Martin's Press, 1995. ISBN: 0312143575, 234 pages.

BRECHT, BERTOLT (1891–1956). Born in Augsburg, Bavaria, Germany, Brecht studied medicine and science and later became a communist. With the advent of Nazis to power in 1933, he was subject to persecution and escaped to Denmark, Finland, and later the United States. He also wrote the story line for Kurt Weill's anti-Nazi *Three Penny Opera* and plays such as *Mother Courage.* After the war he returned to East Berlin and continued to write and publish poetry. Brecht's themes deal with Nazi persecution in general and denial of human rights.

"The Burning of the Books," "I, the Survivor," "1940," and "War Has Been Given a Bad Name." In Hilda Schiff, *Holocaust Poetry*, pp. 8, 127, 17, and 172. New York: St. Martin's Press, 1995. ISBN: 0312143575, 234 pages.

CELAN, PAUL (1920–1969). Born Paul Ancil in Czernowitz, Bukovina (Romania), Celan was raised in a Jewish household; he was exposed to German (spoken in his home), Yiddish (spoken in his community), and Hebrew (spoken in religious school).

In June 1942 Jews from the Czernowitz Ghetto were sent on an infamous forced march to a concentration camp in Transnistria (Ukraine). Within a few months almost all the Jews were shot by the SS. The poet avoided deportation by going into hiding. After being caught, Celan spent almost two years in a Romanian forced labor camp before escaping and fleeing to the Soviet Red Army.

After the war he settled in Bucharest. In 1947 he moved to Vienna, and in 1948 to Paris. During the next twenty years Celan published many volumes of poetry. His works make extensive use of metaphor and other symbolism and have tragic themes. In 1969, at the young age of 49, Paul Celan drowned himself in the Seine River.

"Alchemical," ". . . And No Kind Of," "Aspen Tree," "From the Beam," "From Things Lost," "In the Corner of Time," "Matrix," "Nocturnally Pouting," "Radix," "Sound-Dead Sister-Shell," "Tabernacle Window," "Tenebrae," "There Was Earth inside Them," and "With a Variable Key." In Lawrence L. Langer, *Art from the Ashes*, pp. 603–617. New York: Oxford University Press, 1995. ISBN: 0195077326, 694 pages.

"Death Fugue," "The Jugs," and "Psalm." In Hilda Schiff, *Holocaust Poetry*, pp. 39, 180, and 190. New York: St. Martin's Press, 1995. ISBN: 0312143575, 234 pages.

Breathturn Sun & Moon Classics, No. 74. Translated by Pierre Joris. Los Angeles: Sun & Moon Press, 1995. ISBN: 1557132178, 261 pages.

Collected Prose. Translated by Rosemarie Waldrop. Hanover, NH: Sheep Meadow Press, 1990. ISBN: 0935296921, 67 pages.

Poems of Paul Celan. Edited and translated by Michael Hamburger. New York: Persee Books, 1990. ISBN: 0892551348.

Romanian Poems. Los Angeles: Green Integer Books, 2000. ISBN: 1892295415, 100 pages.

Wolsbohne/Wolf's Bean. Illustrated by Michael Hamburger. New York: William Drenttel, 1997. ISBN: 1884381154, 20 pages.

Del Caro, Adrian. *The Early Poetry of Paul Celan: In the Beginning Was the Word*. Baton Rouge: Louisiana State University Press, 1997. ISBN: 0807122092, 256 pages.

Felstiner, John. *Paul Celan: Poet, Survivor, Jew*. New Haven, CT: Yale University Press, 1995. ISBN: 0300060688, 344 pages.

Floretos, Aris. *Word Traces: Readings of Paul Celan*. Baltimore, MD: Johns Hopkins University Press, 1994. ISBN: 0801845524, 404 pages.

Hollander, Benjamin. *Translating Tradition: Paul Celan in France*. Small Press Distribution, 1988. ISBN: 9990928622.

Lacoue-Labarthe, Phillippe. *Poetry as Experience*. Stanford, CA: Stanford University Press, 1999. ISBN: 0804734267, 680 pages.

Samuels, Clarise. *Holocaust Visions: Surrealism and Existentialism in the Poetry of Paul Celan*. Columbia, SC: Camden House, 1993. ISBN: 187975150X, 134 pages.

COHEN, HELEN DEGAN (dates unavailable). Born in Warsaw, Poland, Helen Degan fled with her family to Belorussia in 1939. After the

Nazi occupation in 1941, the family was held in the ghetto but escaped through the Resistance movement. Helen was hidden by a Catholic woman in the countryside. She did not publish her poems until 1985. Her poem "In Hiding" is autobiographical about a young girl's terror of life in hiding.

"In Hiding." In Jean E. Brown, Elaine C. Stephens, and Janet E. Rubin, *Images from the Holocaust*, p. 59. Lincolnwood, IL: National Textbook Company, 1997. ISBN: 0844259209, 579 pages.

DELBO, CHARLOTTE (1913–1985). See entry on Delbo under Memoirs, Diaries, and Fiction. Her poetry, like her prose, is impressionistic, relating the extreme cruelty the SS inflicted on deportees.

Auschwitz and After. New Haven, CT: Yale University Press, 1995. ISBN: 0300070578, 496 pp. This work combines three books by Delbo: *None of Us Will Return, The Measure of Our Days*, and *Useless Knowledge*. All three contain mostly poetry and prose poetry.

FICOWSKI, JERZY (1924–   ). Born in Poland, Ficowski fought with the Polish Home Army during the war. His poems focused on the tragedy of Jews, Gentiles, and Gypsies under the persecution of the Nazis. His works tell of the travails of the ghetto. After the war he became a well-known poet, translator, and literary critic.

"The Assumption of Miriam," "Both Your Mothers," "I Did Not Manage to Save," and "In Memory of Janusz Korczak." In Hilda Schiff, *Holocaust Poetry*, pp. 36, 83, 86, and 62. New York: St. Martin's Press, 1995. ISBN: 0312143575, 234 pages.

"A Girl of Six from the Ghetto." In Jean E. Brown, Elaine C. Stephens, and Janet E. Rubin, *Images from the Holocaust*, p. 245. Lincolnwood, IL: National Textbook Company, 1997. ISBN: 0844259209, 579 pages.

FRIEDMAN, PAVEL (1921–1944). Born in Prague, Friedman was imprisoned in Theresienstadt at age 23. Little is known about his life. The poem for which he is remembered, "The Butterfly," has been widely anthologized. There is no other record of his work. He was deported to Auschwitz, where he perished on September 29, 1944.

"The Butterfly." Translated into English by Jeanne Nemcova, in Hana Volakova, *I never saw another butterfly . . . Children's Drawings and Poems from Terezin Concentration Camp, 1942–1944*. New York: Schocken Books, 1978. ISBN: 0805241159, 106 pages.

GERSHON, KAREN (1923–1993). Born in Bielefeld, Germany, Karen Gershon arrived in England in 1939 as part of the Kindertransport. Gershon became famous for her poem "We Came as Children" in 1966. Her poems reflect her inner life as a refugee and the emotions of children who left their parents.

"Cast Out" and "The Children's Exodus." In Jean E. Brown, Elaine C. Stephens, and Janet E. Rubin, *Images from the Holocaust*, pp. 75 and 85. Lincolnwood, IL: National Textbook Company, 1997. ISBN: 0844259209, 579 pages.

"I Was Not There" and "Race." In Hilda Schiff, *Holocaust Poetry*, pp. 133 and 161. New York: St. Martin's Press, 1995. ISBN: 0312143575, 234 pages.

The Bread of Exile. London: Victor Gollancz, 1985. ISBN: 0575035994, 184 pages.

Coming Back from Babylon: 24 Poems. London: Victor Gollancz, 1979. ISBN: 0675027193, 55 pages.

My Daughters, My Sisters, and Other Poems. London: Victor Gollancz, 1975. 64 pages.

Selected Poems. London: Victor Gollancz, 1966. 64 pages.

GURDUS, LUBA KRUGMAN (1919–). See entry on Gurdus under Memoirs, Diaries, and Fiction. Gurdus writes of the pain of deportation.

"What Happened That Day." In Jean E. Brown, Elaine C. Stephens, and Janet E. Rubin, *Images from the Holocaust*, p. 452. Lincolnwood, IL: National Textbook Company, 1997. ISBN: 0844259209, 579 pages.

Painful Echoes—: Poems of the Holocaust/from the Diary of Luba Krugman Gurdus. New York: Holocaust Library, 1985. ISBN: 080525059X, 68 pages.

HUCHEL, PETER (1903–1981). Born in Berlin, Huchel studied philosophy and literature and received a prize for his first collection of poems in 1932. He was concerned about the fate of the Jews and the horrors that befell them. At war's end his writings were published extensively in West Germany.

"Roads." In Hilda Schiff, *Holocaust Poetry*, p. 53. New York: St. Martin's Press, 1995. ISBN: 0312143575, 234 pages.

The Garden of Theophrastus and Other Poems. Translated by Michael Hamburger. Manchester: Carcanet New Press; Dublin: Raven Arts Press, 1983. 183 pages.

Selected Poems. Translated by Michael Hamburger. Cheadle: Carcanet Press, 1974. 73 pages.

A Thistle in His Mouth. Selected, translated, and introduced by Henry Beissel. Dunvegan: Cormorant Books, 1987. 117 pages.

KATZENELSON, YITZHAK (1886–1944). See entry on Katzenelson under Memoirs, Diaries, and Fiction.

Belfer, Itzhak, Yitzhak Katzenelson, and Noah H. Rosenbloom. *The Holocaust: Paintings and Drawings. The Song of the Murdered Jewish People.* Jerusalem: Beit Lohamei Haghetaot: Hakibbutz Hameuchad Publishing House, 1995. 112 pages.

KOHN, MURRAY J. (dates unknown). Very little is known about this poet's early life. His mother and sister were killed in the concentration camps. Liberated from Auschwitz in 1945, Kohn eventually immigrated to the United States, settling in Vineland, New Jersey.

The Voice of My Blood Cries Out: The Holocaust as Reflected in Hebrew Poetry. New York: Shengold Publishers, 1979. ISBN: 088400063X, 224 pages.

KORWIN, YALA H. (1923–?). The poet was born in Lvov, Poland. During the Nazi occupation Yala and her family lived in the ghetto until her father found sanctuary on the Aryan side. The family was later denounced, and all except the poet and her sister were killed. The two girls obtained false Christian identity cards and survived the rest of the war working in a German labor camp. Korwin's poems describe the desperate attempts of girls seeking to avoid detection and persecution by the Nazis. After the war Yala lived in France and later in the United States.

"Noemi," "Singing in the Sun," "They Had a System," and "39 Casimir-the-Great Street." In Jean E. Brown, Elaine C. Stephens, and Janet E. Rubin, *Images from the Holocaust*, pp. 53, 45, 41, and 20. Lincolnwood, IL: National Textbook Company, 1997. ISBN: 0844259209, 579 pages.

To Tell the Story: Poems of the Holocaust. New York: Holocaust Library, 1987. ISBN: 0896040917, 112 pages.

KOVNER, ABBA (1918–1987). See entry on Kovner under Memoirs, Diaries, and Fiction. His poetry makes wide use of biblical and Jewish imagery in portraying the tragedy to individuals.

"Far, Far a City Lies." In Hilda Schiff, *Holocaust Poetry*, p. 110. New York: St. Martin's Press, 1995. ISBN: 0312143575, 234 pages.

A Canopy in the Desert; Selected Poems. Translated by Shirley Kaufman. Pittsburgh: University of Pittsburgh Press, 1973. ISBN: 0822932601, 222 pages.

My Little Sister and Selected Poems, 1965–1985. Translated by Shirley Kaufman. Oberlin, OH: Oberlin College, 1986. ISBN: 0932440215 (paperback); 0932440207 (hardback), 159 pages.

Scrolls of Testimony. Translated by Eddie Levinson. Philadelphia: Jewish Publication Society, 2001. ISBN: 0827607105, 191 pages.

Selected Poems [of] Abba Kovner. Translated by Michael Hamburger; selected by Stephen Spender. Harmondsworth: Penguin, 1971. ISBN: 0140421378, 123 pages.

LEVI, PRIMO (1919–1987). See entry on Levi under Memoirs, Diaries, and Fiction. His poetry is autobiographical, depicting the degradation inflicted upon inmates at Auschwitz.

"Reveille," "Shema," and "The Survivor." In Hilda Schiff, *Holocaust Poetry*, pp. 117, 205, and 118. New York: St. Martin's Press, 1995. ISBN: 0312143575, 234 pages.

Collected Poems. Translated by Ruth Feldman and Brian Swann. London; Boston: Faber & Faber, 1988. ISBN: 0571152562 (paperback); 0571152554 (hardback), 78 pages.

Sodi, Risa B. *A Dante of Our Time: Primo Levi and Auschwitz*. New York: Peter Lang Publishing, 1990. ISBN: 0820412198, 124 pages.

MILOSZ, CZESLAW (1911–?). Born in Lithuania of Polish Christian parents, Milosz studied law at the University of Vilnius and first published his poetry in 1933. He was a member of the Polish Underground. His poetry is a memorial to those who perished in the Holocaust. He uses contrast and irony to record the plight of people in the ghettos. After the war Milosz served as a Polish cultural attaché in Paris and Washington, defecting from communist Poland in 1951. In 1960 the poet immigrated to the United States and became a professor of Slavic literature at the University of California (Berkeley). He was awarded the Nobel Prize for Literature in 1980.

"Campo dei Fiori" and "A Poor Christian Looks at the Ghetto." In Hilda Schiff, *Holocaust Poetry*, pp. 167 and 87. New York: St. Martin's Press, 1995. ISBN: 0312143575, 234 pages.

"Dedication." In Jean E. Brown, Elaine C. Stephens, and Janet E. Rubin, *Images from the Holocaust*, p. 556. Lincolnwood, IL: National Textbook Company, 1997. ISBN: 0844259209, 579 pages.

Between Anxiety and Hope: The Poetry and Writing of Czeslaw Milosz. Edited by Edward Mozejko. Edmonton, Canada: University of Alberta Press, 1988. ISBN: 0888641273, 190 pages.

The Collected Poems, 1931–1987. Hopewell, NJ: Ecco Press, 1990. ISBN: 0880011742, 511 pages.

Witness of Poetry. Cambridge, MA: Harvard University Press, 1984. ISBN: 0674953835, 128 pages.

Nathan, Leonard, and Arthur Quinn. *The Poet's Work: An Introduction to Czeslaw Milosz*. Cambridge, MA: Harvard University Press, 1991. ISBN: 0674689704, 178 pages.

NIEMOLLER, MARTIN (1892–1984). Born in Lippstadt, Germany, Niemoller was an ardent anti-communist who first went along with Hitler and his policies. He soon became disillusioned with the Nazi government, however, and eventually became the leader of a group of German Protestant clergy who preached against the Aryanized Protestant Church. His most important poem is entitled "First They Came for the Jews." Expressing regret for the lack of protest by Protestant clergy, Niemoller authored the Stuttgart Declaration, a declaration of guilt. He was arrested by the Gestapo and deported to Sachsenhausen and then to Dachau. After liberation he returned to his career as a cleric in Germany.

"First They Came for the Jews." In Hilda Schiff, *Holocaust Poetry*, p. 9. New York: St. Martin's Press, 1995. ISBN: 0312143575, 234 pages.

PAGIS, DAN (1930–1986). This poet was born in Radautz, Bukovina, Romania. His father left the family and immigrated to Palestine in 1934; his mother died soon after. The boy was raised by his grandparents. Pagis spent three years of his young life in Nazi concentration camps in Transnistria, a Romanian colony in the Southern Ukraine. His poetry is not precise, and allusions to the Holocaust are indirect. Pagis leaves to the reader the challenge of filling in details.

   After the war Pagis joined his father in Palestine. He settled in Jerusalem in 1946, where he received a Ph.D. from Hebrew University. Pagis began publishing his poetry at age 19. He produced more than six volumes of poetry before his early death in 1986.

"Autobiography," "Footprints," "Instructions for Crossing the Border," and "Ready for Parting." In Lawrence L. Langer, *Art from the Ashes*, pp. 586, 593, 591, and 597. New York: Oxford University Press, 1995. ISBN: 195077326, 694 pages.

"Draft of a Reparations Agreement," "Europe, Late," "The Roll Call," "Testimony," and "Written in Pencil in the Sealed Railway-Car." In Hilda Schiff, *Holocaust Poetry*, pp. 132, 6, 43, 47, and 180. New York: St. Martin's Press, 1995. ISBN: 0312143575, 234 pages.

Poems. Translated from the Hebrew by Stephen Mitchell. South Hinksey, Oxford: Carcanet Press, 1972. ISBN: 0856350257, 63 pages.

Points of Departure. Translated by Stephen Mitchell. Philadelphia: Jewish Publication Society of America, 1981. ISBN: 0827602014 (paperback), 123 pages.

Variable Directions: The Selected Poetry of Don Pagis. Translated by Stephen Mitchell. San Francisco: North Point, 1989. ISBN: 0865473846 (paperback); 0865473838 (hardback), 153 pages.

PILINSZKY, JANOS (1921–1981). Born in Budapest, Pilinszky was deported to various concentration camps, including Ravensbruck in 1944. He describes suffering in the camps, very often in spiritual terms, in a rather terse style. At war's end his poetry was published extensively in Hungarian. The poet identified with Holocaust victims throughout his writing career.

"Fable, Detail from His KZ-Oratorio: Dark Heaven," "Harbach 1944," "On the Wall of a KZ-Lager," and "Passion of Ravensbruck." In Hilda Schiff, *Holocaust Poetry*, pp. 52, 48, 51, and 50. New York: St. Martin's Press, 1995. ISBN: 0312143575, 234 pages.

Metropolitan Icons: Selected Poems of Janos Pilinszky in Hungarian and in English. Edited and translated by Emery George. Lewiston, NY: Edwin Mellen Press, 1995. ISBN: 0773490582, 259 pages.

RADNOTI, MIKLOS (1909–1944). Born in Budapest, Radnoti studied briefly in Czechoslovakia after graduation from high school, but he returned home to pursue a doctorate. However, religious restrictions placed upon Jews prevented him from enrolling for courses at the University of Budapest. In response to the restrictions and other anti-Semitic activities, he converted to Catholicism. This action did not save him from the Nazis, however, for they considered converts from Judaism still Jews. Arrested and sent to Yugoslavia, Radnoti became a slave laborer building roads for the Nazis.

In September 1944, already exhausted and in a weakened state, he and others were driven by forced march from Yugoslavia back toward Hungary. In November 1944, too weak and sick to continue, he and others in the same condition were forced to dig a ditch and then were shot and killed, their bodies burned. When Radnoti's remains were later discovered, his last poems were found in the pocket of his clothing. His poetry is descriptive of his condition under the rigors of slave labor and death marches.

"Clouded Sky" and "Postcards." In Hilda Schiff, *Holocaust Poetry*, pp. 24 and 47. New York: St. Martin's Press, 1995. ISBN: 0312143575, 234 pages.

"Dreamscape" (1943–1944), "The Fifth Eclogue" (fragment) (1943), "Floral Song" (1942), "Forced March" (1944), "Fragment" (1944), "Guard and Protect Me" (1937), "In a Troubled Hour" (1939), "Like Death" (1940), "O Ancient Prisons" (1944), "Razglednicas" (1944), "Root" (1944), and "War Diary" (1935–1936). In Lawrence L. Langer, *Art from the Ashes,* pp. 629, 627, 626, 632, 630, 623, 624, 625, 628, 633, 631, and 620. New York: Oxford University Press, 1995. ISBN: 195077326, 694 pages.

Foamy Sky: The Major Poems of Miklos Radnoti. Translated by Zsuzsanna Ozsvath and Frederick Turner. Princeton, NJ: Princeton University Press, 1999. ISBN: 0691069549, 149 pages.

Forced March: Selected Poems. Translated by Clive Wilmer and George Gagnon. Manchester, England: Carcanet New Press, 1979. 62 pages.

33 Poems. Translated by Thomas Orszag-Land. Budapest: Mæcenas, 1992. 124 pages.

Gomori, George, and Clive Wilmer, eds. *The Life and Poetry of Miklos Radnoti: Essays.* New York: Columbia University Press, 1999. ISBN: 0880334266, 200 pages.

RANASINGHE, ANNE (1925–?). Born in Essen, Germany, she was sent to England as part of the Kindertransport in 1939. She was the only member of her family rescued from the Nazis. After the war she became a journalist and married a university professor from Sri Lanka, where she eventually settled. Ranasinghe began writing poetry in 1969. Her poems reflect the agony of her separation from her parents and are an ode to their memory.

"Holocaust 1944." In Hilda Schiff, *Holocaust Poetry*, p. 142. New York: St. Martin's Press, 1995. ISBN: 0312143575, 234 pages.

At What Dark Point. Colombo: English Writers Cooperative of Sri Lanka, 1991. ISBN: 9559069047, 150 pages.

Not Even Shadows. Colombo: English Writers Cooperative of Sri Lanka, 1991. 43 pages.

ROSENFELD, RUTH (1920–1991). Born in Frankfurt am Main, Germany, Ruth Rosenfeld began writing poetry and keeping a diary at the age of 14, in 1934. She escaped to England in 1939, but both her parents perished in the Holocaust. Her poems were written between 1934 and 1939. Although she did not experience the worst the Nazis had to offer, her poetry was often prophetic. She saw the Nazi genocide of the Jews coming. Her poetry reflected a sadness and despair.

Beyond These Shores, 1934–1940: Poems and Diary of a Jewish Girl Who Escaped from Nazi Germany. Translated from the German by Thomas Dorsett. Baltimore, MD: Icarus, 1996. ISBN: 0944806090 (pbk.), 79 pages.

ROZEWICZ, TADEUSZ (1921–?). Born in Radomsko in central Poland to a Catholic family, Rozewicz was involved with the Polish Resistance during the war. At war's end he studied art history at the University of

Cracow. He wrote not only poetry but prose and drama as well. His work has been widely translated, and in 1966 he was awarded the State Prize for Literature First Class, Poland's most prestigious literary award. Rozewicz's poetry describes the horrors of the Nazi occupation suffered by both Jew and Gentile and decries the world's indifference. His poems seem to say "remember us."

"In the Midst of Life," "Leave Us," "Massacre of the Boys," "Pigtail," "Posthumous Rehabilitation," "The Return," "The Survivor," and "What Luck." In Hilda Schiff, *Holocaust Poetry*, pp. 158, 116, 70, 71, 169, 128, 157, and 185. New York: St. Martin's Press, 1995. ISBN: 0312143575, 234 pages.

"The Survivor" and Other Poems. Translated by Magnus J. Krynski and Robert Maguire. Princeton, NJ: Princeton University Press, 1976. ISBN: 069106315X, 160 pages.

Rozewicz, Tadeusz, and Adam Czerniawski. *They Came to See a Poet: Selected Poems*. Chester Springs, PA: Dufour Press, 1991. ISBN: 0856462381, 232 pages.

Unease. Translated by Victor Contoski. St. Paul, MN: New Rivers Press, 1980. ISBN: 0898230136, 156 pages.

SACHS, NELLY (1891–1970). Born in Berlin to an assimilated Jewish family, Sachs was first published in 1921. In 1940 she escaped the Nazis by fleeing to Sweden, where she supported herself by working as a translator. Sachs became an influential opponent of the Nazis, alerting the outside world to the conditions of Jews in the Reich. In 1966 the poet was awarded the Nobel Prize for Literature. Her most well-known poem, containing many stanzas, is "O the Chimneys." Sachs's poetry contains biblical allusions and aims at the heart as well as the mind. She wrote in German, trying to recreate the bitter and tormented world from which she escaped. Many themes include the Holocaust tragedy of mothers and children.

"Already Embraced by the Arm of Heavenly Solace," "A Dead Child Speaks," "O the Chimneys," and "O the Night of the Weeping Children." In Hilda Schiff, *Holocaust Poetry*, pp. 68, 67, 41, and 69. New York: St. Martin's Press, 1995. ISBN: 0312143575, 234 pages.

"Chorus of the Rescued." In Jean E. Brown, Elaine C. Stephens, and Janet E. Rubin. *Images from the Holocaust*, p. 374. Lincolnwood, IL: National Textbook Company, 1997. ISBN: 0844259209, 579 pages.

O the Chimneys: Selected Poems, Including the Verse Play, Eli. Translated from the German by Michael Hamburger. New York: Farrar, Straus and Giroux, 1967. ISBN: 0224612670, 387 pages.

The Seeker, and Other Poems. Translated from the German by Ruth and Michael Mead [and] Michael Hamburger. New York: Farrar, Straus and Giroux, 1970. ISBN: 0374257809, 399 pages.

Bower, Kathrin M. *Ethics and Remembrance in the Poetry of Nelly Sachs and Rose Auslander (Studies in German Literature, Linguistics, and Culture.)* Woodbridge, UK: Boydell & Brewer, 2000. ISBN: 1571131914.

Rudnick, Ursula. *Post-Shoah Religious Metaphors: The Image of God in the Poetry of Nelly Sachs.* New York: Peter Lang Publishing, 1995. ISBN: 0820429295, 296 pages.

SENESH, HANNAH (1921–1944). This poet was born in Budapest into a well-educated, assimilated Jewish family. Fleeing native Hungarian persecution, she left Hungary for Palestine in 1939. In 1941 Senesh joined the Haganah (Jewish self-defense forces), eventually enlisting in the British army in 1943. From January to June 1944 the poet was trained in Egypt as a parachutist. In early June 1944 Hannah was parachuted into Yugoslavia and crossed the border into German-held Hungary. Senesh had a dual mission to establish escape routes for downed airmen and to organize Jewish underground resistance. She was captured on June 9, 1944, and subjected to severe torture in jail in Budapest to reveal the names and locations of other members of her unit. Senesh remained silent, and after a brief reunion with her mother, she was "tried" on October 28, 1944, and executed on November 7, 1944. Her most famous poem is "Blessed Is the Match."

"Blessed Is the Match." In Marie Syrkin, *Blessed is the Match: The Story of Jewish Resistance*, p. 1. Philadelphia: Jewish Publication Society of America, 1947. ISBN: 0827600860, 366 pages.

"One-Two-Three." In Jean E. Brown, Elaine C. Stephens, and Janet E. Rubin, *Images from the Holocaust*, p. 473. Lincolnwood, IL: National Textbook Company, 1997. ISBN: 0844259209, 579 pages.

SLUTSKY, BORIS (1919–?). Born in the Ukraine to Russian Jewish parents, Slutsky served in the Soviet army during the war and witnessed the horrors the Nazis inflicted upon the Jewish people and other nationalities at the front. His poems describe murderous acts against his family in straightforward, almost narrative fashion.

"Burnt" and "How They Killed My Grandmother." In Hilda Schiff, *Holocaust Poetry*, pp. 76 and 30. New York: St. Martin's Press, 1995. ISBN: 0312143575, 234 pages.

Things That Happened (Glas, No. 19). Edited by G. S. Smith. Chicago: Ivan R. Dee, 1999. ISBN: 1566632358, 240 pages.

SUTZKEVER, ABRAHAM (1913–?). Born in Siberia to traditional Jewish parents, Sutzkever was raised in Smorogon near Vilna, Lithuania. In September 1941 fascist Lithuanian police under German supervision captured Sutzkever. He and his wife joined the United Partisan Organization (a Jewish resistance group) and in September 1943 left the ghetto with artist–resistance fighter **Alexander Bogen** and walked more than sixty miles to join a Soviet partisan unit in the forest. Taken to Moscow in March 1944, after Vilna was liberated, they returned home. Sutzkever and his wife immigrated to Palestine in 1947. He wrote in Yiddish, and his work was not published until 1979. His poems reflect life in the Vilna Ghetto. His poetry is sometimes obscure with much metaphor and multiple meanings; at other times it is more concrete. Some poems are intellectual, others emotional.

"Above-in a Death Swordplay," "Black Thorns" (1945), "Burnt Pearls" (1943), "Faces in Swamps" (1942), "For My Child" (1943), "Frozen Jews" (1944), "Grains of Wheat" (1943), "In the Cell" (1941), "Leaves of Ash," "My Every Breath Is a Curse," "Poem about a Herring" (1946), "Resurrection" (1945), "Self-Portrait" (1951), "Serpents of Darkness," "Soon It Will Happen," "Stalks" (1943), and "War" (1939). In Lawrence L. Langer, *Art from the Ashes*, pp. 566, 576, 580, 564, 578, 573, 570, 577, 565, 568, 581, 574, 582, 565, 566, 572, and 563. New York: Oxford University Press, 1995. ISBN: 0195077326, 694 pages.

"A Cartload of Shoes" and "How?" (1943). In Hilda Schiff, *Holocaust Poetry*, pp. 67 and 29. New York: St. Martin's Press, 1995. ISBN: 0312143575, 234 pages.

"Faces in the Swamp," "A Voice from the Heart," "I Feel Like Saying a Prayer," "Burnt Pearls," "I Am Lying in This Coffin," "To the Thin Vein in My Head," "On the Subject of Roses," "For a Comrade." In Marguerite Striar, *Beyond Lament*, pp. 135–147. Evanston, IL: Northwestern University Press, 1999. ISBN: 0810115565, 565 pages.

"1980." In Jean E. Brown, Elaine C. Stephens, and Janet E. Rubin, *Images from the Holocaust*, p. 71. Lincolnwood, IL: National Textbook Company, 1997. ISBN: 0844259209, 579 pages.

Abraham Sutzkever: Partisan Poet. New York: T. Yoseloff, 1971. ISBN: 0498078612, 188 pages.

A. Sutzkever: Selected Poetry and Prose. Translated by Barbara Harshav and Benjamin Harshav. Los Angeles: University of California Press, 1991. ISBN: 0520065395, 433 pages.

Burnt Pearls: Ghetto Poems of Abraham Sutzkever. Translated from the Yiddish by Seymour Mayne. Oakville, Ontario: Mosaic Press/Valley Editions, 1981. ISBN: 0889621411 (paperback); 088962142X (hardback), 51 pages.

Laughter beneath the Forest: Poems from Old and Recent Manuscripts. Translated from the Yiddish by Barnett Zumoff. Hoboken, NJ: Ktav Publishing House, 1996. ISBN: 0881255556, 179 pages.

TAUBE, HERMAN (dates unknown). Born in Lodz, Poland, and orphaned at an early age, the Nazis deported his relatives and Taube survived the camps. The poet describes a past that has disappeared, the traditional Jewish world of Eastern Europe, which he sees as one of beauty and splendor. Taube contrasts this world with images of Majdanek in his poetry of lament and sorrow. He narrates his encounter with people that he met—friends, children, passersby. The poet feels anguish at survivors and other Jews who seem to want to forget both the Holocaust and the Jewish world that once was.

Taube traveled traveled to the United States in 1947 and currently lives in Rockville, Maryland.

"Berlin, Savoy Hotel," "Insects in a Bottle," and "Letter to a Poet." In Marguerite Striar, *Beyond Lament*, pp. 13, 94, 292. Evanston, IL: Northwestern University Press, 1989. ISBN: 0810115565, 565 pages.

Autumn Travels, Devious Paths: Poetry & Prose. Washington, DC: Dryad Press, 1992. ISBN: 0931848849, 222 pages.

Between the Shadows: New and Selected Works. Takoma Park, MD: Dryad Press; Rockville, MD: Jewish Folk Arts Society, 1986. ISBN: 0931848725, 261 pages.

A Chain of Images: Poetic Notes. New York: Shulsinger Brothers, 1979. 180 pages.

Echoes: Poetic Notes. Washington, DC: DIN, 1981. 144 pages.

WIESEL, ELIE (1928–   ). See entry on Weisel under Memoirs, Diaries, and Fiction. Wiesel's biblical allusions in his poetry are applied to the most extreme aspects of the concentration camp experience.

"Ani Maamin" and "Never Shall I Forget." In Hilda Schiff, *Holocaust Poetry*, pp. 194 and 42. New York: St. Martin's Press, 1995. ISBN: 0312143575, 234 pages.

3

Art of the Holocaust

INTRODUCTION

Why, given the nature of the punishment, did the painters continue to paint? In the 1930s the Nazis formulated laws and edicts that dictated the comings and goings, food allowance, livelihood, living arrangements, and statelessness of Jews and other "undesirables." After the Jewish populations were moved into ghettos, the Germans decided who would live to see another day and who would face deportation and death. However, these measures did not and could not destroy the victims' inner strength, the spiritual resistance so many artists exhibited. Artists painted because they wanted to alert the world. They painted because they wanted to memorialize the victims. They painted hoping the scenes they depicted would be a negative example never to be repeated. Using whatever materials they could scrounge, they drew, sketched, and painted on such unlikely canvasses as the backs of postage stamps and on flimsy tissue paper. In some instances they exhibited their work publicly, but most times they worked in total secrecy and at great risk.

What did these creative eyewitnesses see? Through their eyes they recorded the horrors of forced labor, random murder, ghetto life, transit camps, the Resistance, and concentration and death camps. Artists such as Samuel Bak of the Vilna Ghetto, Sara Glicksman-Faitlowitz and Szymon Szerman of the Lodz Ghetto, Esther Lurie of the Kovno Ghetto, Gela Seksztajn, Halina Olomucki and Roman Kramsztyk of the Warsaw Ghetto, and Haim Urison of the Bialystok Ghetto depicted the overcrowding, starvation, random murder, sights, landmarks, and leaders of their respective communities.

Theresienstadt, the so-called model ghetto, was the showplace Nazis used to dupe the International Red Cross with art exhibits, various cultural events, movie theater, cafés, playing orchestras and well-dressed internees strolling the plazas. Of course it was all a lie, for behind the false storefronts lay starving, typhus-infested dead and dying men, women, and children.

In the early 1940s Theresienstadt was set up to be a camp for prominent Jews and Jews who had served in the armed forces during World War I. Almost immediately after their arrival by cattle car from all over Europe, Jewish artists, musicians, and poets were encouraged by the Nazis to produce. An artists' studio was created where Jehuda Bacon, Felix Bloch, Charlotte Buresova, Karel Fleischmann, Bedrich Fritta, Leo Haas, Malvina Schalkova, Otto Ungar, and several others worked at various tasks for the Germans; but more important, they secretly produced hundreds of drawings and paintings detailing the true Theresienstadt. Their collective hope was to pass some of the pieces to the International Red Cross and have them reach the outside world. Somehow the Nazis discovered some of the hidden paintings and many of the artists were tortured, sent to Auschwitz, and gassed.

Children's art was also encouraged in the ghetto as part of its cultural activities. Ludmilla Chladkova, a Theresienstadt inmate, published her works years later in a book about children's art and poetry in Theresienstadt called *I Never Saw Another Butterfly*.

The French Vichy transit camps of Gurs, Compiegne, Drancy, and St. Cyprien held Jews and other Nazi victims until cattle cars arrived to transport the guiltless victims to the death camps in Poland or to slave labor camps. Talented artists such as Osias Hofstatter, Felix Nussbaum, and Karl Schwesig were sent from St. Cyprien to Gurs, where their artistic endeavors were encouraged and two exhibitions were in fact held. In their art these men depicted the atrocious living conditions. They showed the shacks with mud floors, the starvation, and the utter hopelessness of the camps' inhabitants, most of whom were later deported to Auschwitz.

As the Nazi machine trampled Europe, many fled into the forests and mountains to hide. Hermann-Henry Gowa, for example, hid in the mountains of southern France to escape impending arrest. After the war he painted the events he witnessed during the Nazi occupation of France. Nelly Toll went into hiding with a Christian family in Poland. During that time, she painted twenty-nine watercolors of an imaginary life where she was free. Her paintings were based on stories her mother would tell her about children with normal lives. In the dense forests of Eastern Europe some artists joined Resistance or partisan units and were able to strike back at their mortal enemy. Alexander Bogen's unit worked near the Vilna Ghetto, and he was able to move in and out of the ghetto to recruit members for the partisans. Bogen's drawings show the events and horrors he witnessed. Other partisan units worked near Warsaw and Kracow with members Maria Hiszpanska-Neuman and Mieczyslaw Koscielniak. Both were captured and deported to concentration camps.

The French Resistance was integral in saving many Jewish lives, particularly children. France Audoul and L'Abbe Jean Daligault joined partisan units, were arrested, and sent east. Audoul and the Polish artist Maria Hiszpanska-Neuman were sent to Ravensbruck, a concentration camp for women, near Berlin. Audoul depicted the brutality of the SS guards, whereas Hiszpanska-Neuman painted the inmates. Hiszpanska-Neuman's 400 drawings of emaciated and exhausted prisoners were all but lost during the winter of 1945.

As the artist-deportees from all over Europe converged on the Nazi concentration camps and death camps, they continued in their quest to sketch the truth so the outside world would know what happened. Artists such as Dinah Gottliebova-Babbit, Janina Tollik, Alfred Kantor, and David Olere documented their Auschwitz experiences. Gottliebova-Babbitt was assigned to the camp hospital painting portraits of the Gypsy victims of medical experiments performed by the infamous Nazi doctor Josef Mengele. Kantor, Tollik, and Olere sketched drawings of the camp's daily routine. Unlike Gottliebova-Babbitt, their artwork was produced secretly, for discovery would have brought horrible punishment or even death.

Concentration camps Buchenwald, Flossenburg, and Sachsenhausen also housed artists who drew their experiences. Pierre Mania sketched emaciated and beaten fellow Buchenwald inmates, and Jozef Szajna hid twenty drawings of fellow prisoners under his straw cot in the camp hospital. Ota Matousek, an inmate in Flossenburg, sketched drawings of daily life in the camp. Stefan Horski published a book of his paintings depicting camp life in Sachsenhausen. Franciszek Jazwiecki, also an inmate of Sachsenhausen, secretly produced portraits of his fellow prisoners.

As a group these artists of various ages, educational background, and ethnic origin, arrested and held under the most hideous and frightening of conditions, produced vivid and sometimes colorful evidence of the atrocities committed by the Nazis. Through their eyes we cringe at the overcrowded barracks, the brutal sadism, and the unrelenting starvation they faced in ghettos and concentration camps. The SS guards are depicted as giants with bulging muscles or demonic figures in black uniforms. Nothing is left to the imagination—their personal suffering and the suffering of their fellow inmates are etched on paper.

AUDOUL, FRANCE (1894–1977). Audoul was born in Lyon, France, into a family of artists. After the Nazi occupation of France, she joined a newly formed Resistance unit in Toulouse. Arrested by the Gestapo, she was sent to Ravensbruck concentration camp in 1943. She drew scenes of everyday life in the camp. Her drawings show the despair of her fellow inmates and the brutality of the Nazi guards. After liberation, she took her drawings with her, and twenty years later they were published.

Ravensbruck: 150,000 femmes en enfer: 32 croquis et portraits fait au camp 1944–1945. Paris: Le Deporte, 1953.

"Forbidden Prayers" (1944–1945), Ravensbruck, ink. In Janet Blatter and Sybil Milton, *Art of the Holocaust*, p. 162. New York: Rutledge Press, 1981. ISBN: 0831704187. Courtesy Federation Nationale des Deportes et Internes Resistants et Patriotes, Paris.

"The Guard Metes out Punishment" (1944–1945), Ravensbruck, ink. In Blatter and Milton, p. 163. Courtesy Federation Nationale des Deportes et Internes Resistants et Patriotes, Paris.

"The Hell for Women" (undated), Paris, oil on wood. In Blatter and Milton, p. 236. Courtesy Musee de Deux Guerres Mondiales, Paris.

"Shorn" (1944–1945), Ravensbruck, ink. In Blatter and Milton, p. 162. Courtesy Federation Nationale des Deportes et Internes Resistants et Patriotes, Paris.

AWRET, IRENE (dates unknown). Awret was born to a Jewish family in Germany. Before Hitler's rise to power Irene studied art, and after the dictator took control of the government she fled to Belgium, where she continued her studies. After the Nazis invaded Belgium, Awret was held in the transit camp at Malines. She is known for her portraits of fellow internees, many of whom were deported to death camps. Awret successfully hid several of these paintings. After liberation she and her husband immigrated to Israel.

"Before Confiscation" (1943), Malines, watercolor. In Janet Blatter and Sybil Milton, *Art of the Holocaust*, p. 114. New York: Rutledge Press, 1981. ISBN: 0831704187. Courtesy Ghetto Fighters' House, Israel.

"Death Train," watercolor and india ink. In Miriam Novitch, ed., *Spiritual Resistance: Art from the Concentration Camps 1940–1945*, p. 130. Philadelphia: Jewish Publication Society, 1981. Courtesy Kibbutz Lohamei Haghetaot.

"The Search" (1943), Malines, pencil on cardboard. In Novitch, p. 45. Courtesy Kibbutz Lohamei Haghetaot.

"Young Man in Golf Trousers, Seated" (1943), Malines, soft pencil. In Novitch, p. 47. Courtesy Kibbutz Lohamei Haghetaot.

Firster, Richard, and Nora Levin, eds. *The Living Witness: Art in the Concentration Camps*. Philadelphia: Museum of American Jewish History, 1978.

BACON, YEHUDA (1929–?). Born in Ostrava, Czechoslovakia, Yehuda Bacon was deported to Theresienstadt at age 13. He lived in one of the children's homes, Jugenheim L. 417, collective organization housing. At Theresienstadt Leo Haas, Otto Ungar, and Karel Fleischmann taught him to draw and paint. His sketches of fellow prisoners and scenes display a sense of darkness and despair. In December 1943 Bacon and his father were deported to Auschwitz, where his father was killed. After liberation Yehuda settled in Israel. Some of Bacon's paintings were used as evidence in the trial of Adolf Eichmann in Israel in 1961.

"Portrait of a Woman in Auschwitz" (1945), charcoal. In Janet Blatter and Sybil Milton, *Art of the Holocaust*, p. 199. New York: Rutledge Press, 1981. ISBN: 0831704187. Courtesy Ghetto Fighters' House, Israel.

"Self Portrait" (1945), Auschwitz, watercolor. In Blatter and Milton, p. 190. Courtesy Ghetto Fighters' House, Israel.

"The Escape" (1945), charcoal. In Miriam Novitch, ed., *Spiritual Resistance: Art from the Concentration Camps, 1940–1945*, p. 48. Philadelphia: Jewish Publication Society, 1981. Courtesy Kibbutz Lohamei Haghetaot.

"Muselmann" (1945), watercolor and gouache on paper. In Novitch, p. 131. Courtesy Kibbutz Lohamei Haghetaot.

Costanza, Mary S. *The Living Witness: Art in the Concentration Camps and Ghettos*. New York: Free Press, 1982. ISBN: 0029066603.

BAK, SAMUEL (1933–   ). Bak lived in the Vilna Ghetto and at the age of 9 had the first exhibition of his drawings in the ghetto. After escaping he immigrated to Israel, where he studied art. As late as 1999 he resided in the Boston area and has exhibited his work at galleries in the United States, Israel, and Europe.

Bak uses traditional symbols of Jewish learning and faith to bring the Holocaust experience to the observer. He particularly relies on stars, Shabbat candles, Hebrew letters, and the Ten Commandments.

Bak: Myth, Midrash, and Mysticism Paintings, 1973–1994. Boston: Pucker Safrai Gallery, 1995.

A Retrospective Journey: Paintings, 1946–1994. West Bloomfield, MI: Janice Charach Epstein Museum/Gallery, 1994.

Bak, Samuel, and Lawrence L. Langer. *The Game Continues: Chess in the Art of Samuel Bak*. Boston: Pucker Safrai Gallery, 1995. ISBN: 1879985039.

―――. *Landscapes of Jewish Experience: Paintings by Samuel Bak, Essay and Commentary by Lawrence L. Langer*. Boston: Pucker Gallery in association with Brandeis University Press, 1997. ISBN: 0963531824. 125 pages with color illustrations.

Bak, Samuel, and Paul T. Nagano. *The Past Continues*. Boston: D. R. Godine in association with Pucker Safrai Gallery, 1988.

"The Family" (date unavailable), oil on linen. In Nelly Toll, *When Memory Speaks: The Holocaust in Art*, p. 94. Westport, CT: Praeger, 1998. ISBN: 0275955346. Courtesy Pucker Gallery.

"Wall" (date unavailable), oil on linen. In Toll, p. 99. Courtesy Pucker Gallery.

Costanza, Mary S. *The Living Witness: Art in the Concentration Camps and Ghettos*. New York: Free Press, 1982. ISBN: 0029066603.

BARZ, MATHIAS (1895–1982). Born in Dusseldorf, Mathias Barz studied at the Dusseldorf Art Academy as a teenager. In 1925 he married a Jewish woman, Brunhilde Stein. After the Nazis gained power, routine house searches culminated in the destruction and confiscation of several paintings. Constantly harassed, in 1939 the couple was prohibited to paint or exhibit their work. In 1944 they fled into hiding after receiving news of Brunhilde's impending deportation. Barz's colorful paintings depict the sorrow and horror of life under Nazi rule. His wife died in 1965, and Barz died in 1982 in the Netherlands.

"Inferno" (begun in 1945 but never finished), Dusseldorf, oil on wood. In Sybil Milton, ed. and trans., *The Art of Jewish Children, Germany: 1936–1941*, p. 17. New York: Allied Books Limited, 1989. ISBN: 0802225586.

"SS Man" (1979), the Netherlands, oil on cardboard. In Milton, p. 18.

"Working-Class Children" (1926), Dusseldorf, oil on canvas. In Milton, p. 9.

BERLINE, ABRAHAM JOSEPH (1894–1944). Born into a Jewish family in the Ukraine, Berline moved to Paris to study art in 1912. He supported himself as a cabdriver and painted landscapes in his spare time. After the German occupation of France, Berline joined the Resistance. The artist was arrested in 1941 and sent to Compiegne, where he met painter **Isis Kischka**. His paintings depicted everyday life in Compiegne. He was deported to Auschwitz, where he died.

"Internees in the Camp" (1942), Compiegne, pastel. In Janet Blatter and Sybil Milton, *Art of the Holocaust*, p. 103. New York: Rutledge Press, 1981. ISBN: 0831704187. Courtesy Ghetto Fighters' House.

"The Camp of Compiegne" (1941–1942), Compiegne. In Miriam Novitch, ed., *Spiritual Resistance: Art from the Concentration Camps 1940–1945*, p. 129. Philadelphia: Jewish Publication Society, 1981. Courtesy Kibbutz Lohamei Haghetaot.

BERNBAUM, ISRAEL (?–1995). See entry on Bernbaum under Memoirs, Diaries, and Fiction.

My Brother's Keeper: The Holocaust through the Eyes of an Artist. New York: G. P. Putnam's Sons, 1985. ISBN: 0399212426. Paintings of the Warsaw Ghetto in this book are found in the Israel Bernbaum Memorial Shoah Fund of the Holocaust Resource Center, Jewish Federation of Greater Clifton-Passaic, New Jersey.

"Janusz Korczak and His Children on the Way to the Train." In Nelly Toll, *When Memory Speaks: The Holocaust in Art*, p. 43. Westport, CT: Praeger, 1998. ISBN: 02759553406.

BLOCH, FELIX (1915–1944). Born in Vienna, Bloch was interned at Terezin, where he worked with Leo Haas's team of artists in the so-called model camp. In July 1944 he and three other artists were charged with passing anti-Nazi propaganda through his paintings. There are conflicting stories about his death. He was severely beaten in the Little Fortress and believed to have died there; others claim he died on the transport en route to Auschwitz.

"Musicians in Theresienstadt" (undated), sepia wash. In Janet Blatter, and Sybil Milton, *Art of the Holocaust*, p. 95. New York: Rutledge Press, 1981. ISBN: 0831704187. Courtesy Prague State Jewish Museum.

"Transport" (1941), Terezin Camp, wash drawing. In Mary S. Costanza, *The Living Witness: Art in the Concentration Camps and Ghettos*, p. 110. New York: Free Press, 1982. ISBN: 0029066603. Courtesy Prague State Jewish Museum.

"Landscape" (date unavailable), Theresienstadt, watercolor. In Miriam Novitch, ed., *Spiritual Resistance: Art from the Concentration Camps, 1940–1945*, p. 51. Philadelphia: Jewish Publication Society, 1981. Courtesy Kibbutz Lohamei Haghetaot.

BOGEN, ALEXANDER (1916–?). Bogen was born in Lithuania. After the Nazi invasion of Poland, he commanded a Jewish partisan unit in the Narocz Forest and slipped in and out of the Vilna Ghetto to recruit members for the partisans. His drawings recorded the events and horrors he witnessed. Many of these drawings were buried in the woods for safekeeping. When the Vilna Ghetto was going to be destroyed, the partisans tried to rescue key people, one of whom was **Abraham Sutzkever**.

He was taken to Moscow and brought Bogen's drawings with him. They were exhibited in Moscow.

"Child of the Ghetto" (1943), outside Vilna, charcoal. In Janet Blatter and Sybil Milton, *Art of the Holocaust*, p. 127. New York: Rutledge Press, 1981. ISBN: 0831704187. Courtesy Yad Vashem, Israel.

"Holocaust" (undated), Israel, oil. In Blatter and Milton, p. 232. Courtesy Yad Vashem, Israel.

Revolt. Jerusalem, Israel: Yad Vashem, 1974.

"En Route" (1943), location unknown, charcoal. In Mary S. Costanza, *The Living Witness: Art in the Concentration Camps and Ghettos*, p. 122. New York: Free Press, 1982. ISBN: 0029066603. Courtesy Alexander Bogen.

"Partisans, 1943" (1943), in Narocz Forest, charcoal. In Costanza, p. 20. Courtesy Alexander Bogen.

BONIECKI, MARIA ALBIN (dates unknown). Boniecki took part in the September 1939 Polish campaign as a volunteer medic in the Polish Home Army. He was arrested on October 7, 1942, and jailed in Pawiak Prison. On January 18, 1943, he was sent to Maidanek concentration camp. With permission from the Nazis he created a few sculptures from cement. The sculptures were meant to show what the camp looked like, and one of them was the symbol of the Polish Underground ("Tortoise"). Boniecki was released from the camp in 1943 and later moved to the United States.

"Column of Three Eagles" (1944), Maidanek, plaster. In Janet Blatter and Sybil Milton, *Art of the Holocaust*, p. 221. New York: Rutledge Press, 1981. ISBN: 0831704187. Photo courtesy Janina Jaworska, Warsaw.

"Tortoise" (1941–1944), Maidanek, cement sculpture. In Mary S. Costanza, *The Living Witness: Art in the Concentration Camps and Ghettos*, p. 132. New York: Free Press, 1982. ISBN: 0029066603. Courtesy Buchenwald Memorial Museum.

BURESOVA, CHARLOTTE (1940–). Born to a Jewish family in Prague, she began painting at 6 years of age. In the years before the Nazis overran Czechoslovakia, Charlotte painted portraits, still lifes, and flowers. Buresova graduated from the Prague Academy of Art in 1925. Before the artist was deported to Theresienstadt in 1942, she was married to a Gentile attorney. Buresova later divorced her husband in order to save her son from deportation. She escaped transport to Auschwitz because she impressed a Nazi officer who ordered her to paint a picture of the Madonna. She worked in the artists' studio with Leo Haas, Bedrich Fritta, and others. Instead of painting the horrors she witnessed at

Theresienstadt, the artist chose to look at the beauty and sincerity of people and her surroundings. Buresova remained in the camp until three days before liberation. She escaped and made her way back to Prague in the transport car of the Swedish ambassador.

"Child Prayer" (1944), Theresienstadt, watercolor. In Janet Blatter and Sybil Milton, *Art of the Holocaust*, p. 75. New York: Rutledge Press, 1981. ISBN: 0831704187. Courtesy Ghetto Fighters' House, Israel.

"Despair" (1944), Theresienstadt, monotype. In Blatter and Milton, p. 72. Courtesy Ghetto Fighters' House, Israel.

"Mother and Child" (1944), Theresienstadt, monotype. In Blatter and Milton, p. 72. Courtesy Ghetto Fighters' House, Israel.

"Portrait of Gideon Klein" (1944), Theresienstadt, charcoal and watercolor. In Blatter and Milton, p. 72. Courtesy Terezin Memorial Museum.

"Deportation" (1942), Theresienstadt, oil on canvas. In Mary S. Costanza, *The Living Witness: Art in the Concentration Camps and Ghettos*, p. 125. New York: Free Press, 1982. ISBN: 0029066603. Courtesy Ghetto Fighters' House, Israel.

"Ballet Costume Design" (date unavailable), Theresienstadt. In Miriam Novitch ed., *Spiritual Resistance: Art from the Concentration Camps, 1940–1945*, p. 59. Philadelphia: Jewish Publication Society, 1981. Courtesy Kibbutz Lohamei Haghetaot.

"The Cellist" (1943), Theresienstadt, pencil on paper. In Novitch, p. 57. Courtesy Kibbutz Lohamei Haghetaot.

"Deportation, the Last Road" (1944), Theresienstadt, pencil and ink on paper. In Novitch, p. 55. Courtesy Kibbutz Lohamei Haghetaot.

"Portrait of a Child" (1943), Theresienstadt, oil on canvas. In Novitch, p. 133. Courtesy Kibbutz Lohamei Haghetaot.

"Portrait of an Interned Child" (1944), Theresienstadt, aquarelle. In Novitch, p. 61. Courtesy Kibbutz Lohamei Haghetaot.

Toll, Nelly. *When Memory Speaks: The Holocaust in Art*, p. 13. Westport, CT: Praeger, 1998. ISBN: 0275955346.

CAGLI, CORRADO (1910–?). Born in Ancona, Italy, Cagli exhibited his paintings for the first time in 1932 after studying with several Italian masters. He was one of the co-founders of the Second Rome Art Group. In 1939 he was forced to flee by the Italian fascist government, going first to Paris and then on to the United States. He served with the U.S. Army and participated in the liberation of Buchenwald. His sketches of the Buchenwald survivors and the skeletal remains of the deceased are brutal in their honesty. He returned to Italy after the war.

"Child of the Camp" (1945), Buchenwald, pencil. In Janet Blatter and Sybil Milton, *Art of the Holocaust*, p. 228. New York: Rutledge Press, 1981. ISBN: 0831704187. Courtesy Erhard Frommhold, Dresden, Germany.

"Buchenwald" (1945), Buchenwald, pencil. In Blatter and Milton, pp. 228–229. Courtesy Erhard Frommhold, Dresden, Germany.

"The Exodus" (1944). In Miriam Novitch, ed., *Spiritual Resistance: Art from the Concentration Camps 1940–1945*, p. 63. Philadelphia: Jewish Publication Society, 1981. Courtesy Kibbutz Lohamei Haghetaot.

CARPI, ALDO (1886–1973). This artist was born in Milan, his real name Aldo Carpi de Resmini. A master of Italian art, he became a professor at age 26. An antifascist, Carpi produced "The Hurricane Comes," a series of paintings about the horrors of war. He was arrested in 1944 because of this series and deported to Mauthausen concentration camp and its satellite camp, Gusen. The artist would often exchange his sketches with the SS for cigarettes.

Carpi's work detail in the Gusen Pathological Unit made him one of the most important eyewitnesses to the medical experiments carried out at Gusen between 1941 and 1945. He kept a diary hidden under the floor of the infirmary. Some of the pages were hidden in clothing and placed in an urn in the pathology room. Carpi's sketches showed the brutality of the Nazi concentration camp system and the effects the system had on its innocent victims. After liberation he returned to Milan, where he died 1973.

"Corpses in Front of Railroad Station" (1945), Mauthausen, pencil. In Janet Blatter and Sybil Milton, *Art of the Holocaust*, p. 175. New York: Rutledge Press, 1981. ISBN: 0831704187. Courtesy Ghetto Fighters' House, Israel.

"Sick Jewish Prisoner, Dispensary 27" (1945), Mauthausen, pencil. In Blatter and Milton, p. 175. Courtesy Ghetto Fighters' House, Israel.

"Children's Corpses in Front of the Crematorium" (1945), Mauthausen, pencil on paper. In Miriam Novitch, ed., *Spiritual Resistance: Art from the Concentration Camps, 1940–1945*, p. 71. Philadelphia: Jewish Publication Society, 1981. Courtesy Kibbutz Lohamei Haghetaot.

"The Courtyard of the Railway Station, Block 31" (1945), Mauthausen, pencil on paper. In Novitch, p. 65. Courtesy Kibbutz Lohamei Haghetaot.

"The Famished" (date unavailable), Mauthausen, ink on paper. In Novitch, p. 67. Courtesy Kibbutz Lohamei Haghetaot.

"Jews in the Hospital" (1945), Mauthausen, ink on paper. In Novitch, p. 73. Courtesy Kibbutz Lohamei Haghetaot.

"A Little Jewish Boy, Block 31" (1945), Mauthausen, pencil on paper. In Novitch, p. 69. Courtesy Kibbutz Lohamei Haghetaot.

CHLADKOVA, LUDMILA (dates unknown). Chladkova was a child survivor from Theresienstadt.

Blodig, Vojtech. *Ghetto Museum Terezin*. Czechoslovakia: Terezin Memorial Museum, 1991.

Chladkova, Ludmila. *Children from Terezin*. Czechoslovakia: Terezin Memorial Museum, 1989.

————. *Jewish Cemetery in Terezin*. Terezin: Pamatnik Terezin, 1999.

————. *The Terezin Ghetto*. Prague: Publishing House of Nasevojsko [for] the Terezin Monument, 1991.

DALIGAULT, L'ABBE JEAN (1899–1945). Born in France, Daligault became a member of the French Resistance and was arrested in August 1941. After a brief imprisonment he was part of the "Night and Fog" deportation (secret disappearance) to Hinzert camp on September 3, 1942. Daligault's wooden sculptures are of heads and faces of his fellow inmates. He disappeared after being sent to Dachau concentration camp in March 1944.

"Sculptured Face" (1943), Hinzert, sculpted from leg of wooden chair. In Janet Blatter, and Sybil Milton, *Art of the Holocaust*, p. 164. New York: Rutledge Press, 1981. ISBN: 0831704187. Courtesy Musee de la Resistance Besanion, France.

"Magistrate" (1943), Hinzert, plaster. In Blatter and Milton, p. 164. Courtesy Musee de la Resistance Besanion, France.

Peintures et sculptures: Musee de la Resistance et de la Deportation de Besancon. Paris: Editions de la Martiniere, 1996.

ERNST, MAX (1891–1976). Born and raised near Cologne, Germany, Ernst studied philosophy and psychology and taught himself to paint. As a painter he was involved in expressionism, abstractionism, and Dadaism. He moved to Paris in 1922. After 1933 he was in contact with many German refugee artists who also lived in Paris. At the beginning of the war, he was held in the refugee camp of Les Milles, but in 1941 he managed to escape with the assistance of Varian Fry and immigrated to the United States. Ernst returned to France in 1961 and died in Paris in April 1976.

"Apartrides" ("The Stateless") (1939), Les Milles, pencil rubbing with white gouache. In Janet Blatter and Sybil Milton, *Art of the Holocaust*, p. 112. New York: Rutledge Press, 1981. ISBN: 0831704187. Courtesy Staatsgalerie, Stuttgart, Germany.

Max Ernst: Fragments of Capricorn and Other Sculpture, Sedona, Arizona 1948. New York: Arnold Herstand & Company, 1984.

Toll, Nelly. *When Memory Speaks: The Holocaust in Art*. Westport, CT: Praeger, 1998, pp. 29–30. ISBN: 0275955346.

FEDER, AIZIK (1887–1943). Born in Odessa, Russia, Feder was educated in Russian state schools and in traditional Jewish religious schools. In his late teens he joined the revolutionary movement against the Tsar. At age 19 he fled to Berlin to avoid being sent to Siberia and while there studied painting, later moving to Geneva, and finally to Paris. In Paris Feder studied for two years with Henri Matisse. He also worked with painter Otto Freundlich and sculptor Jacques Lipchitz. After the Nazi takeover of France, Feder attempted to reach the local Resistance unit but was arrested. The artist was sent to Drancy, where many of his drawings were completed. He sketched portraits of other inmates in Drancy. In 1943 he was deported to Auschwitz, where he died. Many of his sketches were found by Miriam Novitch and are now housed at Ghetto Fighters' House in Israel.

"Aged Internee" (1943), Drancy, charcoal and pastel. In Janet Blatter and Sybil Milton, *Art of the Holocaust*, p. 101. New York: Rutledge Press, 1981. ISBN: 0831704187. Courtesy Ghetto Fighters' House, Israel.

"Self Portrait" (1943), Drancy, charcoal and pastel. In Mary S. Costanza, *The Living Witness: Art in the Concentration Camps and Ghettos*, p. 69. New York: Free Press, 1982. ISBN: 0029066603. Courtesy Ghetto Fighters' House, Israel.

"Little Blond Boy" (1942), Drancy, color pencil on paper. In Miriam Novitch, ed., *Spiritual Resistance: Art from the Concentration Camps, 1940–1945*, p. 79. Philadelphia: Jewish Publication Society, 1981. Courtesy Kibbutz Lohamei Haghetaot.

"Man Seated, Wearing a Breton Beret" (1942), Drancy, pastel on gray paper. In Novitch, p. 77. Courtesy Kibbutz Lohamei Haghetaot.

"Portrait of a Man with Yellow Star, Reading" (1943), Drancy, color pencil drawing on paper. In Novitch, p. 79. Courtesy Kibbutz Lohamei Haghetaot.

"Young Woman with Book" (1942), Drancy, color pencil drawing. In Novitch, p. 134. Courtesy Kibbutz Lohamei Haghetaot.

FLEISCHMANN, KAREL (1897–1944). Born in Klatovy (Bohemia), Czechoslovakia, Fleischmann was an esteemed dermatologist and lover of the arts. By 1937 the physician had produced several series of lithographs.

He was first interned at Theresienstadt in April 1942 and worked there as a doctor. He later worked with Leo Haas, Yehuda Bacon, Charlotte

Buresova, Bedrich Fritta, and others at the "studio." Most of Fleischmann's drawings from Terezin were of the ghettoized victims and the horrific conditions they were forced to endure. He and his wife were later deported to Auschwitz and sent to the gas chambers upon arrival. The Resistance group in Theresienstadt saved most of his sketches. After liberation Dr. Fleischmann's brother gave the entire collection to the Prague State Jewish Museum.

Firster, Richard, and Nora Levin, eds. *The Living Witness: Art in the Concentration Camps.* Philadelphia: Museum of American Jewish History, 1978.

"Arriving Transport" (1943), Terezin Camp, ink wash. In Janet Blatter and Sybil Milton, *Art of the Holocaust*, p. 87. New York: Rutledge Press, 1981. ISBN: 0831704187. Courtesy Prague State Jewish Museum.

"Effects from Abandoned Apartments" (1943), location unknown, ink and watercolor. In Blatter and Milton, p. 87. Courtesy Prague State Jewish Museum.

"Infirmary for Children" (1942), Terezin Camp, charcoal. In Blatter and Milton, p. 86. Courtesy Prague State Jewish Museum.

"In the Corridor" (1942), Terezin Camp, pencil. In Blatter and Milton, p. 86. Courtesy Prague State Jewish Museum.

"Registration" (1943), Terezin Camp, ink wash. In Mary S. Costanza, *The Living Witness: Art in the Concentration Camps and Ghettos*, p. 112. New York: Free Press, 1982. ISBN: 0029066603. Courtesy Prague State Jewish Museum.

"Untitled" (1942), Terezin, charcoal. In Costanza, p. xvi. Courtesy Prague State Jewish Museum.

"Untitled" (1943), Terezin, pen and ink. In Costanza, p. 15. Courtesy Prague State Jewish Museum.

Karel Fleischmann: Life and Work: Exhibition and the Text of the Catalog Prepared by Marketa Petrasova and Jarmilas Skochova. Czechoslovakia: State Jewish Museum in Prague, 1987.

"Schleusen Hospital" (1942), Theresienstadt, pencil on paper. In Miriam Novitch ed., *Spiritual Resistance: Art from the Concentration Camps, 1940–1945*, p. 83. Philadelphia: Jewish Publication Society, 1981. Courtesy Kibbutz Lohamei Haghetaot.

"Furniture" (1943), Terezin Camp, ink wash on paper. In Lawrence L. Langer, *Art from the Ashes*, p. 683. New York: Oxford University Press, 1995. ISBN: 0195077326. Courtesy Terezin Memorial Museum.

"Registration for Transport" (1943), Terezin Camp, pencil on paper. In Langer, p. 684. Courtesy Terezin Memorial Museum.

"View of Terezin" (1943), Terezin Camp, pencil on paper. In Langer, p. 683. Courtesy Terezin Memorial Museum.

Toll, Nelly. *When Memory Speaks: The Holocaust in Art*, p. 41. Westport, CT: Praeger, 1998. ISBN: 0275955346.

FRITTA, BEDRICH (FRITZ TAUSSIG) (1909–1944). Born in Ivancice, Moravia, Czechoslovakia, Fritta was a commercial artist and painter before the war. He was deported with his family to Theresienstadt in December 1941. The artist was assigned to the technical office, whose task it was to transform Theresienstadt from a fortress to an internment camp. Fritta also worked with his friend Leo Haas in the "model studio." While there, the studio artists (Felix Bloch, Otto Ungar, Charlotte Buresova, and Dr. Karel Fleischmann) together produced a cycle of 150 drawings and sketches detailing Nazi atrocities. The faces of the subjects in Fritta's drawings are blank-eyed and emaciated, based on his daily reality. In July 1944 the paintings were found and Fritta and his family, Bloch, Ungar, and Haas were sent to the Small Fortress and tortured. Fritta's wife died there of starvation.

The artist was deported to Auschwitz on October 26, 1944, with Leo Haas, who carried the desperately ill Fritta on his back. Fritta died in Auschwitz on November 8, 1944. Leo Haas later adopted Fritta's son. Forty-two sketches of his were exhibited in the Manes Gallery in Prague in November 1945.

"Film and Reality" (undated), Theresienstadt, ink. In Janet Blatter and Sybil Milton, *Art of the Holocaust*, p. 84. New York: Rutledge Press, 1981. ISBN: 0831704187. Courtesy Prague State Jewish Museum.

"Fortune Teller" (undated), Theresienstadt, ink. In Blatter and Milton, p. 83. Courtesy Prague State Jewish Museum.

"The Infirmary in the Cinema" (undated), Theresienstadt, ink and wash. In Blatter and Milton, p. 85. Courtesy Prague State Jewish Museum.

"Jewish Prayer" (undated), location unknown, ink. In Blatter and Milton, p. 84. Courtesy Prague State Jewish Museum.

"Life of a Ghetto Prominent" (undated), Theresienstadt, ink. In Blatter and Milton, p. 85. Courtesy Prague State Jewish Museum.

"Lodging in the Attic" (undated), Theresienstadt, ink and wash. In Blatter and Milton, p. 85. Courtesy Prague State Jewish Museum.

"View of Theresienstadt" (undated), ink. In Blatter and Milton, p. 82. Courtesy Prague State Jewish Museum.

"The Old and the Ill" (1943), Theresienstadt, pen & ink. In Mary S. Costanza, *The Living Witness: Art in the Concentration Camps and Ghettos*,

p. 84. New York: Free Press, 1982. ISBN: 0029066603. Courtesy Thomas Fritta Haas.

"Terezin Camp" (1943), pen and ink. In Costanza, p. 114. Courtesy Thomas Fritta Haas.

"Untitled" (1943), Terezin, pen and ink. In Costanza, p. 54. Courtesy Thomas Fritta Haas.

"Accordionist" (undated), Theresienstadt, medium unknown. In Joza Karas, *Music in Terezin*, p. 12. New York: Beaufort Books, 1985. ISBN: 0825302870.

"Concert Hall in Magdeburg Barracks" (undated), Theresienstadt, medium unknown. In Karas, p. 198.

"Terezin Café" (undated), Theresienstadt, medium unknown. In Karas, p. 148.

"At Kavalier" (1943–1944), Theresienstadt, medium unknown. In Lawrence L. Langer, *Art from the Ashes*, p. 693. New York: Oxford University Press, 1995. ISBN: 0195077326. Courtesy Prague State Jewish Museum.

"Hospital in Cinema" (1943–1944), Theresienstadt, medium unknown. In Langer, p. 692. Courtesy Prague State Jewish Museum.

"Kaffeehaus" (1943–1944), Theresienstadt, medium unknown. In Langer, p. 690. Courtesy Prague State Jewish Museum.

"Leaving Transport" (1943–1944), Theresienstadt, medium unknown. In Langer, p. 693. Courtesy Prague State Jewish Museum.

"Life in Terezin" (1943–1944), Theresienstadt, medium unknown. In Langer, p. 691. Courtesy Prague State Jewish Museum.

"Life of a Prominent" (1943–1944), Theresienstadt, medium unknown. In Langer, p. 691. Courtesy Prague State Jewish Museum.

"Shops in Terezin" (1941–1944), Theresienstadt, medium unknown. In Langer, p. 690. Courtesy Prague State Jewish Museum.

"Spectacle at Theresienstadt" (Theresienstadt), 1942–1945, wash on paper. In Miriam Novitch, ed., *Spiritual Resistance: Art from the Concentration Camps 1940–1945*, p. 85. Philadelphia: Jewish Publication Society, 1981. Courtesy Kibbutz Lohamei Haghetaot.

FURTH, VALERIE JAKOBER (1926–?). Furth was born in Munkacs, Czechoslovakia, into an Orthodox Jewish family. When Munkacs was incorporated into Hungary after the Nazi occupation of Czechoslovakia, all anti-Jewish laws and decrees came into effect. The artist relates the story of her family through her paintings—from ghettoization to the horrors of Auschwitz. Furth was assigned to a construction detail in a sub-camp and became a foreman. In April 1945, after the SS had deserted the subcamp, armed guards escorted the inmates to Bergen-Belsen. Although the treatment she and her fellow Auschwitz inmates had endured was harsh, they were shocked and horrified at the condition of the Bergen-Belsen inmates and of the camp itself. Shortly after their transfer, the British liberated them. At war's end the family was reunited and waited in Prague until immigration papers to the United States were granted.

Cabbages & Geraniums: Memories of the Holocaust. Boulder, CO: Social Science Monographs; New York: Distributed by Columbia University Press, 1989. ISBN: 0880339624.

GLICKSMAN-FAITLOWITZ, SARA (1910–?). Born in Lodz, Poland, Glicksman-Faitlowitz attended art school there. Before to the war she was an established painter and had won many awards. During the German occupation, she completed numerous paintings of the Lodz Ghetto, where she was incarcerated. Assigned to work in the Statistics Department, she was instructed to paint dishes showing false food rations to impress the Red Cross inspection team. The artist painted thirteen works in secret. The bridge in Lodz was painted from three different angles: One may be found in Yad Vashem in Israel, another at the Museum of Martyrology in Warsaw, and one at the Lodz Museum. Some of her drawings may be found in the Jewish Historical Institute in Warsaw. After the war she settled in Israel.

"Deportation to Lodz" (1940), Lodz Ghetto, oil on cardboard. In Janet Blatter and Sybil Milton, *Art of the Holocaust*, p. 68. New York: Rutledge Press, 1981. ISBN: 0831704187. Courtesy Yad Vashem.

"The Bridge" (1943), Lodz Ghetto, oil. In Mary S. Costanza, *The Living Witness: Art in the Concentration Camps and Ghettos*, p. 88. New York: Free Press, 1982. ISBN: 0029066603.

"Expulsion" (1943) Lodz Ghetto, pencil drawing. In Costanza, p. 96. Courtesy Yad Vashem.

GOERGEN, EDMOND (dates unknown). An artist from Luxembourg, Georgen became involved in the Resistance movement. After his arrest he was condemned to death, but instead of facing execution he spent three years at Hinzert and Mauthausen. He drew graphic sketches of dead and dying emaciated prisoners at Mauthausen. After the Americans liberated the camp, he returned to Luxembourg.

"Morning Sacrifice" (1944), Mauthausen, pencil. In Janet Blatter and Sybil Milton, *Art of the Holocaust*, pp. 176–177. New York: Rutledge Press, 1981. ISBN: 0831704187. Courtesy Musee de Deux Guerres Mondiales, Paris.

"Study of a Corpse" (1944), Mauthausen, charcoal. In Blatter, p. 176. Courtesy Musee de Deux Guerres Mondiales, Paris.

"Youth in Agony" (1944), Mauthausen, blue pencil. In Blatter, p. 176. Courtesy Musee de Deux Guerres Mondiales, Paris.

Dessins de Mauthausen. Paris: Editions Circle d'Art, 1975.

GOTTLIEBOVA-BABBITT, DINAH (1923–?). Born in Brno, Czechoslovakia, Gottliebova-Babbitt studied art as a youth. After the Nazi occupation of Czechoslovakia, the Jewish artist was deported first to Theresienstadt. She was assigned to work in the art workshop, where postcards of famous paintings were once again transformed into oils.

In 1943 Gottliebova-Babbitt was transported to Auschwitz with her mother and stepbrother. She worked in the camp hospital where Dr. Josef Mengele ordered her to make colored portraits of Gypsy prisoners. These portraits were painted in watercolors provided by Mengele. After the paintings were completed, the Gypsies were gassed and cremated. When the Russians liberated Auschwitz, a prisoner gave some of her portraits to a young Polish boy, whose family donated them to the Auschwitz Memorial Museum. She eventually settled in the United States.

Blatter, Janet, and Sybil Milton. *Art of the Holocaust.* New York: Rutledge Press, 1981. ISBN: 0831704187.

"French Gypsy" (1944), Auschwitz, watercolor. In Mary S. Costanza, *The Living Witness: Art in the Concentration Camps and Ghettos,* p. 48. New York: Free Press, 1982. ISBN: 0029066603. Courtesy Auschwitz Memorial Museum.

"German Gypsy" (1944), Auschwitz, watercolor. In Costanza, p. 44. Courtesy Auschwitz Memorial Museum.

"Polish Gypsy" (1944), Auschwitz, watercolor. In Constanza, p. 45. Courtesy Auschwitz Memorial Museum.

"Portrait of a Dutch Gypsy" (1944), Auschwitz, watercolor. In Costanza, p. 45. Courtesy Auschwitz Memorial Museum.

"Portrait of a Gypsy" (1944), Auschwitz, watercolor. In Constanza, p. 45. Courtesy Auschwitz Memorial Museum.

GOWA, HERMANN-HENRY (1902–?). Born in Hamburg, Germany, Gowa studied art and philosophy at the University of Munich from 1922 to 1924. His anti-Nazi views pushed him to move to France in May 1933. He moved to Nice in 1934, working with various theater groups. In 1941 a large exhibit of his paintings was held at the Galerie Muratore in Nice. In 1942, after the Nazi occupation of France and fearing arrest, Gowa fled to the mountains in southern France. After the war he continued to paint and settled in Berlin. He preferred to use watercolors in his paintings.

"The Retreat" (1941), Nice, mixed media on wood. In Janet Blatter and Sybil Milton, *Art of the Holocaust*, p. 134. New York: Rutledge Press, 1981. ISBN: 0831704187. Courtesy Hermann-Henri Gowa, Berlin.

Dokumentation. Frankfurt am Main: Deutscher Werkbund Hessen, 1987.

HAAS, LEO (1901–1983). Born into a Jewish family in Opava, Czechoslovakia, Haas moved to Berlin in 1922 and stayed until 1924. In 1925 Haas worked as an illustrator in Vienna. He returned to Czechoslovakia in 1926 and worked in his hometown from 1926 to 1938 as a painter, graphic artist, and book illustrator. After the Nazi takeover of Czechoslovakia, Haas was arrested in October 1939 for helping German communists to cross the border illegally.

The artist was first sent to Nisko, near Lublin, and then in 1942 on to Theresienstadt. He was leader of the artists' studio in the technical office along with Bedrich Fritta, Felix Bloch, Otto Ungar, Charlotte Buresova, and Dr. Karel Fleischmann. The group painted a large cycle of paintings depicting daily existence in the camp and hid their works in various places. Some were buried in the ground, and others were hidden behind a brick wall.

Haas and Fritta were sent to Auschwitz, where Haas worked for Dr. Josef Mengele painting twins. From Auschwitz, Haas was sent to Sachsenhausen, and in February 1945 he was evacuated to Mauthausen. On April 13, 1945, he arrived in Ebensee, where the Americans finally liberated him on May 9, 1945.

After the war Haas returned to Czechoslovakia with his newly adopted son, Tommy Fritta (Bedrich Fritta's son). In 1955 they moved to East Berlin, where he drew sketches and worked on several foreign periodicals. Haas was a professor at the Art Academy in Berlin until he died in 1983. Haas's work has been exhibited all over the world.

Firster, Richard, and Nora Levin, eds. *The Living Witness: Art in the Concentration Camps*. Philadelphia: Museum of American Jewish History, 1978.

"Hunger" (1943), Theresienstadt, ink on paper. In Janet Blatter and Sybil Milton, *Art of the Holocaust*, pp. 90–91. New York: Rutledge Press, 1981. ISBN: 0831704187. Courtesy Yidisher Visnshaftlekher Institut (Yiddish Scientific Institute), New York.

"Latrine" (1939), Nisko, pencil. In Blatter and Milton, p. 61. Courtesy Terezin Memorial Museum.

"Laundry Room" (1939), Nisko, pencil. In Blatter and Milton, pp. 60–61. Courtesy Terezin Memorial Museum.

"Living Quarters" (1939), Theresienstadt, pencil. In Blatter and Milton, p. 61. Courtesy Terezin Memorial Museum.

"Mortuary in Theresienstadt" (1943), Theresienstadt, india ink. In Blatter and Milton, p. 88. Courtesy Terezin Memorial Museum.

"Old Women" (1943), Theresienstadt, ink and ink wash. In Blatter and Milton, p. 88. Courtesy Terezin Memorial Museum.

"Portrait of Tommy Fritta" (1943), Theresienstadt, ink. In Blatter and Milton, p. 88. Courtesy Terezin Memorial Museum.

"Prayer" (1939), Nisko, pencil. In Blatter and Milton, p. 59. Courtesy Terezin Memorial Museum.

"Prisoner" (1945), Sachsenhausen, pencil. In Blatter and Milton, p. 210. Courtesy Sachsenhausen Memorial Museum.

"Prisoners with Guards" (1957), Berlin, pen. In Blatter and Milton, pp. 232–233. Courtesy Yidisher Visnshaftlekher Institut (Yiddish Scientific Institute), New York.

"Religious Services" (1943), Theresienstadt, pencil. In Blatter and Milton, p. 89. Courtesy Terezin Memorial Museum.

"Countdown in Terezin" (1943), Theresienstadt, litho pencil. In Mary S. Costanza, *The Living Witness: Art in the Concentration Camps and Ghettos*, p. 106. New York: Free Press, 1982. ISBN: 0029066603. Courtesy Leo Haas.

"Hanging" (undated), Terezin Camp, charcoal. In Costanza, p. 54. Courtesy Terezin Memorial Museum.

"March" (1943), Terezin Camp, drawing. In Costanza, p. x. Courtesy Leo Haas and Terezin Memorial Museum.

"Schrader" (1939), Nisko, pencil drawing. In Costanza, p. 41. Courtesy Leo Haas.

"Slave Labor" (1943), Terezin Camp, grease pencil drawing. In Costanza, p. 63. Courtesy Leo Haas.

"Untitled" (undated), Terezin Camp, litho pencil. In Costanza, p. 7. Courtesy Terezin Memorial Museum.

"Zeichenstube in Terezin" (undated), Terezin, pen and ink. In Costanza, p. 31. Courtesy Terezin Memorial Museum.

"Café in Terezin" (1943–1945), Terezin Camp, ink on paper. In Lawrence Langer, *Art from the Ashes*, p. 678. New York: Oxford University Press, 1995. ISBN: 0963531824. Courtesy Terezin Memorial Museum.

"Drafting/Technical Studio" (1943), Terezin Camp, ink on paper. In Langer, p. 679. Courtesy Terezin Memorial Museum.

"Expecting the Worst" (1943–1945), Terezin Camp, ink on paper. In Langer, p. 680. Courtesy Terezin Memorial Museum.

"The Old and the Ill" (1943–1945), Terezin Camp, ink on paper. In Langer, p. 678. Courtesy Terezin Memorial Museum.

"Scenes of Life in the Ghetto" (1943–1945), Terezin Camp, ink on paper. In Langer, p. 679. Courtesy Terezin Memorial Museum.

Leo Haas: Terezin, 1942–1944. Prague: Oswald, 1983. 28-page book with illustrations about artists in Terezin.

K2-Transit Theresienstadt: Bilder und Dokumente aus Ghettos und Lagen. Rendsburg: Judisches Museum Rendsburg, 1991.

"General Distribution of Food, Post BV" (1944), Theresienstadt, ink on paper. In Miriam Novitch, ed., *Spiritual Resistance: Art from the Concentration Camps, 1940–1945*, p. 91. Philadelphia: Jewish Publication Society, 1981. Courtesy Kibbutz Lohamei Haghetaot.

"To March 4, 1944, With Best Wishes. The Protective Hand" (1944), Theresienstadt, ink and watercolor on paper. In Novitch, p. 91.

Toll, Nelly. *When Memory Speaks: The Holocaust in Art*, p. 41. Westport, CT: Praeger, 1998. ISBN: 0275955346.

HIRSCHBERGER, FRITZ (1912–?). Hirschberger was born in Dresden during World War I to a Galician father and a Czech mother. In 1938 after the completion of his art studies he was arrested by the Gestapo as an undesirable Jewish alien. Hirschberger was forced to cross the border into Poland. After the Nazi invasion of Poland in September 1939, Hirschberger joined the Polish Army. When Poland was defeated and divided he found himself in the Soviet Occupied Zone and was arrested by the Soviet secret police. In 1941 when the Soviets joined the Allies, all Polish prisoners were released and formed the Second Free Polish Corps. He was shipped out to North Africa and participated in the invasion of Italy. Hirschberger eventually immigrated to the United States and settled in San Francisco.

HISZPANSKA-NEUMAN, MARIA (1917–?) Born in Warsaw, Hiszpanska-Neuman studied at the Academy of Fine Arts there. After the German invasion of Poland, she joined the Resistance. Maria was arrested on April 19, 1941, and interned in Radom prison. On April 10, 1942, she was transported to Ravensbruck in Germany and assigned to the harshest labor details. Hiszpanska-Neuman escaped during a forced march in April 1945. Of the 400 drawings she produced in Ravensbruck detailing her exhausted and emaciated fellow prisoners, most were lost after liberation. The artist returned to and lived in Warsaw after the war.

"In the Barracks after Work" (1945), Ravensbruck, india ink. In Janet Blatter and Sybil Milton, *Art of the Holocaust*, p. 158. New York: Rutledge Press, 1981. ISBN: 0831704187. Courtesy Janina Jaworska, Warsaw.

"Stone Carriers" (1944), Ravensbruck, crayon. In Blatter and Milton, p. 159. Courtesy National Museum, Warsaw.

"Ravensbruck Camp" (1944), Ravensbruck, pen and ink. In Mary S. Costanza, *The Living Witness: Art in the Concentration Camps and Ghettos*, p. 80. New York: Free Press, 1982. ISBN: 0029066603. Courtesy Janina Jaworska, Warsaw.

HOFSTATTER, OSIAS (1905–?). Born in Poland, Hofstatter studied in Zurich and Vienna. After the Nazi occupation of Poland, he was arrested, sent to St. Cyprien, and then moved to Gurs (Vichy French internment camps). The conditions were horrible there. The internees lived in shelters with mud and clay floors and were afraid to sleep at night for fear of being eaten by rats. In 1941 he escaped to Switzerland. After the war he immigrated to Israel and became a well-known artist. His works, descriptive of life in St. Cyprien and Gurs, may be found at the Ghetto Fighters' House in Israel.

Firster, Richard, and Nora Levin, eds. *The Living Witness: Art in the Concentration Camps.* Philadelphia: Museum of American Jewish History, 1978.

"Internee" (1940), Gurs, monochrome watercolor. In Janet, Blatter, and Sybil Milton, *Art of the Holocaust*, p. 110. New York: Rutledge Press, 1981. ISBN: 0831704187. Courtesy Ghetto Fighters' House, Israel.

"Gurs Barracks" (1941), Gurs, pen and ink. In Mary S. Costanza, *The Living Witness: Art in the Concentration Camps and Ghettos*, p. 57. New York: Free Press, 1982. ISBN: 0029066603. Courtesy Osias Hofstatter.

"Untitled" (1941), St. Cyprien, pencil on graph paper. In Costanza, p. 119. Courtesy Osias Hofstatter.

"The Camp of Gurs" (1941), Gurs, blue ink and blush on copy book paper. In Miriam Novitch, ed., *Spiritual Resistance: Art from the Concentration Camps, 1940–1945*, p. 93. Philadelphia: Jewish Publication Society, 1981. Courtesy Kibbutz Lohamei Haghetaot.

"Construction of a Railway" (1940), Gurs, soft pencil. In Novitch, p. 95.

HORSKI, STEFAN (1912–?). Little is known of Horski's early life. He was arrested in 1940 and sent to Sachsenhausen. After liberation Horski published a book of paintings showing what life was like in the concentration camps.

"Carrying away the Dead" (1944), Sachsenhausen, watercolor. In Janet Blatter and Sybil Milton, *Art of the Holocaust*, p. 211. New York: Rutledge Press, 1981. ISBN: 0831704187. Courtesy A. Kulisiewicz, Cracow.

Horski, Stefan. *Oranienburg*. Poznan Zarzadem.

JAZWIECKI, FRANCISZEK (1900–1946). Born in Kracow, Poland, Jazwiecki studied at the city's art academy. He was arrested in Cracow in 1940 and thrown into nearby Montelupe prison. The artist was sent to Auschwitz on September 19, 1942, and later to Gross Rosen, Sachsenhausen, Buchenwald, and Halberstadt. He died in October 1946. His paintings, mainly portraits of inmates, are displayed at various concentration camp museums.

"Portrait of Franciszek" (1943), Auschwitz, pencil. In Janet Blatter and Sybil Milton, *Art of the Holocaust*, p. 199. New York: Rutledge Press, 1981. ISBN: 0831704187. Courtesy Auschwitz Memorial Museum.

"Portrait of Janek" age 15 (1944), Sachsenhausen, pencil. In Blatter and Milton, p. 212. Courtesy Auschwitz Memorial Museum.

"Portrait of Italian Prisoner, Dorvilo Pizzignaceo" (1944), Auschwitz, pencil. In Mary S. Costanza, *The Living Witness: Art in the Concentration Camps and Ghettos*, p. 83. New York: Free Press, 1982. ISBN: 0029066603. Courtesy Buchenwald Memorial Museum.

"Self-Portrait" (1944), Auschwitz, pencil and crayon. In Costanza, p. 83. Courtesy Buchenwald Memorial Museum.

KANTOR, ALFRED (1923–?). An 18-year-old art student from Prague, Kantor was sent to Theresienstadt in 1941. Some of Kantor's sketches from Terezin survive because of a friend's bravery. This friend hid them and returned them after liberation. In 1943 Kantor was transported to Auschwitz, where he managed to sketch and draw the horrors he witnessed there to make sure the world knew of the torture the Nazis inflicted on their victims.

Firster, Richard, and Nora Levin, eds. *The Living Witness: Art in the Concentration Camps*. Philadelphia: Museum of American Jewish History, 1978.

The Book of Alfred Kantor: An Artist's Journal of the Holocaust. New York: Schocken Books, 1987. ISBN: 0070332754.

"Distribution of the Soup" (1944), Schwarzheide Camp, pen and ink. In Mary S. Costanza, *The Living Witness: Art in the Concentration Camps and*

Ghettos, p. xxvii. New York: Free Press, 1982. ISBN: 0029066603. Courtesy Alfred Kantor.

"Untitled" (1945), Theresienstadt, watercolor. In Costanza, p. 62. Courtesy Alfred Kantor.

"Two Views of Terezin" (1941), Terezin, colored pencils. In Costanza, p. 109. Courtesy Mary Costanza.

Toll, Nelly. *When Memory Speaks: The Holocaust in Art*. Westport, CT: Praeger, 1998. ISBN: 0275955346.

KARAS-KAUFMAN, OTTO (1915–1944). Born into a Jewish family in Prague, Karas-Kaufman worked as an illustrator before the war. He was deported to Theresienstadt and then on to Auschwitz, where he died in September 1944. His work, depicting scenes of Theresienstadt, largely in watercolor and india ink, are displayed at the Ghetto Fighters' Museum in Israel.

"Faraway Landscape" (undated), Theresienstadt, watercolor. In Janet Blatter and Sybil Milton, *Art of the Holocaust*, p. 75. New York: Rutledge Press, 1981. ISBN: 0831704187. Courtesy Ghetto Fighters' House, Israel.

"Landscape, Railroad Station" (1943), Theresienstadt, watercolor and ink on paper. In Miriam Novitch, ed., *Spiritual Resistance: Art from the Concentration Camps, 1940–1945*, p. 101. Philadelphia: Jewish Publication Society, 1981. Courtesy Kibbutz Lohamei Haghetaot.

"Old Fortress of Theresienstadt" (1942–1945), Theresienstadt, india ink and pen on cardboard. In Novitch, p. 97. Courtesy Kibbutz Lohamei Haghetaot.

"The Railroad Station" (1943), Theresienstadt, india ink and aquarelle on paper. In Novitch, p. 103. Courtesy Kibbutz Lohamei Haghetaot.

"Theresienstadt" (1942), Theresienstadt. In Novitch, p. 99. Courtesy Kibbutz Lohamei Haghetaot.

"Theresienstadt in the Spring" (1943), Theresienstadt, watercolor. In Novitch, p. 140. Courtesy Kibbutz Lohamei Haghetaot.

KIEN, PETR (1919–1944). Born in Warnsdorf, Czechoslovakia, Kien was an artist and musician on the same transport to Theresienstadt as Bedrich Fritta. Prior to Kien's deportation to Auschwitz, he gave his dear friend Helga King a suitcase containing all his Theresienstadt paintings. Helga's mother hid the suitcase. It was later discovered that he wrote short stories and two opera librettos set to music by Victor Ullman. At age 25 he was sent to the gas chambers at Auschwitz. His artwork, mainly portraits of fellow internees, is housed in the Terezin Memorial Museum and Yad Vashem in Israel.

"Women Peeling Potatoes" (1943), Theresienstadt, watercolor. In Mary S. Costanza, *The Living Witness: Art in the Concentration Camps and Ghettos*, p. 73. New York: Free Press, 1982. ISBN: 0029066603. Courtesy Yad Vashem Memorial Museum.

"Bernard Kaff" (undated), Theresienstadt, ink on paper. In Joza Karas, *Music in Terezin*, p. 44. New York: Beaufort Books, 1985. ISBN: 0825302870.

"Carlo S. Taube" (undated), Theresienstadt, ink on paper. In Karas, p. 122.

"Egon Ledec" (undated), Theresienstadt, ink on paper. In Karas, p. xi.

"Fritz Weiss" (undated), Theresienstadt, ink on paper. In Karas, p. 150.

"Gideon Klein" (undated), Theresienstadt, ink on paper. In Karas, p. 72.

"Hans Krasa" (undated), Theresienstadt, ink on paper. In Karas, p. 94.

"Karel Ancerl" (undated), Theresienstadt, ink on paper. In Karas, p. 64.

"Karel Frohlich" (undated), Theresienstadt, ink on paper. In Karas, p. 52.

"Pavel Haas" (undated), Theresienstadt, ink on paper. In Karas, p. 78.

"Rafael Schachter" (undated), Theresienstadt, ink on paper. In Karas, p. 12.

"Viktor Ullmann" (undated), Theresienstadt, ink on paper. In Karas, p. 112.

"Caricature of Dr. Stamm (with Cellist)" (1941–1944?), Theresienstadt, ink on paper. In Lawrence L. Langer, *Art from the Ashes*, p. 687. New York: Oxford University Press, 1995. ISBN: 0195077326. Courtesy Terezin Memorial Museum.

"Caricature of Miss Fischer (with Child)" (1941–1944?), Theresienstadt, ink on paper. In Langer, p. 688. Courtesy Terezin Memorial Museum.

"Portrait of Mr. Stein" (1941–1944?), Theresienstadt, ink on paper. In Langer, p. 686. Courtesy Terezin Memorial Museum.

Kien, Petr, Oliva Pechova, and Pamatnik Terezin. *Petr Kien, 1919–1944*. Czech Republic: Pamatnik Terezin, 1971.

Toll, Nelly. *When Memory Speaks: The Holocaust in Art*, p. 41. Westport, CT: Praeger, 1998. ISBN: 0275955346.

KISCHKA, ISIS (1908–1973). Born in Paris of Russian Jewish immigrant parents, Kischka was an untrained artist who visited libraries and studios to learn artistic techniques. He was arrested by the Gestapo in 1941. Sent to Compiegne, he was later transferred to Drancy, where he stayed until France was liberated in 1944. Many of his sketches are of Compiegne and depict the conditions under which the internees lived.

His works have been exhibited in France, Switzerland, Mexico, and the United States. He died in Paris in 1973.

"The Latrines in Compiegne" (undated), Compiegne, ink on paper. In Miriam Novitch, ed., *Spiritual Resistance: Art from the Concentration Camps 1940–1945*, p. 109. Philadelphia: Jewish Publication Society, 1981. Courtesy Kibbutz Lohamei Haghetaot.

"View of the Compiegne Camp" (undated), Compiegne, ink on paper. In Novitch, p. 109. Courtesy Kibbutz Lohamei Haghetaot.

KOSCIELNIAK, MIECZYSLAW (1912–?). Born in Kalisz, Poland, Koscielniak attended Cracow Academy of Fine Arts. He was drafted into the Polish army in 1939 and wounded. He joined a Resistance unit but was arrested in 1941 and deported to Auschwitz. A guard, after seeing his artwork, had him reassigned to an SS-owned business.

Leaders of the Auschwitz Resistance movement asked Koscielniak to record the atrocities he witnessed at Auschwitz. He sketched the horrors of the camp and depicted the daily life of prisoners. He worked with Francizik Targosz and Bronislaw Czech in Auschwitz using their artwork as messages to the outside world. In January 1945 the artist was deported to Mauthausen. He was liberated by the Americans and eventually settled in Warsaw. Many of his paintings can be found in the Auschwitz Memorial Museum.

"Diary Illustration" (1944), Auschwitz, ink. In Janet Blatter and Sybil Milton, *Art of the Holocaust*, p. 204. New York: Rutledge Press, 1981. ISBN: 0831704187. Courtesy Auschwitz Memorial Museum.

"Diary Illustration" (1944), Auschwitz, ink. In Blatter and Milton, pp. 204–205. Courtesy Auschwitz Memorial Museum.

"Inmate Orchestra" (1943), Auschwitz, ink. In Blatter and Milton, p. 203. Courtesy Janina Jaworska, Warsaw.

"Interior of the Auschwitz Museum" (1942), Auschwitz, oil. In Blatter and Milton, p. 207. Courtesy Auschwitz Memorial Museum.

"Operation [For His Brother on His Name Day]" (1944), Auschwitz, engraving with blue ink. In Blatter and Milton, p. 204. Courtesy Auschwitz Memorial Museum.

"A Prisoner" (1942), Auschwitz, pencil. In Blatter and Milton, p. 206. Courtesy Auschwitz Memorial Museum.

"Prisoners" (1942), Auschwitz, ink. In Blatter and Milton, p. 206. Courtesy Janina Jaworska, Warsaw.

"Return from Work" (1942), Auschwitz, crayon. In Blatter and Milton, p. 206. Courtesy Auschwitz Memorial Museum.

"Ebensee Camp" (1945), Ebensee. In Mary S. Costanza, *The Living Witness: Art in the Concentration Camps and Ghettos*, p. 123. New York: Free Press, 1982. ISBN: 0029066603. Courtesy Auschwitz Memorial Museum.

"Starvation" (1943), Auschwitz, pen and ink. In Costanza, p. 80. Courtesy Auschwitz Memorial Museum.

KRAMSZTYK, ROMAN (1885–1942). Born in Poland, Kramsztyk was a member of the National Institute for Promotion of Plastic Arts in Poland. Just before the outbreak of World War I, the artist exhibited his works widely in London, Venice, and Paris. Kramsztyk was sent to the Warsaw Ghetto, and although he converted to Christianity, he shared the fate of other Jews in the Warsaw Ghetto and was killed in 1942. Some of his sketches salvaged from the Warsaw Ghetto are held in the Warsaw Historical Institute in Poland.

"Jewish Family" (1943), Warsaw Ghetto, charcoal. In Mary S. Costanza, *The Living Witness: Art in the Concentration Camps and Ghettos*, p. 100. New York: Free Press, 1982. ISBN: 0029066603. Courtesy Jewish Historical Institute, Poland.

LANDAU, LEON (?–1945). Little is known of Landau's early life. He worked as an artist and designer for the Royal Theater in Antwerp, Belgium. In 1943 the Jewish artist was arrested, sent to Malines transit camp, and assigned to make signs designating barracks and depots. From Malines he was transported to Auschwitz. Fellow artist **Irene Awrit** saved his drawings. He was later transported to Bergen-Belsen, where he was liberated on April 15, 1945, but he died of typhus shortly after.

"Portrait of a Young Man" (1943), Malines, pencil. In Janet Blatter and Sybil Milton, *Art of the Holocaust*, p. 115. New York: Rutledge Press, 1981. ISBN: 0831704187. Courtesy Ghetto Fighters' House, Israel.

"Distribution of Parcels in the Courtyard" (1943), Malines, oil and gouache on cardboard. In Miriam Novitch, ed., *Spiritual Resistance: Art from the Concentration Camps, 1940–1945*, p. 113. Philadelphia: Jewish Publication Society, 1981. Courtesy Kibbutz Lohamei Haghetaot.

LEVIN, JULO (1901–1943). Levin was born and raised in Stettin, Germany. While attending art school, he was urged by his middle-class Jewish family to quit and instead pursue a career in business. Levin eventually left Stettin, settling in Dusseldorf, where from 1926 to 1932 he was affiliated with the artists' group Young Rhineland and the Rhineland Secession.

In 1933 the artist was arrested and sentenced to forced labor, cleaning streets and cemeteries, for helping emigrants to escape the Nazis. Between the years 1936 and 1938 Levin taught art classes at the Jewish elementary school in Dusseldorf. In 1939 Levin's sister fled to England and his elderly mother moved in with relatives in Berlin. Mrs. Levin was deported in September 1942. Julo Levin was arrested on May 7, 1943, and transported to Auschwitz ten days later. His works were posthumously exhibited in Germany and Israel since 1946.

"My Mother" (1939–1940), Berlin, oil on canvas. In Janet Blatter and Sybil Milton, *Art of the Holocaust*, p. 134. New York: Rutledge Press, 1981. ISBN: 0831704187. Courtesy Mieke Monjau, Dusseldorf.

"Prometheus" (1942–1943), Berlin woodcut. In Blatter and Milton, p. 133. Courtesy Mieke Monjau, Dusseldorf.

"Job" (1933–1934), Dusseldorf, oil on canvas. In Sybil Milton, ed. and trans., *The Art of Jewish Children: Germany, 1936–1941*, p. 15. New York: Allied Books Limited, 1989. ISBN: 0802225586. Courtesy Mieke Monjau, Dusseldorf.

LURIE, ESTHER (1913–?). Born in Liepaj, Lithuania, Lurie studied theater design at the Superior Institute of Decorative Arts in Brussels and at the Academy of Fine Arts in Antwerp from 1931 to 1934. In 1934 Lurie and her family left Europe for Palestine. In 1938 the artist had her first exhibition in Tel Aviv and later returned to Belgium to resume her studies. She visited her sister in Lithuania in 1939 and was caught up in the formation of the Kovno Ghetto. While in Kovno the artist completed over two hundred sketches, most of which were lost. Lurie was urged by the Kovno Jewish Council to document the atrocities occurring in the ghetto. She worked with art student Benzion Josef Schmidt. Their secret works were buried beneath the ground in the cellar of her sister's house and may still be there. In 1944 she was deported to Stutthof and began doing portraits of Nazi guards and their families for extra rations and better supplies. After liberation, upon learning that she spoke seven languages, the Allies asked Esther to be an interpreter. She settled in Israel.

Firster, Richard, and Nora Levin, eds. *The Living Witness: Art in the Concentration Camps*. Philadelphia: Museum of American Jewish History, 1978.

"After the Deportation" (1942), Kovno, watercolor. In Janet Blatter and Sybil Milton, *Art of the Holocaust*, p. 58. New York: Rutledge Press, 1981. ISBN: 0831704187. Courtesy Ghetto Fighters' House, Israel.

"Internee" (1944), Stutthof, pencil. In Blatter and Milton, p. 167. Courtesy Ghetto Fighters' House, Israel.

"In the Ghetto" (1942), Kovno, pen. In Blatter and Milton, p. 58. Courtesy Ghetto Fighters' House, Israel.

"Entrance to the Ghetto, Kovno" (1941–1942), Kovno, pen and ink. In Mary S. Costanza, *The Living Witness: Art in the Concentration Camps and Ghettos*, p. 91. New York: Free Press, 1982. ISBN: 0029066603, Courtesy Esther Lurie, Israel.

"Esther Lurie-Leibitz Camp" (1944), back of cotton paper wrapping. In Costanza, p. 116. Courtesy Esther Lurie, Israel.

"Leibitz Camp" (1944), Leibitz, ink with wood chips. In Costanza, p. 127. Courtesy Esther Lurie, Israel.

"Potato Field" (1941), Kovno, pen and ink. In Costanza, p. 96. Courtesy Esther Lurie, Israel.

"Arrival of a Transport of Deportees in Kovno Ghetto" (1942), Kovno, ink on cardboard. In Miriam Novitch, ed., *Spiritual Resistance: Art from the Concentration Camps, 1940–1945*, p. 121. Philadelphia: Jewish Publication Society, 1981. Courtesy Kibbutz Lohamei Haghetaot.

"Evening Descends" (1941–1956), Kovno, watercolor on paper. In Novitch, p. 142. Courtesy Kibbutz Lohamei Haghetaot.

"Forced Labor" (1942), Kovno, pencil on paper. In Novitch, p. 119. Courtesy Kibbutz Lohamei Haghetaot.

"In the Ghetto of Kovno" (1941), Kovno, pencil on paper. In Novitch, p. 119. Courtesy Kibbutz Lohamei Haghetaot.

"Kovno Ghetto" (1942–1956), Kovno, aquarelle. In Novitch, p. 143. Courtesy Kibbutz Lohamei Haghetaot.

"Wooden Bridge" (1941), Kovno, pencil on paper. In Novitch, p. 119. Courtesy Kibbutz Lohamei Haghetaot.

MANIA, PIERRE (dates unknown). Little is known about Mania's early life. The French artist was sent to the transit camp Compiegne and then deported to Buchenwald in 1943. After liberation he returned to France. His paintings depict the suffering and starvation that inmates at Buchenwald were forced to endure.

"Infirmary Barracks of the Little Camp" (1943), Buchenwald, ink. In Janet Blatter and Sybil Milton, *Art of the Holocaust*, p. 152. New York: Rutledge Press, 1981. ISBN: 0831704187. Courtesy Pierre Mania, Rouen, France.

"The Transport" (1943), Buchenwald, charcoal. In Blatter and Milton, p. 155. Courtesy Pierre Mania, Rouen, France.

"A la Corridre" (1944), Buchenwald. In Mary S. Costanza, *The Living Witness: Art in the Concentration Camps and Ghettos*, p. 58. New York: Free Press, 1982. ISBN: 0029066603. Courtesy Sachsenhausen Memorial Museum.

MATOUSEK, OTA (1890–?). Born in Pilzen, Czechoslovakia, Matousek studied at the Prague Academy from 1910 to 1915. During the 1920s and 1930s Matousek's artwork was widely exhibited. He was arrested by the Gestapo in March 1943 and sent to Flossenburg concentration camp. After liberation a set of sixty-eight sketches depicting everyday life in the camp was exhibited in Prague.

"Prisoners in Flossenburg" (undated), Flossenburg, ink. In Janet Blatter and Sybil Milton, *Art of the Holocaust*, p. 164. New York: Rutledge Press, 1981. ISBN: 0831704187. Courtesy Terezin Memorial Museum.

"Flossenburg Camp" (1943–1945), Flossenburg, wash drawing. In Mary S. Costanza, *The Living Witness: Art in the Concentration Camps and Ghettos*, p. 86. New York: Free Press, 1982. ISBN: 0029066603. Courtesy Sachsenhausen Memorial Museum.

MUSIC, ZORAN (1909–?). Music was born in a small town on the Italian and Austria-Hungary border. After World War I his parents left Italy for Austria to escape Mussolini. Music studied art in Zagreb, living there in the early 1930s. He was arrested in Venice in 1944 for being a part of the Resistance and deported to Dachau. The artist became a slave laborer in an armaments plant. While at his workbench he would tear out sheets of paper from plan books and sketch the camp's conditions. He hid these drawings in the munitions factory, and after it was bombed, the artist was able to find only 35 of the 180 pieces he had completed. When the Americans liberated Dachau, a medic was presented with a drawing sketched by Music. After liberation, Music settled in Vienna. His sketches, mainly of emaciated, corpselike inmates from Dachau, are found at various galleries and museums in France.

Firster, Richard, and Nora Levin, eds. *The Living Witness: Art in the Concentration Camps*. Philadelphia: Museum of American Jewish History, 1978.

"Dachau" (1945), Dachau, ink and rust. In Janet Blatter and Sybil Milton, *Art of the Holocaust*, p. 184. New York: Rutledge Press, 1981. ISBN: 0831704187. Courtesy Zoran Music, Paris.

"Dachau" (1945), Dachau, ink and rust. In Blatter and Milton, pp. 184–185. Courtesy Musee de Deux Guerres Mondiales, Paris.

"We Are Not the Last" (1970), Paris, etching. In Blatter and Milton, p. 231. Courtesy Zoran Music and Galerie de France, Paris.

"Untitled" (1945), Dachau, pencil. In Mary S. Costanza, *The Living Witness: Art in the Concentration Camps and Ghettos*, p. 3. New York: Free Press, 1982. ISBN: 0029066603. Courtesy Dr. Marcus Smith.

"Dachau Camp" (1944), Dachau, pen and ink. In Joseph P. Czarnecki, *Last Traces: The Lost Art of the Holocaust*, p. 56. New York: Atheneum, 1989. ISBN: 0689120222. Courtesy Dr. Marcus Smith.

Grenier, Jean. *Music*. Paris: Le Musee de poche, 1970.

Zoran Music: Galerie Claude Bernard, Paris. Paris: Galerie Claude Bernard, 1983.

NANSEN, ODD (1901–?). The son of a famous explorer, Fridtof Nansen, Odd Nansen helped with the rescue of Norway's 1,700 Jews. The Gestapo arrested him in January 1942 and held him hostage in a Norwegian concentration camp. He was deported to Sachsenhausen and later liberated by the Allies.

"Lorry Fatigue Party" (1944), Sachsenhausen, pen and ink. In Janet Blatter and Sybil Milton, *Art of the Holocaust*, p. 208. New York: Rutledge Press, 1981. ISBN: 0831704187. Courtesy Sachsenhausen Memorial Museum.

Translated by Katherine John. *From Day to Day*. New York: Putnam 1949.

NUSSBAUM, FELIX (1904–1944). Nussbaum was born into a middle-class Jewish family in Osnabruck, Germany. Hitler's rise to power forced the artist to flee Germany, first to Italy and then to Belgium. Upon the German occupation of Belgium, Nussbaum was arrested and sent to St. Cyprien. The artist was deported to Gurs in 1940. He and his wife escaped; recaptured, they were deported to Auschwitz in 1943 in the last wave of Jewish deportations from Belgium. They were killed in Auschwitz in 1944.

In 1971 the Osnabruck Museum posthumously honored Nussbaum with an exhibition of 117 of his paintings. His most famous ones depict the anguish of Gurs.

Berger, Eva, Karl Georg Kaster, and Felix Nussbaum. *Felix Nussbaum: Art Defamed, Art in Exile, Art in Resistance: A Biography*. Woodstock, NY: Overlook Press, 1997. ISBN: 0879517891.

Bilsky, Emily D., Peter Junk, Sybil Milton, and Wendelin Zimmer. *Art and Exile: Felix Nussbaum (1904–1944)*. New York: Jewish Museum, 1985.

Firster, Richard, and Nora Levin, eds. *The Living Witness: Art in the Concentration Camps*. Philadelphia: Museum of American Jewish History, 1978.

"Camp Gurs" (undated), Gurs, pencil and watercolor. In Janet Blatter and Sybil Milton, *Art of the Holocaust*, pp. 110–111. New York: Rutledge Press, 1981. ISBN: 0831704187. Courtesy Leo Baeck Institute, New York.

"Deathdance" (1943–1944), Brussels, oil on canvas. In Blatter and Milton, p. 130. Courtesy Kulturgesch Museum, Osnabruck, Germany.

"Still Life with Doll" (1943), Brussels, oil on canvas. In Blatter and Milton, p. 131. Courtesy Kulturgesch Museum, Osnabruck, Germany.

"The Condemned" (1944), Auschwitz. In Mary S. Costanza, *The Living Witness: Art in the Concentration Camps and Ghettos*, p. 66. New York: Free Press, 1982. ISBN: 0029066603. Courtesy Kulturgesch Museum, Osnabruck, Germany.

"Jew at the Window" (1942). Auschwitz Museum in Germany, painting. In Costanza, p. v. Courtesy Osnabruck Museum, Germany.

"Organist" (1943), Auschwitz Museum in Germany, painting. In Costanza, p. 161. Courtesy Osnabruck Museum, Germany.

OLERE, DAVID (1902–1985). Born into a Jewish family in Warsaw, Olere studied art in Warsaw, Berlin, and Paris. He finally settled in Paris and worked for a film company. After the Nazi invasion of France, the artist was arrested and interned in the Drancy transit camp. Later he was deported to Auschwitz-Birkenau, Mauthausen, Melk, and Ebensee. He tried to escape many times. After liberation in 1945 he returned to Paris and learned that his entire family had been killed. Olere has had exhibitions in Paris, New York, and Chicago. His watercolor and charcoal drawings of Auschwitz-Birkenau camp life are located mainly in the Ghetto Fighters' House in Israel and the Beate Klarsfeld Foundation in France.

Klarsfeld, Serge. *David Olere, 1902–1985: Un peintreau Sonderkommando a Auschwitz*. New York: Beate Klarsfeld Foundation, 1989.

"Christian and Jewish Prayers" (1945), ink and watercolor on paper. In Miriam Novitch, ed., *Spiritual Resistance: Art from the Concentration Camps, 1940–1945*, p. 153. Philadelphia, Jewish Publication Society, 1981. Courtesy Kibbutz Lohamei Haghetaot.

"Forced Labor—Building a Tunnel" (1945), Auschwitz-Birkenau, watercolor and charcoal on paper. In Novitch, p. 149. Courtesy Kibbutz Lohamei Haghetaot.

"The Gold Melters" (1945), Auschwitz-Birkenau, ink and watercolor. In Novitch, p. 149. Courtesy Kibbutz Lohamei Haghetaot.

"Listening to the BBC" (1945), Birkenau, ink and watercolor on paper. In Novitch, p. 147. Courtesy Kibbutz Lohamei Haghetaot.

"Working Kommando (Squad)" (1945), Auschwitz/Birkenau, ink and watercolor on paper. In Novitch, p. 151. Courtesy Kibbutz Lohamei Haghetaot.

"Admission in Mauthausen" (1945), Mauthausen, ink and watercolor. In David Olere, *David Olere—The Eyes of a Witness*, p. 13. Paris: Beate Klarsfeld Foundation, 1989. Courtesy Ghetto Fighters' House and Beate Klarsfeld Foundation.

"Arrival of a Convoy" (undated), location unknown, ink and watercolor. In Olere, p. 89. Paris: Beate Klarsfeld Foundation, 1989. Courtesy Beate Klarsfeld Foundation.

"David Olere Burying the Remains of Children" (undated), Auschwitz, ink and watercolor. In Olere, p. 38. Courtesy Olere family and Beate Klarsfeld Foundation.

"David Olere Punished in the Bunker" (undated), location unknown, ink and watercolor. In Olere, p. 80. Courtesy Yad Vashem Art Museum and Beate Klarsfeld Foundation.

"David Olere Working in a Tunnel at Melk" (1947), Melk, ink and watercolor. In Olere, p. 92. Courtesy Olere Family and Beate Klarsfeld Foundation.

"Destruction of the Jewish People" (1946), location unknown, ink and watercolor. In Olere, p. 96. Courtesy Ghetto Fighters' House and Beate Klarsfeld Foundation.

"The Experimental Injection" (1945), Auschwitz, ink and watercolor. In Olere, p. 83. Courtesy Beate Klarsfeld Foundation.

"The Food of the Dead for the Living" (undated), Birkenau, ink and watercolor. In Olere, p. 86. Courtesy Beate Klarsfeld Foundation.

"For a Crust of Bread" (1946), location unknown, ink and watercolor. In Olere, p. 84. Courtesy Olere Family and Beate Klarsfeld Foundation.

"Gassing" (undated), Auschwitz, ink and watercolor. In Olere, p. 54. Courtesy Beate Klarsfeld Foundation.

"My First Dialogue" (1949), location unknown, ink and watercolor. In Olere, p. 39. Courtesy Olere Family and Beate Klarsfeld Foundation.

"The Oven Room" (1945), Birkenau, ink and watercolor. In Olere, p. 57. Courtesy Ghetto Fighters' House and Beate Klarsfeld Foundation.

"Priest and Rabbi" (undated), Auschwitz, ink and watercolor. In Olere, p. 33. Courtesy Beate Klarsfeld Foundation.

"Selection for Gas Chambers" (1947), location unknown, ink and watercolor. In Olere, p. 29. Courtesy Ghetto Fighters' House and Beate Klarsfeld Foundation.

"Their Last Steps" (1946), location unknown, ink and watercolor. In Olere, p. 25. Courtesy Olere Family and Beate Klarsfeld Foundation.

"Unable to Work" (undated), location unknown, ink and watercolor. In Olere, p. 31. Courtesy Beate Klarsfeld Foundation.

OLOMUCKI, HALINA (dates unknown). Olomucki was born in Warsaw. The Olomucki family lived through the horrors of the Warsaw Ghetto, documenting deportations, the Warsaw Ghetto Uprising in April

1943, and the liquidation of Dr. Korczak's orphanage. Halina Olomucki was deported first to Maidanek and then to Auschwitz, where she worked as a slave laborer in the munitions plant of I. G. Farben painting signs. She was sent to Block 10 (the medical experimentation unit), but when the SS discovered she was an artist they assigned her to draw signs and slogans. She drew secretly and hid her sketches in the barracks bunks. She participated in the October 1944 revolt at Auschwitz that resulted in the destruction of Crematorium III. Despite severe beatings, the co-conspirators never revealed the identities of the others.

When Auschwitz was liquidated in January 1945, Olomucki was marched for two days without food or water to Ravensbruck. After liberation she returned to Poland, and in 1949 she held an exhibition of her works. After living in Paris for several years, in 1972 she settled in Israel with her husband. Many of her drawings depicting scenes from the Warsaw Ghetto and Birkenau (Auschwitz) are housed in the Ghetto Fighters' House in Israel.

Firster, Richard, and Nora Levin, eds. *The Living Witness: Art in the Concentration Camps*. Philadelphia: Museum of American Jewish History, 1978.

"The Elimination of Children and Old People" (1941–1943), Warsaw, pencil on yellowed paper. In Janet Blatter and Sybil Milton, *Art of the Holocaust*, p. 65. New York: Rutledge Press, 1981. ISBN: 0831704187. Courtesy Musee de Deux Guerres Mondiales, Paris.

"In the Ghetto" (1943), Warsaw, charcoal and ink. In Blatter and Milton, p. 64. Courtesy Ghetto Fighters' House, Israel.

"The Liquidation of Dr. Korczak's Orphanage" (1941–1943), Warsaw, pencil on yellowed paper. In Blatter and Milton, p. 65. Courtesy Musee de Deux Guerres Mondiales, Paris.

"Self Portrait after Four Selections" (1943), Auschwitz, pencil. In Blatter and Milton, p. 202. Courtesy Halina Olomucki, Holon, Israel.

"Women Crouching in the Extermination Camp" (1950), Paris, gouache, watercolor, and colored chalk. In Blatter and Milton, p. 232. Courtesy Musee de Deux Guerres Mondiales, Paris.

"Auschwitz Camp" (1944), Auschwitz, charcoal drawing on paper fragment. In Mary S. Costanza, *The Living Witness: Art in the Concentration Camps and Ghettos*, p. 122. New York: Free Press, 1982. ISBN: 0029066603. Courtesy Halina Olomucki, Holon, Israel.

"Boy Selling the Star" (1943), Warsaw Ghetto, charcoal. In Costanza, p. 103. Courtesy Halina Olomucki, Holon, Israel.

"Warsaw Ghetto" (1943), charcoal on tissue. In Costanza, p. 134. Courtesy Miriam Novitch, Israel.

"Women in Birkenau" (1945), Birkenau, soft pencil on transparent paper in poor condition, placed on white paper. In Miriam Novitch, ed., *Spiritual Resistance: Art from the Concentration Camps 1940–1945*, p. 155. Philadelphia: Jewish Publication Society, 1981. Courtesy Kibbutz Lohamei Haghetaot.

"Women Prisoners after Liberation from Birkenau" (1945), Birkenau, charcoal, pen, and brush on yellowish paper. In Novitch, p. 157. Courtesy Kibbutz Lohamei Haghetaot.

"Figures in the Warsaw Ghetto" (1943), Warsaw, soft pencil on transparent paper placed on white paper. In Novitch, p. 159. Courtesy Kibbutz Lohamei Haghetaot.

PANKOK, OTTO (1893–1966). Born in Saam, Germany, Pankok studied at the Dusseldorf and Weimar art academies in 1912 and 1913. In 1914 he was drafted into the army and wounded a year later. In the 1920s he joined the Young Rhineland group in Dusseldorf and knew some of its members Gert Wollheim, Otto Dix, Karl Schwesig, and Julo Levin. In the 1930s Pankok's cycle "Stern and Blume" ("Star and Flower"), containing 150 works, gave him a name in the art world. After the Nazis came to power, the artist was banned from exhibiting his works and his paintings were confiscated. After the war he became a professor at the Academy of Fine Arts.

Pankok, Eva. *Otto Pankok: A Portrait of My Father*. Cincinnati, OH: [s.n.], 1984.

"Goebbels" (1933), Germany, pencil. In Janet Blatter and Sybil Milton, *Art of the Holocaust*, p. 49. New York: Rutledge Press, 1981. ISBN: 0831704187. Courtesy Pankok Museum, Hunxe, Germany.

"The Synagogue" (1940), Berlin, charcoal. In Blatter and Milton, p. 133. Courtesy Pankok Museum, Hunxe, Germany.

"Gypsy Children Behind Barbed Wire" (1936), Dusseldorf, woodcut. In Sybil Milton, ed. and trans., *The Art of Jewish Children: Germany, 1936–1941*, p. 79. New York: Allied Books Limited, 1989. ISBN: 0802225586.

RICHTER, JOSEF (?–1943). Although no early biographical information is available about Josef Richter, it is known that he produced eighteen sketches as a prisoner in the death camp Sobibor. His drawings from 1943 show deportations to Maidanek sketched on a scrap of newspaper, life in the Trawniki camp, and the massacre at the Lublin railroad station in 1943.

A local farmer found the drawings and donated them to Miriam Novitch of the Ghetto Fighters' House in Israel. It is believed that Richter lost his life in the Sobibor inmate revolt.

"Begging for Water from a Small Barred Window in the Train" (1943), Sobibor, pencil. In Janet Blatter and Sybil Milton, *Art of the Holocaust*, p. 222. New York: Rutledge Press, 1981. ISBN: 0831704187. Courtesy Ghetto Fighters' House.

"Deportation" (1943), Sobibor, pencil. In Blatter and Milton, pp. 222–223. Courtesy Ghetto Fighters' House.

"Digging a Grave for a Prisoner Caught Trying to Escape" (1943), Sobibor, pencil. In Blatter and Milton, p. 222. Courtesy Ghetto Fighters' House.

"Sobibor Camp" (1943), pencil drawing on newsprint fragment. In Mary S. Costanza, *The Living Witness: Art in the Concentration Camps and Ghettos*, p. 129. New York: Free Press, 1982. ISBN: 0029066603. Courtesy Ghetto Fighters' House.

RITTERBAND, OLLY (dates unknown). Ritterband was born in Romania; not much is known about her early years. She was imprisoned in Auschwitz, Bergen-Belsen, and Ravensbruck. A survivor, the artist has exhibited her works internationally.

Costanza, Mary S. *The Living Witness: Art in the Concentration Camps and Ghettos*. New York: Free Press, 1982. ISBN: 0029066603.

Will to Survive. Translated by Sean Martin. Copenhagen: Friheds-Museets: Venners Forlage Fond, 1990.

SALOMON, CHARLOTTE (1917–1943). Charlotte Salomon was born and raised in Berlin. In order to escape the Nazis, in 1939 she fled to southern France to the Riviera, then unoccupied by Germany. During her stay there until 1942, she painted 1,325 notebook-sized gouaches along with a textual narration and musical cues. She selected 765 watercolors and arranged them into acts and scenes, entitling her play/operetta, highly autobiographical, "Life or Theater?" Charlotte was captured in her hiding place on the Riviera and taken first to Gurs, a nearby camp, and to Auschwitz where she perished. Charlotte's father and stepmother found her paintings after the war.

Felstiner, Mary Lowenthal. *To Paint Her Life: Charlotte Salomon in the Nazi Era*. New York: HarperCollins, 1994. ISBN: 0060171057.

Charlotte: A Diary in Pictures. New York: Harcourt, Brace & World, 1963.

SCHALKOVA, MALVINA (1882–1944). Born in Prague, Schalkova studied art at the University of Vienna and worked there as an artist until the Nazi occupation. The artist returned to Prague, and in 1941 she and her brother were deported to Theresienstadt. Already a well-known painter, Malvina was conscripted to paint portraits of the SS. Through this venue, the artist was able to obtain materials for her own paintings and to portray the life of the internees. In 1944 Schalkova was sent to Auschwitz, where she was killed. After liberation numerous paintings were discovered hidden behind a double wall. Her paintings, though depicting the harsh conditions of Theresienstadt, are light and show the innocence and spirituality of the subjects. Many of her pieces are found in the Ghetto Fighters' House in Israel.

"Arrival in the Ghetto" (1943), Theresienstadt, watercolor. In Janet Blatter and Sybil Milton, *Art of the Holocaust*, pp. 74–75. New York: Rutledge Press, 1981. ISBN: 0831704187. Courtesy Ghetto Fighters' House.

"Forced Labor" (1943), Theresienstadt, watercolor. In Blatter and Milton, p. 75. Courtesy Ghetto Fighters' House.

"Sleeping Quarters" (1944), Theresienstadt, soft pencil. In Blatter and Milton, p. 72. Courtesy Ghetto Fighters' House.

"Women's Work Shop—Terezin" (undated), Theresienstadt, charcoal. In Mary S. Costanza, *The Living Witness: Art in the Concentration Camps and Ghettos*, p. 22. New York: Free Press, 1982. ISBN: 0029066603. Courtesy Biet Lohamei Haghetaot and Miriam Novitch.

"The Arrival at Theresienstadt" (undated), Theresienstadt, pastel on paper. In Miriam Novitch, ed., *Spiritual Resistance: Art from the Concentration Camps, 1940–1945*, p. 165. Philadelphia: Jewish Publication Society, 1981. Courtesy Kibbutz Lohamei Haghetaot.

"The Artist's Bed in Theresienstadt" (undated), Theresienstadt, watercolor. In Novitch, p. 171. Courtesy Kibbutz Lohamei Haghetaot.

"Courtyard, Always Overcrowded" (undated), Theresienstadt, pencil on paper. In Novitch, p. 175. Courtesy Kibbutz Lohamei Haghetaot.

"Interior with Wooden Bunks" (undated), Theresienstadt, watercolor and pencil on paper. In Novitch, p. 167. Courtesy Kibbutz Lohamei Haghetaot.

"Internee Bathing" (undated), Theresienstadt, watercolor on paper. In Novitch, p. 184. Courtesy Kibbutz Lohamei Haghetaot.

"Internee with Child" (undated), Theresienstadt, watercolor. In Novitch, p. 171. Courtesy Kibbutz Lohamei Haghetaot.

"Internees Working in the Kitchen" (undated), Theresienstadt, pencil on paper. In Novitch, p. 173. Courtesy Kibbutz Lohamei Haghetaot.

"Old Woman Resting" (undated), Theresienstadt, watercolor. In Novitch, p. 185. Courtesy Kibbutz Lohamei Haghetaot.

"Self Portrait" (1944), Theresienstadt, pencil on paper. In Novitch, p. 169. Courtesy Kibbutz Lohamei Haghetaot.

"The Synagogue, Taking Consolation in the Holy Scripture" (undated), Theresienstadt, watercolor on paper. In Novitch, p. 186. Courtesy Kibbutz Lohamei Haghetaot.

"Three Internees" (undated), Theresienstadt, watercolor. In Novitch, p. 175. Courtesy Kibbutz Lohamei Haghetaot.

"Women Working" (undated), Theresienstadt, watercolor. In Novitch, p. 173. Courtesy Kibbutz Lohamei Haghetaot.

SCHLEIFER, SAVIELLY (1881–1943). Born in Odessa, Russia, Schleifer studied at the Odessa Art Academy and in St. Petersburg. Schleifer exhibited his work in Paris in 1905. He returned to St. Petersburg in 1907 and worked as a stage designer. The artist was drafted into the Russian army in World War I and in 1917 founded his own art academy. In 1927 Schleifer and his wife settled in Paris, where he taught art and became a successful painter. He was arrested as a Soviet citizen on June 22, 1941, and interned at Compiegne. Many of his paintings depict everyday life in the internment camp. In 1943 Schleifer was sent to Drancy and then deported to Auschwitz, where he was gassed upon arrival.

"The Watchtower" (1942), Compiegne, watercolor on eggshell lacquered to wood. In Janet Blatter and Sybil Milton, *Art of the Holocaust*, p. 102. New York: Rutledge Press, 1981. ISBN: 0831704187. Courtesy Musee de Deux Guerres Mondiales, Paris.

"Still Life" (1943), Compiegne, watercolor and ink. In Miriam Novitch, ed., *Spiritual Resistance: Art from the Concentration Camps, 1940–1945*, p. 179. Philadelphia: Jewish Publication Society, 1981. Courtesy Kibbutz Lohamei Haghetaot.

SCHWESIG, KARL (1898–1955). Born in Gelsenkirchen, Germany, Schwesig studied at the Academy of Fine Arts in Dusseldorf. A vocal anti-Nazi, he joined the communist party and in 1933 was beaten and jailed. After his release he made his way to Belgium and then to Amsterdam. In 1938 the artist moved to the Pyrenees. After the German invasion of France in 1940, he was arrested and sent to St. Cyprien and Gurs. He joined the communist Resistance movement in Gurs. Art supplies were obtainable in the camp and two large exhibitions were held there in 1941. Felix Nussbaum was one of the exhibitors. The artist worked in the post office drawing descriptions of camp events on the blank margins of real French stamp sheets. Schwesig escaped the Vichy camps but was eventually recaptured and sent to jail in Germany. He was liberated by the Americans in 1945. He died in Dusseldorf.

"Liberte, Egalite, Fraternite" (1941), Gurs, india ink. In Janet Blatter and Sybil Milton, *Art of the Holocaust*, p. 105. New York: Rutledge Press, 1981. ISBN: 0831704187. Courtesy Leo Baeck Institute, New York.

"Prisoner in Barracks" (1940), St. Cyprien, watercolor. In Blatter and Milton, p. 102. Courtesy Ghetto Fighters' House.

"Prisoner on the Seashore" (1940), St. Cyprien, ink. In Blatter and Milton, p. 104. Courtesy Ghetto Fighters' House.

"Stamps" (1940–1943), Gurs, colored ink. In Richard Firster and Nora Levin, eds., *The Living Witness: Art in the Concentration Camps*, p. 40. Philadelphia Museum of American Jewish History, 1978. Courtesy Leo Baeck Institute.

SEKSZTAJN, GELA (1907–1942). Born in Warsaw, the artist exhibited her drawings of Jewish children in 1938. She taught art and painted watercolors mainly of the children inside the ghetto. Deported to Treblinka, she died with her 2-year-old daughter in August 1942.

"Beggar Girl" (1942), Warsaw Ghetto, watercolor. In Janet Blatter and Sybil Milton, *Art of the Holocaust*, p. 66. New York: Rutledge Press, 1981. ISBN: 0831704187. Courtesy Jewish Historical Institute of Warsaw.

"Boy with Basket" (1942), Warsaw Ghetto, watercolor. In Blatter and Milton, p. 67. Courtesy Jewish Historical Institute of Warsaw.

"Girl with Basket" (1942), Warsaw Ghetto, watercolor. In Blatter and Milton, p. 67. Courtesy Jewish Historical Institute of Warsaw.

"Man with Book" (1942), Warsaw Ghetto, watercolor. In Blatter and Milton, p. 66. Courtesy Jewish Historical Institute of Warsaw.

"Man with Glasses" (1942), Warsaw Ghetto, watercolor. In Blatter and Milton, p. 66. Courtesy Jewish Historical Institute of Warsaw.

Toll, Nelly S. *When Memory Speaks: The Holocaust in Art*, pp. 3–4. Westport, CT: Praeger, 1998. ISBN: 0275955346.

SIMON-PIETKIEWICZOWA, JADWIGA (1906–1955). Born in Warsaw, Simon-Pietkiewiczowa studied at the Warsaw Academy of Art. She worked with the Polish Underground in 1939. Arrested by the Gestapo on February 15, 1941, she was held for six months in a Warsaw prison. She was deported to Ravensbruck (mainly a women's camp) on September 22, 1941, and was assigned to making and painting wooden toys. In 1942 Simon-Pietkiewiczowa became ill and twice was put into a punishment bunker. In fall 1943 the artist succeeded in smuggling some of her sketches of fellow prisoners out of the camp and back into Poland. Unfortunately, these drawings were destroyed during the general Warsaw uprising a year later. At the end of 1944 she was so ill that during a "selection" she was chosen for the gas chambers, but friends hid her under several blankets. In April 1945 Jadwiga was evacuated, along with a group of others, to Sweden. The next year she returned to Poland.

"Fellow Prisoners" (1943), Ravensbruck, crayon. In Janet Blatter and Sybil Milton, *Art of the Holocaust*, p. 160. New York: Rutledge Press, 1981. ISBN: 0831704187. Collection of Janina Jaworska, Warsaw.

"Portrait of Janina Peretjathowicz Ill with Pneumonia" (1944), Ravensbruck, pencil. In Blatter and Milton, p. 160. Collection of Janina Jaworska, Warsaw.

"Ravensbruck" (1943), charcoal. In Mary S. Costanza, *The Living Witness: Art in the Concentration Camps and Ghettos*, p. 50. New York: Free Press, 1982. ISBN: 0029066603. Collection of Janina Jaworska, Warsaw.

SZAJNA, JOSEF (1922–?). Born in Rzeszow, Szajna joined the Polish Resistance at the beginning of World War II. After attempting to leave Hungary, he was captured and sent to several prisons, including Tarnow. In July, 1941, after four and one-half months in Tarnow, the artist, weighing just 101 pounds, was deported to Auschwitz. A slave laborer, he was sent to work with construction crews at the Konigsgraben Canal. After he became ill, his friends secretly brought him paper and pencils while he was "treated" in the camp hospital at Birkenau. It was at this time that he unsuccessfully attempted to escape. Szajna was sent to the punishment cells at Auschwitz.

In spring 1944, Szajna was transported to Buchenwald. He became ill again and was sent to the camp hospital, where he drew sketches of his fellow inmates. Twenty of these drawings were hidden under the straw mattress of his hospital cot. The artist was liberated on April 11, 1945. He returned to Poland and continued his education.

"Block 11 in Auschwitz . . . Waiting to Be Called for Execution" (1944), Buchenwald, pencil. In Janet Blatter and Sybil Milton, *Art of the Holocaust*, p. 149. New York: Rutledge Press, 1981. ISBN: 0831704187. Courtesy Janina Jaworska, Warsaw.

"The Roll Call Lasted Very Long . . . My Feet Hurt a Lot" (1944), Buchenwald, pen. In Blatter and Milton, p. 148. Courtesy Janina Jaworska, Warsaw.

"Block 11" (1943), Auschwitz, pencil. In Mary S. Costanza, *The Living Witness: Art in the Concentration Camps and Ghettos*, p. 138. New York: Free Press, 1982. ISBN: 0029066603. Courtesy Auschwitz Memorial Museum.

SZERMAN, SZYMON (1917–1943). Szerman was born in Lodz, Poland. Little is known of his early life. A well-known painter in Poland, Szeman was one of twelve artists employed in the statistics department in the Lodz Ghetto. He perished in the ghetto in 1943. His artwork depicting the conditions of the ghetto is part of the collection of the Ghetto Fighters' House in Israel.

"Transfer to the Ghetto" (1940), Lodz, gouache. In Janet Blatter and Sybil Milton, *Art of the Holocaust*, pp. 70–71. New York: Rutledge Press, 1981. ISBN: 0831704187. Courtesy of Ghetto Fighters' House.

Costanza, Mary S. *The Living Witness: Art in the Concentration Camps and Ghettos*. New York: Free Press, 1982. ISBN: 0029066603.

"In the Ghetto of Lodz—Deportation" (undated), Lodz, pastel. In Miriam Novitch, ed., *Spiritual Resistance: Art from the Concentration Camps 1940– 1945*, p. 181. Philadelphia: Jewish Publication Society, 1981. Courtesy Kibbutz Lohamei Haghetaot.

TARGOSZ, FRANCISZEK (1899–1979). Targosz was born in Lipnik, Poland. Little is known about his early life. The artist was deported to Auschwitz on December 18, 1940. In fall 1941 Auschwitz commandant Rudolf Hoess ordered a museum to be established with Targosz in charge. Working with him were such noted artists as Mieczyslaw Koscielniak and Bronislaw Czech. One of their first tasks was to create fake documentation that would demonstrate the racial inferiority of Gypsies, Jews, and other "undesirables." This work was soon expanded to include the informal production of portraits, greeting cards, cigarette cases, and other small articles used as a form of exchange with the SS. Targosz is credited with saving a number of lives by finding artists alternative work in this museum and keeping them from deadly work details. In January 1945 he was evacuated to Mauthausen, where he was liberated by the Americans. Targosz returned to Poland, where he remained until his death.

Costanza, Mary S. *The Living Witness: Art in the Concentration Camps and Ghettos*. New York: Free Press, 1982. ISBN: 0029066603.

Czarnecki, Joseph P. *Last Traces: The Lost Art of the Holocaust*. New York: Atheneum, 1989. ISBN: 0689120222.

"Horses" (undated), Auschwitz, crayon. In Janet Blatter and Sybil Milton, *Art of the Holocaust*, p. 207. New York: Rutledge Press, 1981. ISBN: 0831704187. Courtesy Auschwitz Memorial Museum.

TOLL, NELLY S. (1935–). See entry on Toll under Memoirs, Diaries, and Fiction.

Behind the Secret Window: A Memoir of a Hidden Childhood during World War Two. New York: Dial Books for Young Readers, 1993. ISBN: 0803713622.

When Memory Speaks: The Holocaust in Art. Westport, CT: Praeger, 1998. ISBN: 0275955346.

Without Surrender: Art of the Holocaust. Philadelphia: Running Press, 1978. ISBN: 0894710559.

TOLLIK, JANINA (1910–?). Born in Janow, Poland, Tollik studied art for three years and also attended the Academy of Fine Arts in Cracow. After 1935 the artist became very well known for her folk art and landscapes. During the Nazi invasion of Poland, Tollik served as a volunteer nurse's aide. In 1940 she joined the Resistance, obtaining false identity cards.

In May 1941 Janina was arrested by the Gestapo and sent to prison in Cracow. Eleven months later she was deported to Auschwitz, where she still managed to obtain materials to sketch and draw. She drew mainly pictures of everyday life in the camp. In October 1944 the artist was transported to Flossenburg and worked as a slave laborer. On May 7, 1945, Tollik and several other prisoners escaped the camp. From 1950 through 1953 the artist lived in Auschwitz (the town) and worked on the book *Never Again*.

"Thirst" (1944), Auschwitz, ink. In Janet Blatter and Sybil Milton, *Art of the Holocaust*, p. 194. New York: Rutledge Press, 1981. ISBN: 0831704187. Courtesy Janina Jaworska, Warsaw.

"The Twenty-four Hour Roll Call" (1946), Poland, gouache. In Blatter and Milton, p. 234. Courtesy Auschwitz Memorial Museum.

"Untitled" (1944), Ravensbruck, pencil. In Mary S. Costanza, *The Living Witness: Art in the Concentration Camps and Ghettos*, p. 62. New York: Free Press, 1982. ISBN: 0029066603. Courtesy Janina Jaworska, Warsaw.

TROLLER, NORBERT (1896–1981). See entry on Troller under Memoirs, Diaries, and Fiction.

Costanza, Mary S. *The Living Witness: Art in the Concentration Camps and Ghettos*. New York: Free Press, 1982. ISBN: 0029066603.

Terezin, 1942–1945: Through the Eyes of Norbert Troller. Essays and Catalog of an Exhibition at the Yeshiva Museum, May 1981–December 1981. New York: The Museum, 1981.

Joel Shatsky, Richard Ives, and Doris Rauch. *Theresienstadt: Hitler's Gift to the Jews*. Chapel Hill: University of North Carolina Press, 1991. ISBN: 0807819654.

UNGAR, OTTO (1901–1945). Born in Husovia, Moravia (Czechoslovakia), Ungar taught painting, mathematics, and geometry in Jewish secondary schools in Brno until 1940. In January 1942 Ungar was deported to Theresienstadt with his wife and daughter. The artist worked in the "art studio" with Bedrich Fritta and Leo Bloch. They worked secretly at night sketching the atrocities the Nazis inflicted on the inmates. In 1944 he and the artists were accused by the Gestapo of passing pictures to the Red Cross about the realities of Theresienstadt. Despite severe torture and punishment, none of the artists gave away any information. The paintings were hidden in a loft and retrieved after liberation by Leo Haas.

Ungar was sent to the Little Fortress in August 1944 and deported to Auschwitz in October. The artist was part of the death march from Auschwitz to Buchenwald in January 1945. He was liberated from Buchenwald in April 1945 and died of typhus in a sanatorium near Weimar in July. Many of his paintings can be found at the Prague State Jewish Museum.

Toll, Nelly S. *When Memory Speaks: The Holocaust in Art*, p. 41. Westport, CT: Praeger, 1998. ISBN: 0275955346.

"After the Arrival of a Transport" (undated), Theresienstadt. In Janet Blatter and Sybil Milton, *Art of the Holocaust*, p. 81. New York: Rutledge Press, 1981. ISBN: 0831704187. Courtesy Terezin Memorial Museum.

"Allegory" (undated), Theresienstadt, gouache. In Blatter and Milton, p. 77. Courtesy State Jewish Museum, Prague.

"Blind People" (undated), Theresienstadt, gouache. In Blatter and Milton, p. 77. Courtesy State Jewish Museum, Prague.

"The Café" (undated), Theresienstadt, gouache. In Blatter and Milton, p. 78. Courtesy Elfrida Ungarova, Brno, Czechoslovakia.

"The Courtyard in Theresienstadt" (undated), Theresienstadt, gouache. In Blatter and Milton, p. 80. Courtesy Terezin Memorial Museum.

"Elderly Woman" (undated), Theresienstadt, gouache. In Blatter and Milton, p. 80. Courtesy Prague State Jewish Museum.

"Line for Food" (undated), Theresienstadt, gouache. In Blatter and Milton, p. 80. Courtesy Terezin Memorial Museum.

"Men in the Attic" (undated), Theresienstadt, watercolor. In Blatter and Milton, p. 77. Courtesy Terezin Memorial Museum.

"Old Man with Soup Bowl" (undated), Theresienstadt, watercolor. In Blatter and Milton, p. 77. Courtesy Terezin Memorial Museum.

"Old Man with Star" (undated), Theresienstadt, gouache. In Blatter and Milton, p. 78. Courtesy Terezin Memorial Museum.

"Polish Children Escorted into Theresienstadt" (1943), Theresienstadt, gouache. In Blatter and Milton, p. 78. Courtesy Elfrida Ungarova, Brno, Czechoslovakia.

"Prayer for a Dead Woman" (undated), Theresienstadt, gouache. In Blatter and Milton, p. 80. Courtesy Terezin Memorial Museum.

"Still Life with Open Window" (undated), Theresienstadt, gouache. In Blatter and Milton, p. 78. Courtesy Terezin Memorial Museum.

"Theater in Theresienstadt" (undated), Theresienstadt, gouache. In Blatter and Milton, p. 79. Courtesy Elfrida Ungarova, Brno, Czechoslovakia.

"Night Burial" (date unknown), Terezin, gouache. In Mary S. Costanza, *The Living Witness: Art in the Concentration Camps and Ghettos*, p. 112. New York: Free Press, 1982. ISBN: 0029066603. Courtesy Yad Vashem.

"Terezin Barracks" (date unknown), Terezin, gouache. In Costanza, p. 104. Courtesy Terezin Memorial Museum.

"Cellist" (undated), Theresienstadt, gouache. In Joza Karas, *Music in Terezin*, p. 192. New York: Beaufort Books, 1985. ISBN: 0825302870.

"Saxophonist" (undated), Theresienstadt, gouache. In Karas, p. 193.

"Old Woman in Nurse's Cape and Kerchief" (1944), Theresienstadt, charcoal. In Miriam Novitch, ed., *Spiritual Resistance: Art from the Concentration Camps, 1940–1945*, p. 204. Philadelphia: Jewish Publication Society, 1981. Courtesy Kibbutz Lohamei Haghetaot.

"Terezin in Winter" (1944), Theresienstadt, watercolor on paper. In Novitch, p. 190. Courtesy Kibbutz Lohamei Haghetaot.

Ungar, Otto, and Oliva Pechova. *Otto Ungar*. Prague: Galerie Vincence Kramare, 1971.

URISON, HAIM (1905–1943). Born in a Jewish shtetl in White Russia, Urison moved with his family to Lodz. In 1928 he went to Paris to study art, returning three years later. In 1936 he went to Warsaw, and in 1938 to Vilna. He had several one-man shows of his paintings, and in 1939 the artist participated in an exhibit back in Warsaw. After the German invasion of Poland, he moved to eastern Poland, which was under Russian rule; but in 1941 he went to visit his ailing mother in the Bialystok Ghetto and became trapped. While in the ghetto he painted portraits of fellow internees. Urison was killed during the mass deportations to Treblinka and Bialystok Ghetto revolt in August 1943.

"In the Ghetto" (date unknown), Bialystok Ghetto, painting. In Miriam Novitch, ed., *Spiritual Resistance: Art from the Concentration Camps, 1940–1945*, pp. 182–183. Philadelphia: Jewish Publication Society, 1981.

"Ghetto Portrait" (1942), Bialystok, gouache. In Janet Blatter and Sybil Milton, *Art of the Holocaust*, p. 55. New York: Routledge Press, 1981. ISBN: 0831704187. Courtesy Ghetto Fighter's House.

VOLAVKOVA, HANA (dates unknown).

I Never Saw Another Butterfly: Children's Drawings and Poems from Terezin Concentration Camp, 1942–1944. Edited by Hana Volavkova; translated into English by Jeanne Nemcova. New York: Schocken Books, 1978. ISBN: 0805241159.

WEISSOVA-HOSKOVA, HELGA (1929–?). Born in Prague, Weissova-Hoskova was already an accomplished painter at age 12 when she and her family were deported to Theresienstadt. She produced paintings about everyday life in Theresienstadt. An uncle of Helga's hid approximately one hundred of her paintings, saving them from destruction. In 1944 Helga and her mother were sent to work in an aircraft factory near Dresden. In April 1945 they were evacuated to Mauthausen and then liberated by the Americans. Weissova-Hoskova became a well-established artist in Prague after the war.

"Chanukah in the Attic of Block L410" (1943), Theresienstadt, india ink. In Janet Blatter and Sybil Milton, *Art of the Holocaust*, p. 91 New York: Rutledge Press, 1981. ISBN: 0831704187. Courtesy Helga Weissova-Hoskova, Prague.

"Cutting down the Third Level of Bunks before the Red Cross Visit" (1944), Theresienstadt, india ink. In Blatter and Milton, p. 91. Courtesy Helga Weissova-Hoskova, Prague.

"Suicide on the Wire" (1945), Prague, ink and ink wash. In Blatter and Milton, p. 26. Courtesy Helga Weissova-Hoskova, Prague.

"Secret School" (1943), Theresienstadt. In Mary S. Costanza, *The Living Witness: Art in the Concentration Camps and Ghettos*. New York: Free Press, 1982. ISBN: 0029066603, p. 75. Courtesy Helga Weissova-Hoskova, Prague.

Volavkova, Hana, ed. *I Never Saw Another Butterfly . . . Children's Drawings and Poems from Terezin Concentration Camp 1942–1944*. Translated into English by Jeanne Nemcova, p. 23. New York: Schocken Books, 1978. ISBN: 0805241159.

WIESENTHAL, SIMON (1908–). See entry on Wiesenthal under Memoirs, Diaries, Fiction.

"Untitled" (1945), Mauthausen, mixed media. In Mary S. Costanza, *The Living Witness: Art in the Concentration Camps and Ghettos*, p. 47. New York: Free Press, 1982. ISBN: 0029066603. Courtesy Simon Wiesenthal, Vienna.

"Untitled" (1945), Mauthausen, mixed media. In Costanza, p. 36. Courtesy Simon Wiesenthal, Vienna.

"Untitled" (1945), Mauthausen, montage. In Costanza, p. 127. Courtesy Simon Wiesenthal, Vienna.

Toll, Nelly S. *When Memory Speaks: The Holocaust in Art*, p. 113. Westport, CT: Praeger, 1998. ISBN: 0275955346.

WYSZOGRAD, MORRIS (1920–?). See entry on Wyszograd under Memoirs, Diaries, and Fiction.

4

Music of the Holocaust

INTRODUCTION

Music is deeply intertwined in the religious and cultural aspects of Jewish life. Prayers and Torah readings are chanted and sung by cantors and rabbis. Songs with lyrics written in Yiddish—the common language of Eastern European Jews—date back 150 years. They tell stories, both humorous and tragic, about local characters, the Czar, daily life in the shtetl (village), and pogroms (organized attacks) staged against them. Many times a tune written in earlier times was recycled with new lyrics to fit the new situation.

In September 1939, after the Nazis conquered Poland, and through the early 1940s as the Nazis pulverized country after country throughout Europe, Jews remaining in those areas became subject to devastating laws and restrictions. The German oppressors sought to control every aspect of their lives. Despite threats of deportation and death, Jews resisted spiritually in any way they could. They continued to pray, to educate their children, and to participate in religious and cultural activities that flourished in both ghettos and concentration camps.

The "model ghetto" established by the Nazis at Theresienstadt was home to several world-class composers, conductors, and musicians whose SS masters ordered them to create operas, concerts, and musical reviews to impress the International Red Cross and present to the outside world a false front of decent treatment of Jews. Internees Viktor Ullmann, Robert Brock, Alice Herz-Sommer, Gideon Klein, Egon Ledec, Rafael Schachter, Hans Krasa, David Grunfeld, and others met their demands but also produced numerous musical pieces they freely performed for other inmates. Some musicians viewed their incarceration in Theresienstadt as time to practice and perfect their craft. In fall 1944, however, Ullmann, Krasa, Schachter, Ledec, and many other well-known musicians were deported to Auschwitz and murdered. The musicians left in the ghetto were mainly Danish citizens still under the protection of their king or they were Jews of mixed marriages.

The musicians interned in Eastern European ghettos provided the tortured inhabitants with a precious few hours of pleasure. The ghetto songs also served other purposes: They documented ghetto life and upheld tradition. The ghetto had street singers who performed in makeshift concert halls in coffeehouses and libraries. Their street songs emphasized hunger, corrupt administration (anti-Judenrat sentiment), a hope for liberation, and sometimes a call for uprising. Most songs consisted of lyrics attached to preexisting melodies. Mordechai Gebirtig, of the Krakow Ghetto, wrote songs that depicted life under the Nazi thumb. Hirsh Glik of the Vilna Ghetto in Lithuania composed martial music inspired by the heroism displayed by the young people who participated in the Warsaw Ghetto Uprising. Liuba Levitska, also of Vilna, became a heroine as she sang her most famous song, "Two Little Doves," in the death pits at Ponary.

There were renditions of traditional Jewish selections. Music always played a part in Sabbath ritual and holidays, particularly Passover and Yom Kippur. These musical themes expressed hopelessness, helplessness, and revenge.

There were orchestras of prisoner-musicians at the five extermination camps. The unfortunate musicians had to play as their fellow inmates went to work or were marched to the gas chambers. Auschwitz-Birkenau had six orchestras, including an all-female one. One orchestra had 120 performer-inmates. The suicide rate among the musicians was very high.

The compositions, lyrics, and music written during the Holocaust show that even under the worst, most horrific conditions, a people's desire to bring humanity and beauty to the world shines through. Hitler failed miserably in his efforts to stifle Jewish musicians from creating and performing their music. Although the victims perished in the gas chambers of Auschwitz and the death pits of Ponary, their legacies live on in the poignant music they produced.

ALLEN-SHORE, LENA (1919–   ). Born in Krakow to wealthy Jewish parents, Allen-Shore was hidden by Polish Catholics with her brother, Adam. As a preteen she was deported to Majdanek concentration camp. After liberation she studied at the University of Paris and then at the Canadian universities of Montreal and McGill. She received her doctorate at Dropsie College of Jewish Studies. She moved to Philadelphia, where she became a senior research fellow at the University of Pennsylvania of Social Work. She married and had one son. Dr. Allen-Shore established her own Allen-Shore Center of Continuing Educating affiliated with Gratz College, located just outside Philadelphia. She is the author of a number of short works dealing with the Holocaust experience and the poem "The Little Shoes & the Cry from Warsaw," which she made into a cantata. The cantata was presented before Pope John Paul II.

The Little Shoes & the Cry from Warsaw. Rockville, MD: Schreiber Publishing, 1983. ISBN: 0884000958. 25 pages.

ANCERL, KAREL (1908–1973). Born in southern Bohemia, Ancerl graduated from the Prague Conservatory, mastering conducting and composition. Before his imprisonment in Theresienstadt he was conductor at the Liberated Theater in Prague. During his internment he worked with several musicians and groups of musicians, assisting them in fine-tuning their craft. After liberation he returned to Prague and in the late 1960s became conductor of the Toronto Symphony.

Karas, Joza. *Music in Terezin.* New York: Beaufort Books, 1985. ISBN: 0825302870. 223 pages.

ARANYI, JULIETTE (1912–1944). Born in Slovakia, Aranyl was a child prodigy who began playing piano as a toddler and studied in Bratislava and Vienna. Aranyi performed at concerts at age 6. She was deported to Theresienstadt and then to Auschwitz, where she perished.

Karas, Joza. *Music in Terezin.* New York: Beaufort Books, 1985. ISBN: 0825302870. 223 pages.

ART, MUSIC & EDUCATION AS STRATEGIES FOR SURVIVAL: THERESIENSTADT, 1941–1945. Anne D. Dutlinger, ed. Brooklyn, NY: Herodias, 2000. ISBN: 192874611X. 204 pages. Describes the work of several artists in various mediums. From architect Walter Gropius, artist Paul Klee, and graphic designer Friedl Dicker, the book encompasses artwork, essays, and photographs in order to educate the reader about Holocaust artists.

BERMAN, KAREL (1919–?). Born in Bohemia, Czechoslovakia, Berman was an operatic performer forced to assume a Gentile name in order to work after the German occupation of the Sudetenland. Because Jewish musicians were not permitted to perform publicly, concerts were held clandestinely in private apartments or dwellings. After his deportation to Theresienstadt, Berman participated in various performances and conducted the girls chorus. In September 1941 he was deported to Auschwitz. Almost immediately he was sent to Germany to work as a slave laborer in an aircraft factory. Berman later survived a forced march and was liberated near Dachau by the Americans in April 1945.

After liberation the singer returned to his home in Prague only to find that all but one of his relatives had been killed in the concentration camps. He continued his singing and became active in the recording and television industries. While in Theresienstadt he wrote three compositions: "Poupata," Four Songs for Bass & Piano; "Terezin," Suite for Piano; and Three Songs for High Voice & Piano.

Karas, Joza. *Music in Terezin*. New York: Beaufort Books, 1985. ISBN: 0825302870. 223 pages.

BIRDS ARE DROWSING: FOR MIXED CHOIR (SATB) AND PIANO. Melody by Leyb Yampolsky; choral arrangement Joshua Jacobson. Leyb Yampolsky. New York: Transcontinental Music, 1995. 6 pp. (1 score). Words in romanized Yiddish; also printed as text in romanized Yiddish with English translation.

BROCK, ROBERT (1905–1979). Born in Bohemia, Brock was a famous conductor before his arrest and incarceration in Theresienstadt. His first official duty in the "model ghetto" was to pull the hearse with other inmates that brought bread into the ghetto and to remove the bodies for burial. After a period of time Brock was reassigned to the orchestra as a conductor. As the end of the war approached, the Nazis invited Red Cross officials to inspect the ghetto and ordered the conductors to come up with a suitable program to impress them. With Brock conducting, the orchestra played and the chorus sang a cleverly disguised version of the Czech national anthem. After liberation he became conductor at the Grand Opera and a professor at the Academy of Musical Arts, both located in Prague.

Karas, Joza. *Music in Terezin*. New York: Beaufort Books, 1985. ISBN: 0825302870. 223 pages.

BROYDO, KASRIEL (?–1945). Author and director of theater revues and concerts in the Vilna Ghetto, Broydo was arrested and deported to a concentration camp near Riga. The Germans drowned him and others on a barge in the Baltic Sea in 1945.

CARVED IN COURAGE. Sylvia Glickman. Bryn Mawr, PA: Hildegard Publishing Co., 1997. 45 pages (1 score). Commemorates the bravery of the Danish people who helped save Denmark's Jewish population from the Nazis.

CRADLE OF FIRE: FIVE SETTINGS OF HOLOCAUST SONGS FOR TREBLE CHOIR AND ORCHESTRA. Michael Isaacson, with English adaptations by Samuel Rosenbaum. New York: Transcontinental Music Publications, 1988. 36 pages (1 vocal score). Yiddish or English words.

DEUTSCH, PETER (1901–1965). Born in Berlin, Deutsch wrote music for German films before moving to Denmark in 1929. In Denmark Deutsch composed several solo and orchestral pieces and was the former conductor of the Royal Orchestra in Copenhagen. The composer arrived in Theresienstadt in October 1943 on a transport with other Danish Jews. He organized an orchestra, and they performed many concerts. In fall 1944 most of the men had been deported to death camps except for the Danes who were still under the protection of their king. In April 1945 the Danish prisoners were released into the custody of the Red Cross and taken to Sweden. Deutsch returned to Denmark and resumed his work as a composer.

Karas, Joza. *Music in Terezin.* New York: Beaufort Books, 1985. ISBN: 0825302870. 223 pages.

FREUDENFELD, RUDOLF (1921–?). Born in Prague, Freudenfeld put together arrangements for a children's chorus prior to his deportation to Theresienstadt. In July 1941 Freudenfeld's father celebrated his fiftieth birthday. To commemorate the occasion, the opera *Brundibar* was to be performed. Eventually all the participants were rounded up and sent to Theresienstadt. While there, Freudenfeld conducted all the performances of *Brundibar*. He was later deported to Auschwitz. After liberation he returned to Prague, changed his name to Franek, and became director of a secondary school.

Karas, Joza. *Music in Terezin.* New York: Beaufort Books, 1985. ISBN: 0825302870. 223 pages.

FROHLICH, KAREL (1917–?). Born in Moravia, Frohlich studied at the Prague Conservatory. In 1940 and 1941 he gave solo performances under an assumed name to avoid arrest by the Nazis. He arrived in Theresienstadt in 1941, smuggling in both his violin and viola. Frohlich joined the musical community there, participating in variety shows and other performances. The musician joined three other prisoners, forming the Terezin Quartet. In October 1944 Frohlich and two other members of the group were deported to Auschwitz. He was later sent to Buchenwald and liberated by the Americans. Of the quartet, only Frohlich survived. After liberation in 1945 he became a concertmaster in Prague and went to Paris to continue his studies. In 1948 he and his wife immigrated to the United States.

Karas, Joza. *Music in Terezin*. New York: Beaufort Books, 1985. ISBN: 0825302870. 223 pages.

GEBIRTIG, MORDECHAI (1877–1942). Born in Krakow, Poland, Gebirtig became a carpenter. Taking the pen name Bertig, he wrote music and lyrics that coincided with the world around him. His music was about the Jewish way of life in Krakow. After the Nazi invasion of Poland in 1939, his music took on a much darker tone. His song "Es Brent" ("On Fire") tells the story of a burning village. His compositions were about simple Jewish folk and his poems (he wrote about one hundred) were sung in theaters, in halls, at public meetings, and on the street. In 1942 Bertig was arrested by the Gestapo and on June 4 of that year killed in Krakow.

"Ver Der Ershter Vet Lakhn" ("Who Will Be the First to Laugh"). In Eleanor Mlotek, and Joseph Mlotek, *Songs of Generations: New Pearl of Yiddish Songs*, pp. 13–15. New York: Workmen's Circle. ISBN: 1877909653. 303 pages.

"Es Brent." In Jerry Silverman, *The Yiddish Songbook*, pp. 184–185. Briarcliff, NY: Stein and Day Publishers, 1983. ISBN: 0812861302 (paperback); ISBN: 0812828291 (hardback). 207 pages.

Krakow Ghetto Notebook. Fort Washington, NY: Koch International Classics, 1994.

Schneider, Gertrude. *Mordechai Gebirtig: His Poetic and Musical Legacy*. Westport, CT: Greenwood Publishing Group, 2000. ISBN: 0275966577. 224 pages.

GERUT, ROSALIE. *We Are Here* [Sound Recording]. Milton, MA: Rosalie Gerut & Friends, 1988, 1 sound cassette: analog. Principally songs; includes instrumental pieces. The songs sung in Yiddish, English, and Hebrew include lyrics written by Holocaust survivors.

"GETO LID" ("Ghetto Song"). In Jerry Silverman, *The Yiddish Song Book*, pp. 192–193. Leyb Opeskin. Briarcliff, NY: Stein and Day Publishers, 1983. ISBN: 0812861302 (paperback); ISBN: 0812828291 (hardback). 207 pages.

GLIK, HIRSH (1920–1944). Glik was born in Vilna, Lithuania. In April 1943, when the Nazis began the first round of deportations in the Vilna Ghetto, Glik escaped and joined a partisan unit. He was inspired to write his music by the heroic young people in the Warsaw Ghetto Uprising. The musician was captured in the final wave of the liquidation of the ghetto and sent to a concentration camp in Estonia. He managed to escape in 1944 and rejoin the Resistance, but he was killed while fighting the Nazis in the woods nearby.

"Zog Nit Keynmol" ("Never Say"). In Jerry Silverman, *The Yiddish Song Book*, p. 203. Briarcliff, NY: Stein and Day Publishers, 1983. ISBN: 0812861302 (paperback); ISBN: 0812828291 (hardback). 207 pages. A Jewish partisan song sung in the Vilna Ghetto.

"Shtil, di Nacht" ("Still, the Night"). In Jerry Silverman, *The Yiddish Song Book*, p. 202. Briarcliff, NY: Stein and Day Publishers, 1983. ISBN: 0812861302 (paperback); ISBN: 0812828291 (hardback). 207 pages. A Jewish partisan song sung in the Vilna Ghetto.

Glickman, Sylvia. *The Walls Are Quiet Now*. Bryn Mawr, PA: Hildegard Publishing Company, 1993, 31 pp. (1 score). For orchestra. It reflects the emotions evoked by the memorial wall outside the Grunwald S-bahn station in Berlin. The wall honors the memory of the Jews of the city who were sent to concentration camps.

GRUNFELD, DAVID (1915–1963). Born in Ruthenia, Grunfeld moved with his family to Prague and studied music until the Germans occupied the country. While incarcerated in Theresienstadt, he sang in many operas and was one of the more well known people in the ghetto. After liberation he immigrated to the United States and became a performer using the name David Garen. In 1961 he became a cantor in New York. While incarcerated he co-wrote a piece for string quartets with Zikmund Schul.

Karas, Joza. *Music in Terezin*. New York: Beaufort Books, 1985. ISBN: 0825302870. 223 pages.

Terezin Music Anthology. Vol. 4, *Al S'fod*. Terezin Music Memorial Project, Yad Vashen, Jerusalem, Israel, 1998. Includes works by David Grunfeld. Musicians: Emilie Berendsen, Milada Cejkova, and Naftali Herstik.

HAAS, PAVEL (1899–1944). Haas was born in Brno, Moravia. In his early teens he enrolled in the Music School of the Philharmonic Society. When he was 17, he was drafted into the Austrian army. After World War I he resumed his musical studies. In the years before World War II Haas wrote several patriotic compositions celebrating the new independent Czech Republic. Sent to Theresienstadt, Haas wrote "Al S'fod" for Men's Chorus; "Study" for String Orchestra; and "Four Songs to the Text of Chinese Poetry" for Bass & Piano. He participated in the shows and concerts the prisoners arranged. The musician was deported to Auschwitz and gassed.

Karas, Joza. *Music in Terezin.* New York: Beaufort Books, 1985. ISBN: 0825302870. 223 pages.

HERZ-SOMMER, ALICE (1903–?). Born in Prague, Herz-Sommer studied at the German Music Academy and performed in many piano recitals around the country. Deported to Theresienstadt, she continued to give recitals and concerts, particularly after the men had been transported to Auschwitz in 1944. After liberation she continued her musical career in Czechoslovakia before immigrating with her young son to Israel.

Karas, Joza. *Music in Terezin.* New York: Beaufort Books, 1985. ISBN: 0825302870. 223 pages.

HIDDEN HISTORY, SONGS OF THE KOVNO GHETTO. Washington, DC: United States Holocaust Memorial Museum, 1997.

THE HOLOCAUST: AN UPRISING IN THE GHETTO: A TONE POEM. David Finko. Philadelphia: Dako Publishers, 1985. 50 pages (1 score). For orchestra.

I NEVER SAW ANOTHER BUTTERFLY: SIX SONGS FOR SOPRANO AND SAXOPHONE. Based on poems by Pavel Friedman, Koleba, and Franta Bass. Lori Laitman. Washington, DC: Arsis Press, 1998. 25 pages (1 score). Text from the anthology *I Never Saw Another Butterfly*, which consists of the poetry of children interned in Theresienstadt.

KALISCH, SHOSHANA (dates unknown). Shoshana Kalisch was born in Galanta, Czechoslovakia. Taken with her parents and sister and three brothers to Auschwitz-Birkenau, she was the only one who survived. A number of years after the war, she recalled songs the girls sang in the barracks and made a record of them. She was encouraged by her husband, Victor Kalisch.

Kalisch, Shoshana, with Barbara Meister. *Yes, We Sang!: Songs of the Ghettos and Concentration Camps.* New York: Harper & Row, 1985. ISBN: 0060912367 (paperback); ISBN: 0060154489 (hardback). 160 pages (1 score). For voice and piano. English and romanized Yiddish words. Original text of Yiddish songs, pp. 151–157.

KACZERGINSKY, SHMERKE A. (dates unknown). "Itsik Vitnberg." In Jerry Silverman, *The Yiddish Song Book*, pp. 188–189. Briarcliff Manor, NY: Stein and Day Publishers, 1983. ISBN: 0812861302 (paperback); ISBN: 0812828291 (hardback). 207 pages. The song is about Itsik Vitnberg, a Vilna shoemaker who became a leader of the United Partisan

Organization. He was arrested by the Gestapo in July 1943 but managed to escape. The Nazis threatened to destroy the entire Vilna Ghetto and kill all its inhabitants unless Vitnberg turned himself in. Hoping to save the lives of others, he capitulated, but within two months the ghetto was destroyed anyway.

KACZERGINSKY, SHMERKE, AND BASYA RUBIN. "Yugnt-Himn" ("Youth Hymn"). In Jerry Silverman, *The Yiddish Song Book*, pp. 198–199. Briarcliff, NY: Stein and Day Publishers, 1983. ISBN: 0812861302 (paperback); ISBN: 0812828291 (hardback). 207 pages. This hymn, by a poet and ghetto partisan fighter, encouraged Jewish youth from the Vilna Ghetto to hold their heads up high and fight back against their mortal enemy. Kaczerginsky also collected and preserved many ghetto songs.

KAFF, BERNARD (1905–1944). Born in Brno, Moravia, Kaff studied piano in his hometown and later in Vienna and Berlin. He toured Europe, playing many new compositions, and then taught piano in Austria for eleven years. After his incarceration in Theresienstadt, he became the first musician to give a piano recital. In October 1944 he was deported to Auschwitz, where he died.

Karas, Joza. *Music in Terezin*. New York: Beaufort Books, 1985. ISBN: 0825302870. 223 pages.

KAPLAN, PEYSAKH (?–1943). Born in Poland, Kaplan was incarcerated in the Bilaystok Ghetto. A writer, composer, and music critic, he wrote a song documenting the shooting murder by the SS of 5,000 Jews on the Sabbath of July 12, 1942. He died in the Bialystok Uprising of August 1943, a response to mass deportation.

KLEIN, GIDEON (1919–1945). Born in Moravia, Klein graduated from music school in 1939 and went on to study piano composition. He became an integral part of the Jewish musical community in Theresienstadt, both composing and performing. Klein was deported east to the death camps and died. While incarcerated in the ghetto he wrote the following: "Trio" for Violin, Viola & Cello; "Fantasia and Fugue" for String Quartet; "Sonata" for Piano; "Madrigal" (text by F. Villon) for 2 Sopranos, Alto, Tenor & Bass; "Madrigal" (text by F. Holderlin) for 2 Sopranos, Alto, Tenor & Bass; "Old Folk Poetry" for Men's Chorus. Klein arranged the following: "Wiegenlied" for Soprano & Piano; "Bachuri Leantisa" for Women's Chorus.

Karas, Joza. *Music in Terezin*. New York: Beaufort Books, 1985. ISBN: 0825302870. 223 pages.

KLING, PAVEL (1928–?). Born in Opava, Kling showed brilliance as a child violinist studying in Brno, Vienna, and Prague. After being incarcerated in Theresienstadt, he continued his violin studies with **Karel Frohlich** and played in the orchestra and in chamber ensembles. After liberation the violinist spent several years in Japan as a concertmaster, eventually immigrating to the United States. He joined the Louisville Symphony Orchestra and taught at the university there.

Karas, Joza. *Music in Terezin.* New York: Beaufort Books, 1985. ISBN: 0825302870. 223 pages.

KOCZANOWICZ, ZBIGNIEW (dates unknown). Koczanowicz wrote a poem "Piesn Obozowa" ("Camp Song") turned into a song at Falkensee, a subcamp of Sachsenhausen, where Zbigniew was a prisoner. This camp song, using Koczanowicz's poem and a nineteenth-century folk song, was later set to an original melody by another prisoner, Ludwig Zuk Sharszewski. The song-poem tells what it means to be a concentration camp prisoner. The song is played on the U.S. Holocaust Museum's website.

KRASA, HANS (1899–1944). Born in Prague, Krasa graduated from the German Music Academy in Prague and worked as a vocal coach. He began composing music as a child, and most of his works have been performed in major European cities. In the late 1920s to early 1930s, the musician composed a few operas and musical scores, some of which were performed in the United States.

He arrived in Theresienstadt in April 1942 and almost immediately began composing. In 1944 he was ordered by the SS to compose a musical piece to impress the Red Cross, who were coming to inspect the ghetto. *Brundibar*, an opera for children, was played that day, and shortly after the visit Krasa was deported to Auschwitz and killed. While incarcerated Krasa composed other pieces as well: "Passacaglia and Fugue" for Violin, Viola & Cello; "Dance" for Violin, Viola & Cello; "Theme with Variations" for String Quartet; "Three Songs" for Baritone, Clarinet, Viola & Cello.

Karas, Joza. *Music in Terezin.* New York: Beaufort Books, 1985. ISBN: 0825302870. 223 pages.

Terezin Music Anthology. Vol. 3, *Hans Krasa: Brundibar.* Terezin Music Memorial Project, Yad Vashem, Jerusalem, Israel, 1996. Musicians: Ivan Kusnjer, Ora Shiran, Allan Leiman, Michael Kugel, Ludmila Cermakova, Milada Cejkova, Carmela Leiman, Felix Nemirovsky, and Ilan Schul.

KULISIEWICZ, ALEKSANDER (1918–?). Born in Krakow, Poland, Kulisiewicz studied to be a musician. Imprisoned at Sachsenhausen concentration camp, he collected, composed, and performed songs secretly. After he was caught, the Gestapo punished him by injecting him with diptheria. An antidote was smuggled in for him, and although he survived, his voice was damaged.

Songs from the Depths of Hell. Washington, DC: Folkways/37700, 1998.

LAKS, SZYMON (1901–1983). Born in Warsaw, Laks was a student of both mathematics and musical composition. Before leaving Poland in 1925, he became a conductor. Traveling to Paris, the musician enrolled in the Polish Conservatory and joined the several other young Polish conductors and musicians there. During the Nazi occupation of France, Laks was deported to Auschwitz, where he adapted the three Warsaw polonaises. After liberation by the Red Army, he returned to Paris, where he died.

Kapelmeester van Auschwitz: Muziek uit Andere Wereld. Leuven: Kritak, 1991. ISBN: 9063033753. 136 pages.

Music of Another World. Translated by Chester A. Kisiel. Evanston, IL.: Northwestern University Press, 2000. ISBN: 0810118025 (paperback); 0810108429 (hardback). 141 pages.

LASKER-WALFISCH, ANITA (1925–?). Born in Germany, Lasker-Walfisch studied the cello. She was deported to Auschwitz in 1942. The conductor of the female orchestra there, Alma Boset, the niece of Gustav Mahler, accepted her into the orchestra. She played marches morning and evening for the work details that marched out. She and other members of the orchestra were sent to Bergen-Belsen. The British liberated her in 1945.

"My Century," BBC World Service. Broadcast August 9, 1999.

LEDEC, EGON (1889–1944). Born in eastern Bohemia, Ledec graduated from a prestigious music school in Prague and joined the Czech Philharmonic. After World War I Ledec was promoted to associate concertmaster. Incarcerated in Theresienstadt, the musician performed as a soloist and composed waltzes, marches, and pieces for violin and piano. In October 1944 Ledec was deported to Auschwitz and murdered. While in Theresienstadt he composed "Gavotte" for String Quartet.

Karas, Joza. *Music in Terezin*. New York: Beaufort Books, 1985. ISBN: 0825302870. 223 pages.

LEVITSKA, LIUBA (dates unknown). A folk and opera singer in the Vilna Ghetto, Levitska sang her most famous song "Two Little Doves" (written by Y. L. Cahan) in a concert held shortly after the mass murder of 1,500 Vilna Jews. When the Nazis took Levitska to Ponary (the death pits outside Vilna) to be killed, she sang this song right until the end.

Mlotek, Eleanor, and Joseph Mlotek. *Songs of Generations: New Pearl of Yiddish Songs*, p. 34. New York: Workmen's Circle, 1988. ISBN: 1877909653, 303 pages.

PARTISANS OF VILNA [SOUND RECORDING]. Michael Alpert, Adrienne Cooper, Irena Klepfisz, Henry Sapoznik, and Josh Waletzky (musicians). Chicago: Flying Fish, 1989. 1 sound disc: digital; 4¾ inch. Twelve songs written and sung by members of the Jewish Underground in the Vilna Ghetto. The music is an expression of the suffering, rage, heroism, and pride the partisans experienced. The songs are sung in their original languages.

PEPPENHEIM, LEO (1896–1982). Born in Amsterdam, Peppenheim studied music in Cologne and made his conducting debut in 1916. Peppenheim worked closely with several German opera companies until the Nazis came to power. He returned to Holland in the late 1930s. Deported to Theresienstadt with other Danish Jews, he conducted the orchestra and participated in many performances. After his release he resumed his conducting duties in various Dutch and German orchestras. He retired in 1975, living in Arnheim.

Karas, Joza. *Music in Terezin*. New York: Beaufort Books, 1985. ISBN: 0825302870, 223 pages.

RED PETALS IN THE SNOW: FOR SOLO VOICE (HIGH) AND PIANO. Based on a poem by Dora Teitleboim. Helen Medwedeff Greenberg. New York: Transcontinental Music, 1995. 9 pages (1 score). Words in romanized Yiddish.

REMEMBER THE CHILDREN, SONGS FOR AND BY CHILDREN OF THE HOLOCAUST [SOUND RECORDING]. Gary Bodiger, Zalmen Mlotek, Henry Sapoznik, Lorin Sklamberg, and Jeff Warschauer (musicians). Washington, DC: United States Holocaust Memorial Museum, 1991. 1 sound disc: digital, stereo, 4¾ inch plus booklet. Nineteen songs sung and written by Jewish children, victims of the Nazis, who were forced to live under the most wretched conditions in the ghettos of Eastern Europe. Several of the songs were never recorded and reveal the anguish the children endured.

RISE UP AND FIGHT—SONGS OF THE JEWISH PARTISANS. Washington, DC: United States Holocaust Memorial Museum. The eighteen selections are performed by Theodore Bikel, Frieda Anuch, and Noble Voices.

ROSE, ALMA (1906–1944). Alma came from a musical family. She was the niece of the famous conductor–composer Gustav Mahler. Her father, the concertmaster of the Vienna opera, taught her to play the violin. Alma studied at the Vienna Conservatory and the Vienna State Academy. In 1932 Alma formed the Vienna Waltzing Girls, the first women's orchestra in Austria. With the aggression by Hitler, the Nazis caught up to her and deported her to Auschwitz. In 1942 Alma became the formulator and conductor of the concentration camp's women's orchestra until her death by disease in 1944.

Newman, Richard. *Alma Rose: Vienna to Auschwitz*. Portland, OR: Amadeus Press, 2000. ISBN: 1574670514.

RUDNITZKY, LEAH. "S'Dremlin Feygl" ("Birds Are Dozing"). In Richard Silverman, *The Yiddish Song Book*, pp. 196–197. Briarcliff, NY: Stein and Day Publishers, 1983. ISBN: 0812861302 (paperback); ISBN: 0812828291 (hardback). 207 pages. A ghetto lullaby.

SCHACHTER, RAFAEL (1905–1944). Born in Romania, Schachter came to Prague after World War I to study music, graduating with degrees in composition, conducting, and piano. He arrived in Theresienstadt with the first wave of Jewish "volunteers" in November 1941. The cultural life of the ghetto was initiated by two men—Schachter and Karel Svenk. They teamed up early in 1942 and co-produced many shows. Schachter also collaborated with composer **Gideon Klein** in the formation of new and expanded choral groups that sung in the various languages of the ghetto.

In 1943 the composer produced an opera entitled *Terezin Requiem*. Shortly after its critically acclaimed debut, almost the entire chorus was deported to concentration camps. In 1944 the SS ordered Schachter to conduct *Requiem* for the International Red Cross. He complied and was severely rebuked by many in the artistic community for cooperating with the Nazis. He was deported to Auschwitz in October 1944. Accompanying him on the transport were Karel Ancerl, Viktor Ullmann, Hans Krasa, Egon Ledec, and Bernard Kaff, to name a few. They were killed immediately upon their arrival.

Karas, Joza. *Music in Terezin*. New York: Beaufort Books, 1985. ISBN: 0825302870. 223 pages.

SCHOENBERG, ARNOLD (1874–1951). Born in Vienna, Schoenberg was a self-taught composer. He experimented with new ultramodern theories and techniques. The composer developed an atonal, twelve-tone system. From 1925 to 1933, Schoenberg taught at the Prussian Academy of Arts in Berlin. In 1933 the Nazis had two charges against him—he was Jewish, and his musical system was "degenerate." Dismissed from his position, Schoenberg fled to America. His works then took on a Jewish theme. *A Survivor from Warsaw* is based on a true story during the beginning of the Warsaw Ghetto Uprising. The atonal, twelve-tone piece opens when the ghetto defenders sing the "Shema Israel," the watch word of the Jewish faith.

A Survivor from Warsaw. Op. 46, Czech Philharmonic Chorus. Album, *The Last World War.* Prague: Musician Bona, 2000.

SCHUL, ZIKMUND (1916–1944). Born in Germany, Schul studied musical composition in his homeland before fleeing to Prague to escape the Nazi persecution of Jews. Although he had no money or employment, he continued his studies. His acquaintance with the family of Rabbi Lieben brought him a job he both needed and enjoyed. Schul's duty was to transcribe ancient Hebrew manuscripts. In November 1941 he was sent to Theresienstadt.

He began composing almost immediately upon his arrival in the ghetto. Schul maintained his interest in Hebraic themes and melodies, using them frequently in his music. The composer became a friend and confidant of **Viktor Ullmann**. Schul contracted tuberculosis in spring 1944 and died in June. While interned in the ghetto he composed: "Schicksal," Song for Alto, Flute, Viola & Cello; "Two Chassidic Dancers" for Viola & Cello; "Duo" for Violin & Viola; "Finale" from "Contana Judaica" for Men's Chorus & Tenor Solo.

Karas, Joza. *Music in Terezin.* New York: Beaufort Books, 1985. ISBN: 0825302870. 223 pages.

SH'MA: FOR TENOR SOLO, CHORUS, OBLIGATO PIANO, AND ORCHESTRA. Andy Vores. Brookline, MA: A. Vores, 1995. 134 pages (1 score). Text from poems by Dunash Ben Labrat, Primo Levi, Yitzhak Katzenelson, Uri Zvi Greenberg, and Lena Allen-Shore.

SINGING FOR SURVIVAL: SONGS OF THE LODZ GHETTO, 1940–45. Gila Flam. Urbana: University of Illinois Press, 1992. ISBN: 0252018176. 207 pages. An in-depth look at the cultural life of the Lodz Ghetto in Poland. Survivors recall the music and performances of those dark days. The majority of the songs have not been seen or performed since the ghetto was liquidated.

THE SONG OF THE MURDERED JEWISH PEOPLE. Moravian Philharmonic. Zlata Razddin. Based on poet Yitzhak Katzenelson's work.

SONGS FROM THE GHETTO. Morris Rosenfeld and Leo Wiener. New York: Irvington Publishers, 1976.

SONGS OF THE GHETTOS [SOUND RECORDING]. [*Bet Iohame ha-geta'ot*] Israel: Hed Arzi, 1976. 1 sound disc: analog, 33⅓ rpm, stereo. Sung in English; translated presumably from Hebrew and Yiddish.

STEINER-KRAUS, EDITH (1913–?). Born in Vienna, pianist Steiner-Kraus began performing in the early 1920s. After studying music in Berlin, she moved to Prague and performed on the radio. Incarcerated in Theresienstadt, she continued performing, playing an all-Bach recital and several pieces by Franz Schubert. Steiner-Kraus collaborated with many other musicians. In fall 1944 her husband was deported to Auschwitz, where he was killed. After liberation she immigrated to Israel, where she continued her career as a performer.

Karas, Joza. *Music in Terezin.* New York: Beaufort Books, 1985. ISBN: 0825302870. 223 pages.

STERNHEIM, NOKHEM (1879–1942). Born in Galicia, a region in southeastern Poland and northwestern Ukraine, Sternheim composed several folk songs until he was killed by the Nazis.

"Sorele." in Eleanor Mlotek, and Joseph Mlotek, *Songs of Generations: New Pearl of Yiddish Songs*, pp. 53–55. New York: Workmen's Circle, 1988. ISBN 1877909653. 303 pages.

SZPILMAN, WLADYSLAW, AND WILM HOSENFELD. *The Pianist: The Extraordinary Story of One Man's Survival in Warsaw, 1939–45.* New York: Picador USA, 1999.

TEN BROTHERS: FOR MIXED CHOIR (SATB) AND PIANO. Folk song adaptation by Martin Rosenberg; choral arrangement by Joshua Jacobson; piano arrangement by Mordecai Sheinkman. Martin Rosenberg. New York: Transcontinental Music, 1995. 14 pages (1 score).

TROUPIANSKI, YANKL (1909–1944). A Jewish composer and music teacher in Yiddish schools in Warsaw and Vilna, Lithuania, Troupianski was deported to the death camps and killed.

"Mir Kumen On" ("We Are Coming"). In Eleanor Mlotek and Joseph Mlotek, *Songs of Generations: New Pearl of Yiddish Songs*, pp. 18–19. New York: Workmen's Circle, 1988. ISBN: 1877909653. 303 pages.

20 SONGS OF THE GHETTOS: ARRANGED FOR VOICE AND PIANO; ISSUED ON THE TWENTIETH ANNIVERSARY OF THE WARSAW

GHETTO UPRISING, 1943–1963. Henech Kon. New York: Congress for Jewish Culture, 1963.

ULLMANN, VIKTOR (1898–1944). Born in Silesia, Ullmann studied music in Vienna and composition at the Prague Conservatory. After World War I Ullmann moved to Prague, continuing his musical education. He conducted a performance in December 1921 at the New German Theater. The musician left Prague for a year, becoming the music director of an opera house. Upon his return he gave private lessons and wrote reviews for newspapers and other periodicals. In 1935 Ullmann composed an opera featuring a chorus and symphony orchestra.

In September 1942 Viktor was incarcerated in Theresienstadt, where he was assigned as a music critic and concert rehearsal manager. He completed many important works as a composer and reviewed several others. He is probably the most famous of all the composers and musicians held at Theresienstadt. In October 1944 he was deported to Auschwitz, where he was killed. While interned in Theresienstadt this prolific composer wrote the following: Third String Quartet; Sonata No. 5 for Piano; Sonata No. 6 for Piano; Sonata No. 7 for Piano; *Der Kaiser von Atlantis*, opera, full score and vocal score; "Three Songs" for Baritone and Piano; "Herbst" for Voice, Violin, Viola & Cello; "Der Mensch und sein Tag" for Voice & Piano; "Two Chinese Songs" for Voice & Piano; "Holderlin Lieder" for Voice & Piano; "Brezulinka," Three Songs for Voice & Piano; "Wendla im Garten" for Voice & Piano; "Abendphantasie" for Voice & Piano; "Immer in Mitten" for Mezzo-soprano & Piano; "Chansons des Enfants Française" for Voice & Piano; "Three Songs" for Children's Chorus; "Three Songs" for Women's Chorus; "Two Songs" for Women's Chorus; "Three Songs" for Men's Chorus; "Two Songs" for Mixed Chorus.

Karas, Joza. *Music in Terezin.* New York: Beaufort Books, 1985. ISBN: 0825302870. 223 pages.

Terezin Music Anthology Vol. 1, *Ullmann: Piano Sonatas.* NY: Koch International, 1991. Terezin Music Memorial Project, Yad Vashem, Jerusalem, Israel. Musicians: Marcel Bergman, Robert Kolben, Edith Kraus, Ora Shiran, Eliakum Salzman, and Miriam Hartman.

"UNTER DI CHURVES FUN POLYN" ("Under the Ruins of Poland"). In Richard Silverman, *The Yiddish Song Book*, pp. 186–187. Itsik Manger and S. Beresovsky. Briarcliff, NY: Stein and Day Publishers, 1983. ISBN: 0812861302 (paperback); ISBN: 0812828291 (hardback). 207 pages.

WALDA, DICK, AND LEX VAN WEREN. *Trompettist in Auschwitz.* Amsterdam: De Bataafsche Leeuw, 1989.

WE ARE HERE: SONGS OF THE HOLOCAUST IN YIDDISH & SING-ABLE ENGLISH TRANSLATION. Eleanor G. Mlotek and Malke Gottlieb. New York: Workmen's Circle, 1983. ISBN: 0686408055. 104 pages.

WEBER, ILSE (1903–1944). Ilse was deported to Terezin where he composed songs for singers in the cabaret there. The composite title was *Stimmen Aus Theresienstadt.*

We're Riding on Wooden Horses. Fort Washington, NY: Koch International Classics, 2001. This CD contains Weber's songs sung by fellow inmates Karel Svent, Martin Roman, Otto Skutecky, Evald Weiss, and Adolf Strauss.

WINDSONGS: POETRY BY CHILDREN AT TEREZIN, CZECHOSLOVAKIA, WHO WERE PRISONERS OF THE NAZIS IN THE CONCENTRATION CAMP OF THERESIENSTADT: SONG CYCLE FOR VOICE AND PIANO. Larry Zimmerman. New York: Transcontinental Music Publications, 1992. 23 pages (1 score).

YIDDISH SONGS OF THE HOLOCAUST [SOUND RECORDING]. Narrated and performed by Ruth Rubin, New York: R. Rubin, 1987, 1 sound cassette: analog. Rubin presents a lecture-recital where she discusses Yiddish songs and poetry by Holocaust victims.

ZIPPER, HERBERT (1904–?). Born to a Jewish family in Vienna, Zipper studied at the Academy for Music and the Performing Arts in Vienna, where he met his future wife, Trudi Dubsky. He accepted a position as Kapellmeister in Dusseldorf and also taught there. With the takeover by the Nazis, he fled to Vienna. After the annexation, the Gestapo arrested him and deported Zipper to Dachau and later to Buchenwald. At Buchenwald he met Jara Soyber, and they composed "Dachaulied" ("Dachau Song"), which became famous among the victims of the Nazi regime. Released in 1939, he fled to Paris. After the Nazis occupied France, he fled to the Philippines, accepting a position in the Symphonic Orchestra of Manila. He married Trude in 1939. Surviving the war in the Pacific, the Zippers came to the United States, where he was active as a composer, conductor, and music teacher.

Schwarz, Birgit. *The Quiet Invasion Continues: Herbert Zipper: A Life of New Beginnings.* Vienna: Austrian Information Service, 1993.

5

Videos of the Holocaust Experience

INTRODUCTION

The videos examined here focus on survivors. The films may have been made by a survivor, feature a survivor, or include survivor testimonies. Most videos of the Holocaust experience are documentaries whose intent is to inform the viewer. Some videos feature just a single survivor such as Simon Wiesenthal, Gerda Klein, or Marek Edelman in a format that includes an interview and a narrator who recaps the highlights of the survivor's life.

Videos have now taken the place of films because of the ease in presentation. They provide valuable information to the viewer. Most often videos present archival material, which offers the viewer a clearer picture of the historical events. The videos portray the fear, agony, suffering, death, and destruction of the Holocaust years. Care was taken in these entries to run the gamut of pre-Holocaust to post-Holocaust years and to provide a variety of experiences within the years 1933 to 1945. The videos provided serve the purpose of awareness, to keep memories alive, and, perhaps for those participating, may act as a catharsis. Each entry identifies the title, running time, whether color or black and white, the appropriate age level for viewers, and the distributor.

Other interview videos are based on a survivor's retelling experiences already told in a book. Fania Fenelon, for example, essentially repeats on video what is contained in her book *Playing for Time*. Inge Auerbacher recounts her experiences at Theresienstadt in *All Jews Out*, based on her book *I Am a Star*. Likewise, Kitty Hart's book *Kitty—Return to Auschwitz* is the basis of her video of the same title.

Some videos recount the experiences of non-Jewish peoples persecuted by the Nazi regime. For instance, *Jehovah's Witnesses Stand Firm* describes the persecution of a Christian religious sect; *Persecuted & Forgotten (The Gypsies of Auschwitz)* recounts the genocide of the Roma.

The courage of Righteous Gentiles, those Christians who risked their lives to save Jews, is the subject of yet other videos. These include a revisitation to the site of rescue. Rescued individuals generally interview either the rescuers or the eyewitnesses to the rescue. Thus, Ruth Hartz in *A Legacy of Goodness* returns to central France to interview the children of the parents (eyewitnesses) who sheltered her. Pierre Sauvage returns to LeChambon, France, to interview his boyhood rescuers. In *The Other Side of Faith* the principal figure returns to Poland with his rescuer—in this case his wife, who married him soon after the war, but not before rescuing a number of other Polish Jews. In each case the rescuer says, "It was the right thing to do," confirming the implicit moral message that one ought not be a bystander to injustice. In this category is included the feature-length movie *Au Revoir Les Enfants*, which features a priest rescuer in a fictional account of a survivor who is sheltered as a boy in a Catholic boarding school. Louis Malle, the producer, was himself a boy sheltered in such a school. Also in this category, *The Visas That Saved Lives* recreates Japanese diplomat Sugihara's story as related by his wife and son present in Lithuania when Sugihara granted Jewish refugees visas to escape death.

A few videos lament U.S. failure to rescue Holocaust victims and criticize U.S. immigration and refugee policy. In *America and the Holocaust: Deceit and Indifference* viewers sympathize with Kurt Klein and his desperate efforts to rescue his parents in Nazi Germany as the U.S. State Department delays. Viewers also sympathize with passengers aboard the S.S. *St. Louis* as they frantically seek a place to land in *The Double Crossing: The Voyage of the St. Louis*.

Videos may focus on the arts and on the artists who bore witness to the horrors of the Holocaust. *The Music Survives* is narrated by and tells about composers banned in the Third Reich. *My Brother's Keeper* describes the Warsaw Ghetto Uprising as seen through the paintings of the artist-narrator.

Jewish resistance, and resistance in general, both spiritual and physical, is explored. *Partisans of Vilna* reveals bravery against terrible odds. *The Triumph of Memory* shows that Gentiles who resisted the Nazi invaders also experienced the horrors of the concentration camps. And *Faith Amid the Flames* presents very religious Jews who hold on to their faith despite Job-like persecution.

Videos that take viewers into the heart of the death camps include *Kitty—Return to Auschwitz* and *One Survivor Remembers*, which provide graphic details of the culmination of the Final Solution. *The Last Seven*

Months of Anne Frank completes the well-known Anne Frank story. These videos provide photos from the past and document the horrible train ride to the camps.

In such videos as *The Double Crossing, The Camera of My Family,* and *The Lost Children of Berlin,* German Jews show how they were once well integrated in German society but then became isolated and were later persecuted as criminals. Their film technique involves incorporating testimony from survivors with present-day, archival, or private footage submitted by the survivors.

Films not only provide viewers with straight narrative but also raise the question, Can the Holocaust happen again? German Jews believed themselves to be highly integrated and much-valued citizens of Germany until the Nazi storm broke that illusion. Films on the partisans and on the Resistance highlight the difficulties in fighting back against tremendous odds, and films that deal with rescuers point out how ordinary people rose above petty routine and fear to commit heroic acts. Through both kinds of film, the viewer is compelled to consider what he or she would do in the face of gross injustice. It remains for documentaries and films made by nonsurvivors to look into the minds of the Nazis and collaborators to understand the dark forces and perverted ideas that fired the engine of mass murder called the Holocaust.

ALL JEWS OUT
Documentary. 82 min./Color/B&W. Ages 10+. The National Center for Jewish Film.

This documentary by Holocaust survivor Inge Auerbacher outlines the story of the Jewish Auerbacher family from the German town of Goppingen. It includes home movies of the family from the 1930s and follows Inge through her deportation to the ghetto of Theresienstadt in Czechoslovakia, where she was imprisoned for three and one-half years. (See entry on Auerbacher in Memoirs, Diaries, and Fiction.)

AMERICA AND THE HOLOCAUST: DECEIT AND INDIFFERENCE
Documentary. 87 min./Color/B&W. Ages 14+. PBS Video.

This video relates the painful story of America's failure to respond to the plight of Jews in the 1930s, a time when Jews could still leave the Reich. A good part of the video is focused on Kurt Klein, a Jewish refugee who found haven in America. However, he tries in vain to save his mother and father left behind in Germany. The storyline traces the United States' official policy of delay and perfidy toward the desperate refugees, whose life in Germany was becoming more and more precarious. Klein makes all kinds of efforts to procure a visa for his trapped parents. By the time the visa is approved, the elder Kleins have disappeared. Although despondent over his parents, Klein joined the American army. Eventually he liberated a concentration camp, where he met he future wife Gerda Klein. (See entry on Gerda Klein under Memoirs, Diaries, and Fiction.)

AU REVOIR LES ENFANTS
Feature Film. 102 min./Color. Ages 14+. Social Studies School Service.

Louis Malle, a survivor by hiding in Vichy France, produced this movie of Jewish boys at an exclusive Catholic boys school in Vichy France during the Nazi occupation. The tale parallels that of Malle, who was sheltered in such a school. A courageous French priest, the headmaster, shelters the Jewish boys at the school, who are integrated with the other students. However, an older boy, part of the custodial force, betrays the Jewish boys to the Gestapo. German soldiers burst into a classroom while class is in session and single out the boys. They march the Jewish boys and the righteous headmaster away, presumably to doom. The Catholic boys stand at attention as the troupe is led away and say goodbye. The film ends as the priest says, "Au revoir les enfants."

THE CAMERA OF MY FAMILY
Documentary. 18 min./Color/B&W. Ages 11+. Anti-Defamation League.

This video recounts the story of Catherine Hanf Noren, a professional photographer who was born in Germany and left with her parents in 1938. The storyline is based on her book by the same title. Her Jewish family lived in Germany for generations and considered themselves Jews only by religion. Her grandparents became collectors and distributors of German ethnic goods. Her father settled in the town of Dachau and owned a fabric business. Male members of the family were very patriotic and volunteered to fight in World War I. Noren finds old photographs of her grandmother and traces her roots back in Germany with narration about still photos. There are no shocking or horrific pictures. All are of family life through generations; interspersed is the history of the rise of Nazism and the persecution of the Jews.

THE CHILDREN OF IZIEU
Documentary. 28 min./Color/B&W. Ages 16+. National Center for Jewish Film.

In 1944 the Gestapo head in Lyon, Klaus Barbie, sent two vans to the French village of Izieu. Their mission was to deport the children of the orphanage located there to their deaths. In the raid forty-four Jewish children ranging in age from 4 to 17 and five adults were thrown into the vans and disappeared. The video interviews immediate eyewitness neighbors and two Izieu children who were hidden and escaped this deportation.

CHOOSING ONE'S WAY—RESISTANCE IN AUSCHWITZ-BIRKENAU
Documentary. 30 min./Color. Ages 16+. Ergo Media.

The focus of this documentary is a little-known story of rebellion inside the Jewish annex of Auschwitz known as Birkenau. Gunpowder was smuggled to the Jewish workers by women who were working as slave laborers at a nearby munitions factory. The conduit was Jewish heroine Roza Robota, who had contact with both the crematoria work detail and the munitions workers. Crematorium Number 4 was successfully blown up; unfortunately, the resisters were all shot. The film features interviews with thirteen eyewitness survivors of the camp and rare footage which contributes to the piecing together of this remarkable heroism.

DIAMONDS IN THE SNOW
Documentary and reconstruction. 59 min./Color/B&W. Ages 13+. Cinema Guild.

Three women born in Bedzin, Poland, recall a childhood of hiding from the German invaders and narrate how Polish-Christian rescuers, Righteous Gentiles, saved their lives near the southern German border. The story of this destroyed Jewish community is developed through interviews, archival film, and photos. The reconstruction of the event informs viewers about Jewish communal life in Bedzin and provides a background for the biography of the three women.

THE DOUBLE CROSSING: THE VOYAGE OF THE ST. LOUIS
Documentary. 29 min./Color/B&W. Ages 16+. Ergo Media.

With the blessing of Adolf Hitler the luxury liner *St. Louis* sailed from Hamburg, Nazi Germany, on May 13, 1939, with 936 Jewish refugees on board bound for freedom in Havana, Cuba. The passengers believed they were escaping the terrible persecution in Nazi Germany, but the Cuban government refused them entry into the country. Even though 734 of the refugees held quota numbers for eventual admission into the United States, the U.S. State Department denied them refuge and refused to budge from the official restrictive immigration policy. Archival footage plus numerous interviews with survivors of the *St. Louis* recapture the event. One interviewee, Liesl Loeb (nee Joseph), recalls the frantic efforts of her father, Joseph Joseph, the chairman of the *St. Louis* Passenger Committee.

FAITH AMID THE FLAMES
Documentary, interview, and reconstruction. 30 min./Color. Ages 15+.
Eventful Enterprise.

This video focuses on one strictly Orthodox Jew and his story to illustrate
the spiritual resistance of Orthodox Jews during the Holocaust. The film
records the faith and testimonies of observant Jews, who risked their
lives to maintain their faith in the ghettos and concentration camps. In
one scene an observant Jew offers a prayer stating how good it is to be
a Jew. A fellow inmate asks, "How can you say that when you are suffering so in the concentration camp?" The reply was "Because I am not
a Nazi." The film also deals with the moral struggle the leading rabbis
endured in order to answer faithfully many of the questions on Jewish
law brought out by the Holocaust.

FREEDOM IS NOT A GIFT FROM HEAVEN: THE CENTURY OF SIMON WIESENTHAL
Documentary. 60 min./Color. Ages 15+. Ergo Media.

Simon Wiesenthal himself tells this Nazi hunter's story. The documentary shares his thoughts and his history at various Holocaust sites. Wiesenthal speaks also before German high school students, narrating his
experiences at various camps and his liberation from Mauthausen. Wiesenthal relates how he became a Nazi hunter and how he was able to
track down SS murderers. He explains why it is necessary to learn about
the Jewish genocide and why after all these years it is important to bring
escaped Nazi war criminals to the bar of justice.

INTO THE ARMS OF STRANGERS: STORIES OF THE KINDERTRANSPORT
Documentary. 122 min./Color/B&W. CD. Ages 11+. Amazon.com.

In the nine months prior to the outbreak of World War II in Europe,
10,000 children from greater Germany, all under age 17, left permanently
for England without adult supervision. This was known as the Kindertransport. Children left behind their parents (who often met their doom
in camps), homes, possessions, and even their childhood. This documentary, replete with individual testimonies, tells the story of their anguish,
their heartbreak, and their adjustment. Parents try to put on a happy
face as they wish their children goodbye, following their offspring as
long as they can along the tracks. There are many flashbacks in color
from the present as former deportees recollect, with black-and-white archival movies focusing on the Germany, Austria, and England of 1938–
1939. Some parts are in German. A narrator helps to fit the parts together
while a musical score in the background adds drama.

JEHOVAH'S WITNESSES STAND FIRM AGAINST NAZI ASSAULT

Documentary. 78 min./Color. Ages 14+. Watch Tower Bible and Tract Society of New York.

When Hitler came to power in 1933, there were approximately 20,000 Jehovah's Witnesses living in Germany. They were arrested and sent to concentration camps for refusing to salute the Fuhrer and refusing to fight for the Third Reich. This video features ten historians from Europe and North America and over twenty Jehovah's Witness survivors who tell the story of the persecution of the Witnesses by the Nazis.

KITTY—RETURN TO AUSCHWITZ

Documentary. 82 min./Color. Ages 15+. Social Studies School Service.

Kitty Hart, an Auschwitz-Birkenau survivor, was interned in the death camp when she was 16 years old. She returns to the site with her grown son to tell him and others of her experiences and to try to understand what happened there. She describes each aspect of the camp. She walks the viewer through the gate to the unloading platform; describes the selection process; describes those who went to the crematoria and those who went to the barracks. She takes the viewer to the ramshackle and unsanitary barracks and to the latrine area. In graphic terms she describes the horrendous inhumane treatment of the inmates and her two-year experience.

THE LAST SEVEN MONTHS OF ANNE FRANK

Documentary. 75 min./Color /B&W. Ages 15+. Simon Wiesenthal Center.

Based on the book by the same title, this documentary follows the book in telling what happened to Anne Frank after her arrest in the attic. The video focuses on six teenage girls who went through the camps Westerbork, Auschwitz, and Bergen-Belsen with Anne, yet managed to survive. They relate the deplorable ride on the freight train to Auschwitz; their encounter with the infamous Dr. Joseph Mengele, the Nazi camp physician and experimenter on children; and the horrendous conditions at the camps. They reveal the heartbreaking details of the final days of the Frank sisters, Margot and Anne, and how they suffered from scabies and typhus. Sadly, they explain, after Margot died Anne, believing all her family dead, became despondent, and clad only in a blanket, she succumbs. Unknown to Anne, her father, Otto, survived, the only one in the family to do so.

A LEGACY OF GOODNESS

Documentary. 30 min./Color & B&W. Ages 10+. Social Studies School Service and Your Name Is Renee Institute.

This video follows the storyline of Ruth Hartz's book *Your Name Is Renee.* Ruth Hartz returns to Albi, in south-central France, and locates two sisters, children of the family Fedon who sheltered her during the war years from the pro-Nazi Vichy government and the Nazi occupiers. The parents had died, but their children, now grandmothers, were Ruth's babysitters and remember the experience well. The video moves largely by interview in the family garden of the rescue home. When French is used exclusively, subtitles are employed. Hartz is the narrator-interviewer. Photos from the time (1943–1944) are shown. Ruth was moved after nine months to a convent-orphanage. Only the mother superior knew of Ruth's true situation, and she kept the secret. Photos of that experience are included. As is the case with many rescuers, when asked why they helped save Jews, they answered, "Because it was the right thing to do."

THE LONELY STRUGGLE: LAST HERO OF THE WARSAW GHETTO UPRISING
Documentary. 60 min./Color. Ages 15+. Ergo Home Video Media.

Marek Edelman, presently a cardiologist in Lodz, Poland, is the sole surviving member of the leadership of the Warsaw Ghetto Uprising. The survivor provides an insider's account of the 600 Jewish young people who rose up against the Nazis on April 19, 1943. He expresses in the long interview his disappointment in the lack of support by other ghetto residents, by Polish supporters, and by the outside world. Edelman was an important figure in Solidarity's fight against Communist oppression in Poland.

THE LOST CHILDREN OF BERLIN
Documentary. 50 min./Color. Ages 14+. The Shoah Foundation.

In April 1942 the Gestapo closed the last Jewish school in Berlin. Fifty-four years later fifty former students traveled from all over the world to attend its reopening. Many of the attendees had no idea that the others had survived the Holocaust. The video uses the testimony of the survivors to document Jewish life in Berlin during the war years. These survivors relate how they were able to survive even after Kristallnacht and the massive attempt to murder all the Jews. In their testimonies they recall the dangers they encountered, not only from Nazi authorities but also from zealous Hitler Youth. Whereas at first they were traumatized by the separation and discrimination shown to them, they enjoyed the comfort of being in a Jewish school and in a completely Jewish environment. The males actually bragged how they protected the female Jewish students from the Hitler Youth.

MUSIC OF AUSCHWITZ
Documentary. 16 min./Color. Ages 13+. Anti-Defamation League of B'nai B'rith.

Morley Safer of *60 Minutes* introduces us to Fania Fenelon, author of *Playing for Time*. Fenelon was a member of the all-female prisoners' orchestra that made music to pacify the new arrivals into a sense of calm and to give relief to Nazis after long days and nights of killing. Sometimes the orchestra was made to play as other prisoners were being gassed or executed. Fenelon contrasts the Nazis' love of music and culture with the inhumanity of their treatment of innocent people. She attributes her ability to sing *Madame Butterfly* to her survival in the Auschwitz inferno. (See entry on Fenelon under Memoirs, Diaries and Fiction.)

THE MUSIC SURVIVES
Documentary. 35 min./Color & B&W. Ages 15+. Decca.

This video narrates the Nazi attempt, right from the beginning of their regime in 1933, to eliminate what they called "degenerate art." Excerpts, particularly from the works of composers who had already blazed trails of innovation during the 1920s, are included. Berthold Goldschmidt, a refugee composer, narrates some of the story. Interjected are scenes of Hitler, Nazi book burning, comments by Goebbels, and the Final Solution. Mentioned are victims of concentration camps, composers Viktor Ullmann, Pavel Haas, Erwin Schilhoff, and Franz Schreker. The video points out how damaging the purge was to both German culture and the future productivity of the banned artists, although a few became productive in Hollywood. Along with the video, a seventy-three-minute CD plays the music of eleven banned composers.

MY BROTHER'S KEEPER
Documentary. 25 min./Color. Ages 10+. Clearvue.

Survivor and artist Israel Birnbaum relates scenes of the Holocaust, particularly the story of the Warsaw Ghetto and the plight of Jewish children in a series of dramatic paintings. The scenes are basically from his own work also entitled *My Brother's Keeper*, where he concentrates on the destruction of the Warsaw Ghetto. Birnbaum developed this presentation in order to explain the Holocaust to the children of New York City. A CD for Mac and Windows contains the full text of Birnbaum's book as well as the paintings. (See entry on Birnbaum in Memoirs, Diaries, and Fiction.)

ONE SURVIVOR REMEMBERS
Documentary. 39 min./Color. Ages 14+. Direct Cinema Limited.

Survivor Gerda Weissman Klein, author of the book *All but My Life*, recalls the major events of her life. This includes the shock of the German occupation of Poland in 1939 and her deportation to the concentration camps. She recalls her experience as a slave laborer and the murderous death march in winter 1945. Her eventual liberation was by Lieutenant Kurt Klein, in charge of an American military unit (see video entry: *America and the Holocaust: Deceit and Indifference*), whom she married. The video is augmented through a series of interviews, photographs, and footage shot in the actual locations of her memories. (See entry on Klein in Memoirs, Diaries, and Fiction.)

THE OTHER SIDE OF FAITH
Documentary. 27 min./Color. Ages 13+. Documentaries International Film and Video.

This video tells the story of Josef Burzminski and Stephania Podgorska. The latter rescued thirteen Jews during the time of the German occupation of Poland. The couple, Josef and Stephania, now married, go back to the site of the rescue, Przemysl, in 1995 and describe the events and places during wartime. Josef had escaped from a cattle train in 1942 and sought refuge with Stephania and her sister. The older sister worked for Josef's father. She decided to shelter him, his brother, and eleven other escaped Jews at a house in the country. The SS requisitioned the house, but thinking only the two girls were residents, they permitted the sisters to reside on the top floor. Stephania arranged for the thirteen Jews to hide for two and one-half years on the upper floor by building a false wall. Stephania, a devout Catholic, believed Mother Mary guided her. She risked her life and the life of her sister, Helena, and was in constant danger until liberation by Soviet soldiers. The video comes with a discussion guide.

PARTISANS OF VILNA
Documentary. 130 min./Color /B&W. Ages 16+. American Home Video.

Aviva Kempner, a Vilna partisan herself, produced this feature-length documentary consisting of forty interviews in English, Hebrew, and Yiddish. Among the interviewees are the Resistance leaders Abba Kovner, leader of the Vilna partisans, and Chaika Grossman, leader of the Bialystok revolt. The material covers the Nazi German occupation period in the Baltic countries, 1941–1944. Rare photos of ghetto and forest fighting are interspersed with survivor testimonies. Included are scenes of firefights, sabotage, and other acts of resistance. Survivors also discuss moral issues relating to resistance, including the guilt of leaving relatives and loved ones behind in the ghetto and the effects of partisan activities on their later lives.

PERSECUTED & FORGOTTEN (THE GYPSIES OF AUSCHWITZ)

Documentary. 54 min./Color. Ages 15+. EBS Productions.

A group of German Roma (Gypsies) survivors return to Auschwitz and come to terms with the horrors they experienced. Through personal accounts, the viewer learns about a genocide that is not too well known. The viewer is told about the "Gypsy Police," who arrested Gypsies in Germany and Austria, and learns about the Institute for Racial Hygiene administrated by Dr. Robert Ritter, a German psychiatrist responsible for genealogical research and compiling a national racial census of Roma and Sinti (the ethnic group inside Germany and Austria) that led to their imprisonment and liquidation. Some of the Gypsies interviewed lament the discrimination they still experience today.

A PLACE TO SAVE YOUR LIFE—THE SHANGHAI JEWS

Documentary. 22 min./B&W. Ages 14+. Filmmakers Library.

The documentary relates the story of about 17,000 European refugees mostly from Nazi-controlled Austria and Germany who left to escape persecution. They were joined by an established Shanghai Jewish population of about 10,000. The Japanese had occupied this port city in November 1937 and in late 1938 had offered Jews a safe haven without any entry visa. Although the Japanese forced the Jews into a ghetto, they ignored German demands for Jewish deportation. The video features interviews with survivors together with archival photographs of the Shanghai ghetto. Included are former refugees who came as religious school students, embracing the entire Mir Yeshiva.

SHOAH

Documentary. 570 min./Color/B&W. Ages 16+. Paramount Home Videos.

The narrator, director, and producer of this film is Claude Lanzman, who went to the sites of the major concentration camps and filmed them as they are today. The video is an assemblage of Holocaust witnesses: survivors of these camps and even Nazi functionaries who perpetrated crimes. The Polish villagers who resided near the death camps seemed to show little emotion as Lanzman interviewed them. The Jewish survivors recalled the horror of their wives and children designated for the gas chambers. One segment films the recently deceased Jan Karski, the Gentile Polish Underground courier, who relates how he escaped the

Warsaw Ghetto, viewed a death camp, and made a futile attempt to alert Allied leaders and an incredulous Supreme Court Justice Felix Frankfurter.

THERESIENSTADT—GATEWAY TO AUSCHWITZ
Documentary. 60 min./Color/B&W. Ages 11+. American Film & Video Association.

Survivors who were children in Theresienstadt during the war tell their stories. They recall their friendships, the children's opera *Brundibar*, and even stealing food because of rampant hunger. This video is interspersed with original inmate artwork and photographs. Seeking to create a false impression for the International Red Cross and for propaganda purposes, the Nazis permitted cultural activities and a children's village inside Theresienstadt. In reality for most prisoners the camp was a transit point on the way to Auschwitz. Fifteen thousand children under 15 years of age were incarcerated in the "model ghetto" and only 150 survived.

THE TRIUMPH OF MEMORY
Documentary. 29 min./Color/B&W. Ages 16+. PBS Video.

This video is made up of interviews with three Gentile Nazi concentration camp survivors, all Resistance fighters. The interviewer and narrator himself, Arnost Lustig, is a survivor of Theresienstadt and a well-known Holocaust fiction writer. The Gestapo sent Frenchman Pierre Troadec to Mauthausen after his capture for rescuing downed American fliers. Reider Dittman was sent to Buchenwald for sabotaging two German shops in Norway; he reveals that Nordic prisoners were treated far better than all other nationalities. Czech Resistance fighter Vera Laska is a well-known author of serious Holocaust works; she relates how she hid Jews and fought until sent to Auschwitz. Irina Kharina, the only one who spoke in her native tongue, Russian, relates how she fought as a Soviet Red Army partisan behind the German lines.

TSVI NUSSBAUM—A BOY FROM WARSAW
Documentary. 50 min./B&W. Ages 16+. Ergo Media.

This documentary relates the story of the famous Warsaw Ghetto picture of a 9-year-old boy with his hands up and an SS soldier near him with rifle ready. That boy, Tsvi Nussbaum, tells the story of his survival and new life in Israel as a medical doctor. The film examines Tsvi's imprisonment in Bergen-Belsen and the aftermath. Tsvi explains how he survived it all, his luck in being an exchanged Jew for a Palestinian German national, and how he feels about the murderers who took four generations of his family. An Orthodox Jew, Dr. Nussbaum contrasts his worldview with that of his Nazi persecutors.

THE VISAS THAT SAVED LIVES
Documentary. 115 min./Color. Ages 15+. Ergo Media.

One summer morning in 1940 Chiune Sugihara, Japan's consul-general in Lithuania, awoke to the sound of over 200 desperate Jews crowding outside the consulate. They were hoping to obtain visas to anywhere that would take them from certain death at the hands of the Nazis. Defying diplomatic orders, Sugihara issued an estimated 1,600–3,500 visas from August to September 1940, saving over 2,000 lives. The video uses flashbacks and some reenactments by professional actors to tell the story of the Righteous Gentile. The video interviews the wife and son, present in Kovno, Lithuania, who bemoan that the Japanese government dismissed Chiune Sugihara and persecuted him until his death. Only recently did the Japanese government rehabilitate his memory.

WEAPONS OF THE SPIRIT
Documentary. 38 min./Color. Ages 11+. (Classroom Version) Anti-Defamation League.

Filmmaker, director, and writer of this film, Pierre Sauvage was born and protected in the village of Le Chambon, a farming community of 5,000 Protestants in central France. Led by their pastor, the inhabitants rescued 5,000 Jews during World War II. In this full-length version, Pierre Sauvage returns to the scene of his birth and interviews the heroic natives who saved his and his parents' lives. The interviews reveal simple people with great humanity and courage who make little of their wartime deeds.

More information can be found in the book by Philip Hallie, *Lest Innocent Blood Be Shed: The Story of the Village of Le Chambon and How Goodness Happened There* (New York: Harperperennial Library, 1994). Interviews are augmented by the personal reflections of Sauvage. There is also a conversation between Bill Moyers and the filmmaker. A shortened school version (thirty-eight minutes) without the interview and the opening scene of a long train ride is available and suitable for younger teenagers.

Index

About the Authors

PHILIP ROSEN is the Educational Director of the Goodwin Holocaust Museum and Holocaust Education Center at Cherry Hill, New Jersey. He is also adjunct professor in Holocaust Studies at West Chester University in Pennsylvania. Dr. Rosen has interviewed many survivors and liberators and visited the sites of concentration camps in Europe. He is the co-author (with Eric Epstein) of *Dictionary of the Holocaust: Biography, Geography, and Terminology* (Greenwood, 1997) and a member of the curriculum committee of the Commission of the Holocaust of New Jersey.

NINA APFELBAUM has worked in the publishing field as a copywriter, proofreader, and production manager. She has served as Dr. Rosen's assistant at the Holocaust Awareness Museum for six years and proofread his book *Dictionary of the Holocaust*.